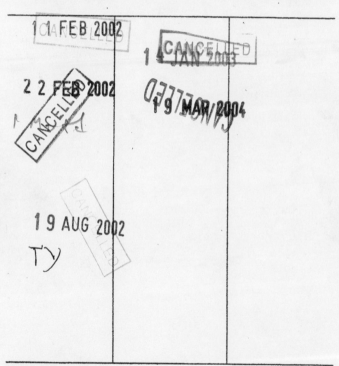

Reviving the Muse:

Essays on Music
After Modernism

Reviving the Muse:

Essays on Music After Modernism

edited by Peter Davison

First published in Great Britain in 2001

Claridge Press Ltd
Horsell's Farm Cottage, Brinkworth, Wilts. SN15 5AS
Reg no. 02119177
www.claridgepress.com
info@claridgepress.com

Printed and bound by Antony Rowe, Chippenham, Great Britain.

Cover Design: Claridge Press
Cover illustration from M. K. Čiurlionis *Sea Sonata (Sonata no. 5 — finale)* held in the M. K. Čiurlionis Art Museum in Kaunas, Lithuania.

CIP data for this title is available from the British Library.

ISBN No: 1-870626-54-0 (hbk)

Musicology

Contents

Preface   1

1   True Authority:
     Janáček, Schoenberg and us
     Roger Scruton   7

2   Schopenhauer and Music:
     a musician's approach
     Menno Boogaard   31

3   '. . . the madness that is believed . . .'
     a re-evaluation of the life and work of
     Arnold Schoenberg
     Peter Davison   55

4   Chromatic Engineering:
     'unnatural' musical intervals and the fate
     of the hexachordal modes
     Robert Walker   83

5   Modernism and After
     Robin Holloway   93

6   Form and Meaning:
     the inner life of music
     Robin Walker   112

7   *Reviving the Muse*
    Peter Davison   120

8   *Recreating the Classical Tradition*
    John Borstlap   149

9   *Renewing the Past:*
    some personal thoughts
    David Matthews   199

10 *Old Practices, New Ideals: the symphony*
    orchestra in the modern world
    John Boyden   213

11 *Looking Sideways for New Music*
    Edward Pearce   232

12 *Building Blake's 'Jeruslaem'*
    Sir Ernest Hall   247

    Biographical Notes on Contributors   263

    'Sea Sonata (Sonata no. 5 — finale)'
    by M. K. Čiurlionis
    Publisher's Note on the Cover Illustration   267

    Index   269

Preface

I find myself introducing this collection of essays, after listening to the great surge that concludes Janáček's *Sinfonietta*. This cascade of fanfares provokes the kind of response that in my youth made me interested in music at all, and I am impressed that, even after countless hearings, this deep stirring of energy in myself is still possible. It is a reaction that is sadly rare in music written since the Second World War, with a few notable exceptions, such as Britten's moving *War Requiem*. This lack of music infused with such a vital energy may not be a complete picture, but there is little evidence to the contrary. It is, on the other hand, hard to believe that the talent and will for an invigorating new music does not exist. If the muse no longer sings, it must be because *we* have silenced her, and our task must be to liberate her once again.

One of the motives of the modernist movement of the early twentieth century was to protect 'high art' from a corrupted popular culture. Modernism was a desperate measure for desperate times. The renewal of the moral and spiritual purpose of high art, and thereby the redemption of European culture as a whole, was sadly not achieved. In the end, any sense of a renaissance collapsed in the codification of revolutionary ideas, which were absorbed into the safe haven of academia. It thus became possible for anyone with a wild idea, claiming to break new ground, to find some official approval. In our own times the nightmares of the early modernists have come to pass. The global consumerist culture, with its pseudo-democratic market-place, discriminates against any claim of superior enlightenment which would validate high art. Such art only survives by accepting its equivalent status with all other kinds of entertainment, becoming the desirable object of the same consumers who purchase computers, package holidays and motor cars.

The early modernists not only failed to defend high art but, by taking refuge in academia, they demonstrated no capacity for leadership. They tragically, and perhaps unavoidably, contributed to the collective aberration that destroyed so much in the last century. The market of consumers applauds the marginalising of troublesome artists and musicians with their uneconomic means and apparently elitist ends. A 'lucky' few have been kept on artificial life-support by the meagre grants of governments, whose loyalty to modernist orthodoxy stems from the same guilty motive that offers social security to other casualties of consumerism. There is also a wish to diminish the artist's relevance to real life — a pact for silence, which modernism happily maintains.

This collection of essays does not express a coherent philosophy or theory of music. The aim is simply to stimulate debate and question the assumptions that currently govern the criticism, composition and promotion of new music. There is no attempt to replace one orthodoxy with another. Much of what is written is personal and subjective, encompassing many shades of opinion. However, there is nothing arbitrary about the choice of authors. Roger Scruton's authoritative and ground-breaking book, *The Aesthetics of Music*, illuminates several of the essays, and his own contribution illustrates the crucial point that music is a means of spiritual and moral renewal. The first part of this book addresses the theoretical, philosophical and historical issues behind our current predicament. However, the last fifty years have also taught us that the question of new music cannot be entirely addressed through the posturing of brilliant analytical minds. Too often dazzling intellects have demonstrated little understanding of music as a language of feeling and transcendence. For this reason, I have included several essays by active and renowned composers, who provide refreshing insights based upon their actual experience and methods of working.

The post-war existential gloom that pervaded most cultural speculation in the last century has to be adapted to a different context, even if it records a trauma that cannot be ignored. The utterances of Schoenberg, Adorno and their successors have entrenched a climate of despair and existential crisis as a norm. The origin of this '*Angst*' was in the over-ripe climate of late-Romanticism. Indeed, many of the aesthetic and theoretical conflicts of the last century seem to begin with the towering and controversial figure of Richard Wagner, and perhaps it is to him that we have to return in some way to resolve many of our cultural problems. The overpowering psycho-spiritual effect of his music almost created a new aesthetic religion, and we have needed the entire duration of the last century to be able to assess his work in a perspective that neither overrates nor diminishes its extraordinary achievement.

In contemporary concert life, the repertoire familiar to and appreciated by the public is shrinking. There is a danger of stagnation in both the performance and interpretation of this narrowing canon of works. We badly need an injection of new music, whether by reviving lost and neglected masterpieces from the past, or by the advent of a more approachable kind of contemporary composition. The current situation is the result of the alienation of the mainstream concert-goer, who has taken refuge in the old and familiar: a polarised response to the aggressive attack of the new. Much as intellectuals may despise the concert-going public's taste or lack of it, this audience forms the main arena for judgement, where cultural assimilation takes place. In the longer term, it is where posterity makes itself heard. Critics, bureaucrats and theorists will not have the final say.

So, despite the obstructive background of our secular, consumerist and globalised society, the fundamental question is whether new music with an unashamedly European accent can break through the confusion and climate of cynicism to touch people once again. Contemporary music has ceased to connect with what might be called the core of an educated and civilised society, and it rarely seems to draw upon the natural impulses and feelings that are the true source of creative endeavour. The spontaneity and subjectivity of good music-making have been badly damaged by market-pressures and the impact of advancing technology, in both performance and composition. This book asks: how did this come about, how inevitable is it, can we connect with the public again ? Finally, it looks forward to a society with music at its the heart, in Sir Ernest Hall's personal and practical affirmation of music's power to transform the self and the society around us.

Doubtless some will consider many of these ideas intellectually regressive, too idealistic or backward-looking, but such categories are a matter of fashion. Being undogmatic and eschewing cultural pessimism are radical acts in the current climate. However, this book does not dismiss outright the modernist experience or deny its right to exist, nor does it posit a glib or 'new-age' optimism as an alternative. It is a plea for freedom, spontaneity, imagination and expression in music, but one which recognises the physical and psychological limitations of the human being.

We live in a period of transition. For the young composer trying to find a voice, there seems little guidance through the maze of ideologies and practices. This book attempts to show that there are still some authoritative bases for the art of music, and that its cultural importance should not be underestimated. Music is the natural language of the muse, who tells us we are all bound by a universal spirit. She tells us of our need to grow and offers meaning in the face of our mortality. Without recognition of these things, great music cannot be created, and our lives, individually and collectively, become impoverished. Music can express our potential and stimulate development towards it, and for this reason it offers hope. To neglect music is to forget our deeper selves.

Acknowledgements

I would like to thank Roger Scruton for his energy and commitment in bringing this book to fruition. He has long expressed himself with courage and wisdom in these matters, against the tide of opinion. I would also like to thank Sir Ernest Hall for his generous support, and the members of the Albany discussion group, whose comradeship and stimulus encouraged me to make this collection and who have provided much of its content.

Peter Davison
West Kirby, Wirral
November 2000

1

True Authority:
Janáček, Schoenberg and us

Roger Scruton

There is an experience that is familiar to all of us, and central to the
value of art, which we might characterise as a sense of necessity,
of an absolute rightness in some artistic gesture, a perception that
'it could not have been otherwise'. We have this experience, even
though we know full well that it *could* have been otherwise, that,
in the very detail that strikes us as imbued with an ineluctable
necessity, the artist is exercising complete freedom of choice, and
lesser talents might have proceeded in quite another way without
disaster. Hence our recourse to metaphors: we are not speaking of
a real necessity, but of a necessity of the heart — a necessity that
seems to reveal an order and rightness whose meaning lies in us.
This experience is, we might say, an encounter with authority, and
it has much in common with the encounters that command
obedience in life.

Kent says to Lear: 'You have that in your countenance which I
would fain call master.' 'What's that?' asks Lear, and Kent replies:
'Authority'. In art as in life authority answers our questions: it is
the self-authenticating presence that silences doubt. During the
first decades of the last century composers and critics were full of

such doubt, and anxious to discover the authority who would overcome it. It is a cliché to say that the tonal language had become a
cliché; but like every cliché it has a core of truth. After Wagner and
Debussy it seemed impossible to return to the diatonic melodies
and tonal polyphony of the romantics: these things had lost their
innocence, which meant that they had ceased to be genuine
expressions and become sentimental, parts of a complicitous game
of pretence. Tonality was kitsch.

'Kitsch' is a Central European word for a phenomenon that
flourishes everywhere, but which reached a poignant self-
awareness in Central Europe at the end of the nineteenth century.
For the artistic revolutionaries of the late Habsburg Empire kitsch
was the artistic nemesis of the Austro-Hungarian settlement, the
proof that a civilisation had been eaten away by emotional
termites, and stood veneering its own emptiness and on the brink
of collapse. Nothing in the decaying order had real authority;
everything was a laughable pretence. The artistic revolutionaries
did not seek popularity, since it was precisely the kowtowing to
popular culture, they thought, which had cheapened the artistic
language, brought it down from the liturgical to the commercial
level. They wanted to *command* respect, not to court it.

Schoenberg perfectly exemplifies that attitude, both in his
music, and in the theoretical writings through which he explained
and rationalised the twelve-tone technique. Schoenberg also illustrates an important distinction — that between the person with
authority and the authoritarian. The authoritarian is the one who
hides behind rigid edicts and peremptory commands. He fortifies
himself with systems, rules, and rubber stamps, in order to conceal
the arbitrariness of his actions. The authority, by contrast, is the
one who spontaneously does what is right, and whose actions and
example elicit our approval because they seem to emerge
ineluctably from a free and understanding nature. The contrast
between the two kinds of character is displayed, it seems to me, in
that between Schoenberg and Janáček.

Both Schoenberg and Janáček were great teachers, and both
divided their lives between composition and public-spirited

musical enterprises. Both were theorists, and both bequeathed to posterity deep and difficult textbooks on the nature of harmony. And of course both were central Europeans, caught up in the turmoil of events that led to the collapse of the Austro-Hungarian Empire and to the political vacuum into which Nazism and Communism poured their nihilistic poisons. And although Janáček belonged to the generation prior to Schoenberg, he was a late developer, and found his musical identity exactly at the same time as Schoenberg.

The contrast between the two composers illustrates a wider division within the civilisation from which they both emerged — the division between the centralising, cosmopolitan culture of Vienna, and the national revival that had become the principal source of light in the Slavonic and Hungarian provinces. Schoenberg's sense that tonality was exhausted, and that the romantic language at which he was so consummate a master had nothing more to say, reflected the parochial concerns of Vienna, where a tired Empire, presided over by a tired Emperor, had consumed without remainder its accumulated capital of hope. Nothing was left, the intellectuals believed, save officialdom, anonymous routines, and the impersonal jurisdiction that was spread over a vast hinterland of strangers. By contrast, Janáček's ability to catch from his native Moravian air the freshest tonal harmonies, and the palpitating fragments of original and life-enhancing melody, reflected the hopes and longings of a new country — or rather a country newly discovered, rejoicing in the sense of locality, of being here and now and not (like Vienna) anywhere and anywhen.

The impenetrable bureaucracy of Kafka's *Trial* and *Castle* reflects the old order of Vienna in terminal decline — an order in which inviolable procedures and inscrutable laws conceal the arbitrariness and will-lessness of the power that imposes them. The hollowness of this cosmopolitan order is placed dramatically before us also by Musil, in *The Man without Qualities*. Musil shows the individual conscience, surrounded by a society kept in place by meaningless routines. In this demoralized order the conscience becomes subjective, vacillating, profoundly unsure of anything save its own impressions. The man without qualities is in fact a man without substance, a subjectivity without a self.

In *Young Törless*, Musil, himself born in Bohemia, describes the youth of a cosmopolitan aesthete, educated in a school which stands so much apart from the surrounding farms and villages that their inhabitants appear, to the boys who stare from the windows, scarcely human. Only once, when Musil refers to one of these troglodytic creatures as bearing a name which, in the local language, means 'he came hurrying'do we have an inkling that this is a place where Czech is spoken (for presumably, though the author does not say so, the name is Pospíšil). Musil's despair at the emptiness of cosmopolitan Vienna goes hand in hand with a refusal to acknowledge the existence of anywhere else. His sights pass from everywhere to nowhere, without finding the somewhere that counts. And the everywhere and the nowhere are one, namely Vienna, on the brink of self-destruction.

It is this nowhere that is rejected by the cynical soldier Švejk, even though, being a Pražan, he has no somewhere to offer in exchange for it, apart from his local pub. Janáček too rejected both the everywhere of old Vienna, and the nowhere to which it led. But his somewhere was both imagined and real. Nothing was further from his heart than the cynicism of Hašek; he had re-imagined Moravia, not as it was, but in a higher and purer version of itself, a version in which the locality and its people were idealized objects of love. Two momentous results of this were his folk-song arrangements, and his collection of speech melodies. Both of these fed his conception of music, as an expression of feeling, intimately tied both to speech and to dance: to be judged like speech for its truth, and like dance for its life. Hence music, for Janáček, could not be detached from its social context — any more than speech or dance could be detached. Music is a form of immediate communication and togetherness, and its roots are to be found in a people, a place and a time.

Of course, such an attitude is possible only in certain places and certain times. Janáček was the inheritor of Smetana and Dvořák, and the active participant in a movement of national revival that reached to the humblest regions of society — even to the house-maid, Marie Stejskalová, whose garrulous reminiscences, recorded by Marie Trkanová, give such a vivid picture of the changes through which the people of Brno, and the Janáček household in particular, then lived. It was possible to regard folk-song and folk-poetry, folk-festivals and folk-religion, as genuine expressions of community in which all the sacred episodes — youth, courtship, marriage, childbirth, nurture, mourning — were sincerely expressed and marked with the stamp of a place and a time.

No such thing was true of Vienna. In place of folk music and folk dances there was the music of the café and the dance-hall — some of it sophisticated, in the manner of the Strauss family, much of it degenerate. The sentimental song and the waltz had seized the popular imagination, and serious composers had become wary of 'the spirit of the people' when its voice was so often near to schmalz. Only Mahler would sometimes risk it — and he drew as much on his native Moravia as he did on Vienna, when it was nec-essary for 'the people'to get a look in. As for Schoenberg, it is very clear from his theoretical writings that he blamed the decay of tonality as much on the eruption of its debased popular forms as on the exhaustion of post-Wagnerian harmony. The people appear in his music not as a self-renewing moral community, the fount of innocent joy, but as a bewildered crowd. Indeed no work of art matches *Moses und Aron* in this respect — a portrait of the crowd as a degenerate monster, a collective denial of God, wandering in need of a redemption that must come, if it comes, from outside. For Janáček the imagined community was not a crowd at all, but a kind of person, radiant with divine life, not the recipient of redemption but its source.

As I remarked, both Janáček and Schoenberg were theoreti-cians. Neither of them is an easy read. Nevertheless, there is an immediate and all-important distinction between them, which is that Schoenberg is abstract, generalising, systematising, whereas Janáček is intuitive, concrete, and reluctant to explain. He is concerned above all with how we hear music, and with the relations between harmonies and notes as they are experienced. His theory of the moment of chaos, which ensues when the notes of one chord hang over into the beginning of the next, and so form a binding or *spletná*, is a theory of what we hear, a kind of deep psychology of musical connection. Likewise his idea that common chords can retain their identity even when 'thickened' with other notes, or even when another and rival chord 'percolates'into them — this is again a theory of what is heard, and a very interesting one. Chords were, for Janáček, musical individuals, whose identity was not cancelled when they were mixed, but which continued to exist through changes in the overall harmonic texture. The common chords of the major and minor scales never lost their truth for him, for it was a heard truth — a truth of phenomenology. The triads had an innocent life of their own, and if, in vulgar contexts, they could be abused, the fault lay in the contexts, not the chords. It would never occur to Janáček to dismiss a chord entirely, on the grounds that it had 'become banal'. But this is precisely what Schoenberg did, in relation to the diminished seventh. (See *Harmonielehre*, pp. 288-9.) No chord, for Janáček, was banal in itself, or incapable of being refreshed by returning it to its source, in the music of humanity. Throughout Janáček's music we find the simplest of tonal harmonies, juxtaposed with harmonies taken from the modernist repertoire, used not in any systematic or rule-governed way, but because they sound right — both musically and emotionally.

This 'sounding right'is not the same as being right according to some system or rule. For the authoritarian personality, however, nothing less than system will do; without it, he feels entirely unprotected. It is in this way, I believe, that we should understand Schoenberg's break with tonality. Schoenberg saw tonality as a system — a set of rules for the combination of notes, a musical grammar, which had exhausted its expressive potential. The solution was not to add new chords and new melodic and rhythmic shapes to the system, for this could never remove the fundamental pollution, which lay in the system itself. The rules, which once had set us free, were now constraining us, forcing us towards falsehood and schmalz. So it is the rules that must be changed. We must devise a new system for the combination of notes, a new musical grammar, which would enable us to do the same kind of thing that tonality enabled us to do, but without making the tonal sounds. Thus emerged the serial technique, and composition with twelve notes, each treated as equal, so that none could emerge as a tonic, and no chord could be sidetracked into the old patterns of tension and resolution that were the routine of tonal harmony.

This famous experiment was an act of aggression towards the popular ear. Schoenberg hated the audiences of contemporary Vienna, he despised the easy-going popular culture that was symbolised for him by the common chords of tonality. Although, as his arrangements of Strauss waltzes indicate, he had an ironical and sophisticated love of the old Viennese culture, he was also appalled by the sight of ordinary human enjoyment. He devised erudite concerts at which clapping was outlawed, and in which works were attended to in the same frame of mind as a surgical operation.

Furthermore, Schoenberg's new system was designed to have the same trans-national and universal character as the one which it replaced. Music was not to be renewed, as Janáček sought to renew it, by being returned to a community and a locality where song and dance still lived. It was to be reconstructed in the terms laid down by the old imperial idea, but somehow rescued from the decadence and exhaustion of empire.

Schoenberg thereby opened the way to what could be called the routinisation of modernism. To write new music, on the Schoenbergian model, it was not necessary to look for the community to which your music was addressed, and from whose heart-beats you took your primary inspiration. It was enough to devise a system, a code, which would cancel the arbitrariness of the sounds, by organising them in accordance with another, inaudible, grammar. The method could be applied anywhere, and in any frame of mind. And so long as the old expectations, enshrined in the experience of tonality, were frustrated, and so long as the inner logic of the result could nevertheless be revealed to the rational and enquiring mind, the result would be music — new, meaningful music, cured of banality by being rescued from the crowd. This was the aspect of Schoenberg's thinking which was to have such a far-reaching and, in my view, deleterious effect. Principal among those who took up the serialist doctrine was Theodor Adorno, who welded the revolutionary musical syntax to revolutionary politics, to form a peculiarly intoxicating substitute for authority. Adorno managed to deceive not only himself but a whole generation of radical critics into thinking that the artistic avant-garde, as Schoenberg had envisaged it, stood side by side with the revolutionary vanguard, in opposition to the false consciousness and ideology of bourgeois society. The rejection of tonality was also an emancipation, parallel to, and part of, the emancipation of society from the capitalist system.

Schoenberg's approach to music made listening hard. But it made composing easy. Only a few practitioners of serialism had the genius of Schoenberg or Berg, who were able to reconcile the mad mathematics of the system with another, and more musical organisation, which had nothing to do with the serial order (unless the serial order was itself founded, as in Berg's Violin Concerto, on tonal harmonic principles). For lesser talents, the adherence to the *a priori* system failed to conceal the arbitrariness of the result. Nevertheless, they were fortified against criticism by the erudition of their theory. For many decades after the triumph of Schoenberg it was difficult to criticize the modernist experiments: each came fully armed in doctrine, and the more arbitrary the sounds, the deeper must be their real musical meaning — so at least it was assumed. Moreover, the adroit propaganda of Adorno, Ernst Bloch and Hanns Eisler, which had identified serialism with left-wing politics, and its opponents with the Nazi critics of *entartete Kunst*, made it almost dangerous to question the prevailing orthodoxy.

Thus it was that a whole generation of critics failed to notice that many of the modernist sound effects had themselves become banal — far more banal than the diminished seventh chord, since they belonged to no coherent language that could inject them with musical meaning. (Examples: cluster chords on the upper wood-wind, multiple percussion with no rhythm to emphasize, jagged lines of pseudo-melody, punctuated by super-saturated dissonance on the brass — clichés of alienation, reliably rewarded by those who pay the piper.)

Tonality is not a system, in the sense that the serial method is a system. It does not proceed from a set of *a priori* rules for the organisation of notes, but from an empirical understanding of the way things sound, and of the gravitational forces that set up mutual attraction and repulsion between the notes of a scale. Such rules as can be given for tonal composition are not rules of grammar, but *a posteriori* generalisations, records of past successes, which together form a tradition, rather than a language or a code. Tonality is rooted in the way things sound, and is therefore infinitely open to experiment. If the diminished seventh sounds banal, then drop it, or change the context so that it regains some of its freshness (as in Berg's *Lyric Suite*, first movement, measure 15): that is the correct response to Schoenberg's strictures.

The same should be said of the fundamental building blocks of tonal harmony. If the major triad is a cliché, then try spreading it over five octaves, as Janáček does; try thickening it with the discordant second sounding quietly in the alto, and the tonic and mediant clustered in the bass, as in so many places in Janáček's lyrical operas. Try placing it in a new context — under a pentatonic melody, for example, as in Ex.1, the last and greatest episode in the *Diary of One who Disappeared*:

Ex. 1. 'S Bohem'

If the change from major to minor sounds too cheap, re-make the minor third as part of a whole-tone sequence, as in the next strophe of the melody from the *Diary*:

Ex. 2. *ditto*

And if you need to stand at one remove from the key for a moment, without sliding into another, use whole-tone chords, as Puccini does in *Madama Butterfly*, or as Janáček does, for example in Ex. 3 from *On an Overgrown Path*. There is nothing daring about these experiments, nor do they imply some new harmonic system. But they have a naturalness and freshness that rescues them from Schoenberg's dismissive strictures.

Ex. 3. *Overgrown Path*

Purists will not, of course, be satisfied. They will point out — and rightly — that the great achievement of the Western musical tradition has been to produce organized and extended musical structures, in which musical material is not merely stated, but developed melodically, harmonically and rhythmically to create an impression of organic growth and the sense of an ending. Of course Schoenberg was wrong to think of tonality as a set of rules; even more wrong to think that he could find an equivalent in his per-mutational system. But he was not wrong to think of tonality as permitting large scale relations and audible development, or in identifying these facts as essential to the power of classical music. What does Janáček offer us instead? And if he offers nothing except brilliant flashes and enigmatic fragments, why should we take him as our model? Why not follow Schoenberg at least in this: in searching for a comprehensive musical order, which will facilitate the great arches of musical thought that are familiar to us in Mozart or Brahms?

It is of course wrong to suggest that Janáček's music contains no development: as John Tyrrell has argued, the paradigm of theme

Ex. 4. 'S Bohem'

and variations is always at work in his musical thinking. The concluding song of the *Diary* provides a vivid illustration, and it is worth pausing to examine it (Ex. 4). The theme is stated in its quasi-pentatonic version, in D-flat major. The first variation follows at once, in D-flat minor, but with that strange whole-tone accompanying phrase. The piano varies this phrase, and then, in a diminished version, establishes it as a running whole-tone background to the melody in its original version, this time in canon with the bass line. The melody is repeated in unison, with a new variant of the concluding phrase. The accompanying figure is now transposed to the bass, with the melody, in a new variant, sounding in E major/E minor, until the piano breaks in with a magical abbreviation of the theme in demi-semi quavers, now in A-flat minor, the crucial concluding phrase being used to take the music into its heart-stopping peroration in E-flat major, in which the various fragments are rearranged as a surging accompaniment to the singer's cry. The song is in fact a masterpiece of musical organisation, all the more remarkable in that the material from which it is constructed is chosen not for its structural potential, but for its expressive power: the folk-like melody — which has already appeared in the context of Zefka's seductive appeal — and the three-note phrase with its repeated note and whole-tone prolongation.

Of course, the critic will not be satisfied with such examples: this is organisation, certainly, but organisation at the micro-level. What about the larger scale? Janáček's instrumental works rely on repetition, ostinato and accompanying figures; the melodic lines consist of short, poignant phrases; the keys are often sustained (as in the example just given) for no more than a few bars and modulate unpredictably and often wildly, in order to attain some desired effect; there is little in the way of counterpoint, and the whole effect is one of episodes and interruptions, as in the string quartets or the *Sinfonietta*, with timbre, colour and rhythm making much of the running. Are these not signs that musical structure, and long-term musical thought, are here being pushed into the background, in favour of those quick grasps at the heart-strings of which Janáček was such a master?

It is a real question. But far from showing the weakness of Janáček, it points to his achievement, in cutting the living parts of tonality free from the parts which had ossified or died. If the only way to continue the great tradition of structural thinking was by means of the caricature proposed by Schoenberg, in which intellectual order replaced the order perceived by the ear, then this was a sign that the tradition of structural thinking was dead. But it was not a sign that tonality was dead, only that tonality must be severed from the symphonic project, and re-made as a more plastic, more impressionistic idiom. That was what Janáček did.

The symphonic project, as we find it in Brahms, for example, depends upon lengthy themes, carefully prepared changes of tonal centre, contrapuntal organisation, and a direction of phrases, melodies, sections and movements towards their end. Janáček rejected all those features. His musical practice, like his musical theory, concentrates on the atomic particles of musical meaning: chord-sequences and melodic phrases, together with the multi-layered rhythmic organisation that he called *sčasovaní*. His themes are short, pregnant gestures; shifts of key are abrupt and colouristic, seldom establishing a tonal centre; organisation depends upon repetition and small-scale variation rather than counterpoint; and the emphasis throughout is on beginnings rather than endings. The Janáček theme is usually moving away from rather than towards its most vital moment — in just the way that human gestures erupt and then die away — as in Examples 5 and 6. (Note the wholly characteristic one-beat empty bar which comes

Ex. 5. 'V Mlhách'

Ex. 6. *Overgrown Path*

at the end of these melodies, and in which they die away. This bar is an integral part of the melodic structure, like the bar of silence that ends Beethoven's 5th Symphony.)

Ex. 7. *Overgrown Path*

Ex. 8. *ditto*   Ex. 9. 'S Bohem'

Janáček's figures tend to contain repeated notes, as in Examples. 7, 8 and 9, creating two beginnings without an ending. His melodies often set out, in Slavonic fashion, from the downbeat; his greatest moments are announcements rather than conclusions, like the trumpet call that summons back the introductory fanfare of the *Sinfonietta* to conclude the work — to conclude it, in fact, with its beginning. And even in the final bars he may start something new — as in the conclusion of Act 2 of *Kat'a*, in which the music suddenly slips out of the composer's favourite erotic region of D flat-A flat, and ends on a radiant E major chord, but one in which we hear a new beginning, as the mediant weaves in and out of major and minor — the seeds of tragedy in the midst of joy.

This emphasis on beginnings means that cross rhythms arise as spontaneously in Janáček as they do in ordinary life; phrases burst out and cut across each other like speech in the market place. The typical Janáček sound reminds one less of a carefully disciplined gathering, in which each person is dedicated to the collective task, than of a passionate and intimate conversation, in which voices break out under the pressure of some inner urgency, and in which harmony is achieved in spite of the many voices and not because of them. This is dramatic music par excellence, and it is organised according to dramatic rather than symphonic demands. This is as true of the string quartets and the *Sinfonietta* as it is of the operas and the *Glagolitic Mass*. And because Janáček was a great drama-tist, his music hangs perfectly together, achieving heights of expression which entirely justify the passage work that leads towards and away from them. In a sense he was the opposite of Wagner. While Wagner achieves dramatic intensity by symphonic means, Janáček achieves symphonic intensity through drama. It is thus that we hear, for example, the great second act of *Kat'a*, and the equally sublime peroration to the *Makropulos Case*.

This has, I believe, a great bearing on Janáček's importance for us, in our current historical predicament. Schoenberg's experiment with serial organisation was an attempt to reconnect modern music to the great tradition of symphonic utterance. The new music was to be as organised and as authoritative as the tonal symphony, with the same kind of organic inter-dependence among its parts, and the same depth of structure. It was to be an exercise in sustained musical thought, requiring the very same intense, objective and analytical audience that might listen in silence to a symphony of Brahms. The assumption was that the traditional concert audience would be reborn, and music once again assume its place at the heart of a metropolitan culture. The enterprise failed not merely because the serial system remained a merely intellectual device, with no ability to address the ear, but because the audience to which Schoenberg addressed himself could not be created anew. It belonged to a particular cultural moment, and that moment was passing. The routinisation of modernism in our time reflects this fact. The modernist novelties are not the spontaneous results of a dialogue between composer and audience: they take place in a void, like abstract thought-experiments, appealing more to curiosity than to an established emotional need. Only by elaborate artifice, involving state patronage, a carefully nurtured establish-ment of insiders, and those pretentious commentators who one might call hypocritics and who monopolize the quality press, can something like a modernist audience be brought into being.

The transformation of the audience that was occurring in

Schoenberg's day reflected the increasing mobility of society, the ready availability of music, the democratisation of taste, and the shortening of attention span that is the inevitable concomitant of modern life. The great chamber works of Brahms are addressed to people who move more slowly, and at a greater distance from one another, than we do. They contain tenderness, longing, and passion: but all are recollected in tranquillity, and set at a distance by the patient musical thought that sits, as it were, in judgement upon them. A modern composer could not write in such a way; to do so would be to falsify the rhythms of his psyche. Tenderness, longing and passion still exist: but they are intense, momentary and as it were thought-resistant. You can stay at Brahms's level of musical objectivity only if you purify music of its reference to life, and remake it as an intellectual exercise. And you can fortify this exercise with theories and commentaries and systems and rules; but it will never achieve the authority of art. Instead it will be an authoritarian mask, behind which lies a frozen or an anxious sensibility.

It is in these terms that we should understand the achievement of Janáček. His venture towards the folk culture of Moravia was not merely a repudiation of metropolitan Vienna. It was an attempt to discover the elements from which a true modern music could be made — a music that would appeal to the modern ear directly, using devices that touch what is most spontaneous and immediate in our understanding of musical form. Janáček's interest in speech melodies, *nápěvky*, derived from the view that the true units of musical meaning exist at the micro-level: the whole state of the organism, as he put it, and every phase of spiritual activity may be revealed in speech-melodies. (See Bohumír Štědroň, *Janáček ve vzpomínkách a dopísech*, p.138.) If we need to revitalize tonality, then we should look for those points where life and melody coincide. It is here, in speech melody, that musical discovery and musical invention must begin.

Moreover, the elements of musical order still retain their appeal. Even in the accelerated conditions of modern life — and especially in those conditions — people understand repetition;

they understand the rhythmical figure; they respond to the pure intervals of fifth and fourth; their attention can be captured by strophic melodies and dance rhythms. To use these as your raw materials is not to cheapen music, but to begin from the point where music makes contact with life. Of course, there is always a risk of banality; but one reason for returning to the old folk culture is that it shows these devices in their pure and uncorrupted form, before they have 'become banal' through losing their real-life context. It was this pure material that was reworked by Janáček, and which set limits to his style without, however, cramping it. He wrote in such a way that, even in the midst of the most angular phrases and dissonant harmony, he could regain at a step the lilt of folk melody and the clarity of a tonal chord. And by organising his music dramatically, with the strophic song as his model, he prepared himself for the great change which came over the audience in the twentieth century — the change from a culture of cool, objective listening, to one of audio-visual involvement. The *Diary* showed clearly that Janáček was moving in time to his potential audience, by presenting a song-cycle which can also be staged, with off-stage effects and an opportunity for theatrical lighting.

The gains, for Janáček, were not merely aesthetic. At the same time as capturing a new kind of audience, he was able to communicate a moral vision. In contrast to the despair and emptiness expressed by Schoenberg's *Erwartung*, for example, the operas of Janáček are vindications of human life. His characters — his women especially — are real, lovable and the objects of the most compelling sympathy. This sympathy animates the music, and forms a kind of halo around the characters as they move on the stage. Even a tragic fate like Kat'a's seems to confirm the value and worthwhileness of the life that leads to it. For it provides Kat'a with the opportunity to capture our hearts, and to show us that she is what she ought to be, and suffers through no fault of her own.

It is worth saying something here about the moral vision conveyed in Janáček's works. There are those who find, in the instrumental music as much as the operas, a message of rebellion

— a desire to cast off the strictures of an oppressive religious morality, to live freely and to love by impulse. They see those frightening stepmother figures — the Kostelnička and Kabanicha — as embodiments of a sclerotic moral order, against which the young heart makes its futile bid for freedom. And they connect all this with the composer's passion of Kamila Stösslová, and the unhappiness of his marriage to a conventional church-going bourgeoise. Did he not say, in response to the critic who welcomed the *Glagolitic Mass* as an affirmation of Christian faith, that he was no believer?

And yet the ear tells quite another story. We meet Kat'a first in intimate conversation with Varvara, telling the girl about her life before marriage, and how the church was the most important part of it: 'Já k smrti ráda chodila do kostela' — leading at once to the tenderest of music (Ex. 10), in which you hear the character-forming force of Kat'a's piety.

Ex. 10. *Kat'a Kabanová*

All that precedes this passage, incidentally, is a supreme vindication of Janáček's account of *nápěvky*. Kat'a's whole organism, and all the phases of her spiritual life, are contained in the little bursts of ingenuous melody that she breathes above the orchestra. The music tells us that Kat'a's religion has been an education of the emotions, a preparation for the very passion that would have fulfilled her, had life been kind, but which will in the event destroy her. Moreover, the only explanation that Boris gives of his love for Kat'a, when confiding in Kudrjáš, shows that he too sees Kat'a's piety as the centre of her being and the source of her irresistible appeal: 'if only you could see her at her prayers, what an angelic smile plays on her cheeks, and the light which shines from them!' And again we hear what is being said far more clearly in the music than in the words. Boris has been lifted out of the ordinariness of his being by this encounter with the spark of God in Kat'a. (It was Janáček who said of *From the House of the Dead*, that it endeavours to show the 'spark of God'even in the lowest of human life.)

To put the point directly: Janáček was aware that a folk-culture cannot exist without religion, that religion is not so much a set of doctrines as a habit of piety, and that its meaning lies in the practices which instal it in human hearts. If we must go to folk-culture for our paradigms of passion, then we must acknowledge that passion is here dependent upon its religious context. This truth is brought home in another way by *The Makropulos Case*. Emilia Marty's longevity has deprived her of passion because all piety has died in her: by playing at God she has lost Him. Alone of the characters on stage, she is without the spark of God — although she miraculously regains it as she dies.

Janáček's invocation of the Marian processional at Frýdek in *On an Overgrown Path* shows how deeply, for him, were the ideas of beauty and piety intertwined. The dramas of Jenůfa, Kat'a and the young man who disappeared involve characters formed by faith and prepared for passion by their religious routine. One by one the characters in the Tsarist gulag reveal the spark of God that lives in them, and which was planted there in some forgotten child-

hood. The masterly libretto that Janáček wrote for this opera owes
its success precisely to the religious impulse which it allows constantly to shine through the music and cancel the sense of failure.

I mention this because it brings to the fore the underlying
honesty and realism of Janáček's vision. He did not sentimentalize
the folk culture whose melodies and rhythms he drew upon, but
saw it as a whole — a complete form of life, in which the
consolations of community were obtainable only because the
discipline of religion had been internalized by those admitted to
membership. Consolation has a social cost, and it is a heavy one.
The discipline of religion may be a source of innocent joy; but it
also confronts the individual who is tempted from its path with
tragedy. To put it another way: religion in Janáček is not abstract,
theological or universal. It is local, immediate, the voice of the
very community that is being invoked by the music. Its meaning is
given, not by doctrine, but by the lives that are led under its
tutelage — lives that may be tragic as well as fulfilled, and where
the tragedy and the fulfilment derive from a common source.

Once again the contrast is with Schoenberg, in whose works
religion plays a large and imposing role, but for whom faith was a
matter of abstract and universal doctrine, addressed to a wandering
people, a crowd without place or time. The failure of Schoenberg's
Moses to communicate this theological faith to a people bent on
idolatry parallels the failure of Schoenberg's abstract serialism to
win an audience. Neither Moses nor Schoenberg is able to win
through to the human heart — the heart that exists in the here and
now, and which is fulfilled not by abstract laws or a universal
culture, but by the concrete customs and rituals of a community
rooted in a place and a time.

The sceptic will say that, even if Schoenberg has no authority
for us now, the same must be true of Janáček. For the community
that he invokes in his music has long since vanished from the
world. Folk-music is a thing of the past, and pop, our modern
vernacular, is either antinomian or sentimental, and in neither case
able to supply the soundworld of innocence that Janáček found in
his native Moravia. In a world where the sexual revolution has

made all options easy and affordable, the very possibility of a drama like Kat'a's is ruled out. In such a world alienation is the fundamental fact, and whatever we think of Janáček's music, it is a supremely unalienated music: a music of acceptance, at every point affirming that life is worthwhile. The appeal of the modernist avant-garde lies surely in the fact that it does not presuppose the spontaneous social order to which Janáček constantly returns us; it is not addressed to a community, but to the individual, who experiences through the music the alienation that reigns in his heart. For such an individual, it is Schoenberg and not Janáček who must be his guide. Hence, in so far as we notice a genuine modernist audience emerging in our conditions, it is an audience of sceptical individualists, urban, unattached, and without any real religious convictions.

Such a sceptical rejoinder is, however, too quick. The community invoked in Janáček's music no longer existed at the time when he wrote. And it had always been, in part, an 'imagined community', brought alive by its own story-telling, and dependent not only on large-scale subsidy from Vienna, but also on an element of literary make-believe. The national revival in the Czech lands was in part a work of the imagination. The Czechs were learning to live by an idea of themselves, and of their country. From the beginning music had played a vital part in this project. Janáček's music, like Dvořák's, was not derived from the community portrayed in it: it was an attempt to create that community as a musical idea. And that, in part, is why it is so inspiring, and why it still has such authority for modern people. They hear in this music the working out of an ideal — not a metaphysical or mythical ideal, but an ideal of human community. Janáček's authoritative gestures are really gestures of sympathy, towards situations which are idealized by the very act of sympathising. In this way Janáček constantly reminds us of our human potential: we too, while the music works on us, rise above our self-involvement, and reach outwards to others, idealizing them in our surge of fellow-feeling.

And here lies the significance of the devices on which Janáček draws: repetition, rhythmic figures, folk melodies, *nápěvky mluvy* and altered diatonic harmonies. All of these are addressed directly to the ear: they are anti-theoretical, even populist in their meaning. Even if it is only a few musically educated people who appreciate this music, the image it creates is of an inclusive community, united by a common culture and a common moral code.

Whether you can write music in this way now is, of course, a controversial question. But I shall conclude with a few observations. First, art is an act of communication, which makes no sense without a real or imagined audience. And in imagining the audience, you are imagining the community which idealizes them and to which they aspire. In a world of short attention-spans and information overload, this audience cannot be captured by Schoenberg's method. It is still questionable whether the avant-garde can obtain a real audience; too often those present in the concert hall seem like a pseudo-audience, or at any rate an audience of pseuds. The true goal, by contrast, is to win the audience over, to entice them to join you in the imaginative project.

Secondly, we must respect the devices that Janáček made such vivid use of: repetition, dance rhythm, diatonic phrases and tonal harmonies. For us these are the perennial symbols of community, and without them we succeed in expressing only solipsistic emotions. If we venture towards dissonance, then we should follow the examples of Janáček, Bartók and Stravinsky: we should contrast the dissonant chord with the chord that wholly or partially resolves it. Schoenberg wanted us to reject that contrast. He hoped for 'the emancipation of the dissonance' in which no chord would be heard as intrinsically more harmonious than any other. But by emancipating dissonance you also lose it. There are dissonances in Strauss and Mahler that are far more excruciating than anything in Schoenberg, precisely because they are departures from the tonal path. The point of dissonance is that it brings tonality to life; and Janáček's way of doing this was exemplary.

Finally melody and the melodic phrase. Music without melody is in danger of being a mere sound effect — maybe an interesting sound effect, but nevertheless an effect which is one of sound and not of music. Composers today need to rediscover the art of creating melodies, for these are the true musical protagonists, the actors on the stage of music, whose life-stories are told by the notes. And again Janáček sets an irreproachable example. His melodies, taken from the rhythm of human speech, and at the same time imbued with a tradition of song and dance, were entirely unsentimental — images of sincere human utterance, as though compelled from the heart rather than put together from a repertoire of formulae. That such melodies were within the reach of composers even in the most recent past is clear from Britten, Messiaen and Tippett. Are we to assume that the store of them is finite, and that we have now scraped the barrel clean? Surely not.

Those are only suggestions, and I do not doubt that the problems posed by the attempt to follow Janáček's example are at least as great as the problems posed by the attempt to follow Schoenberg. However, I cannot help feeling that the most important thing for all of us is to decide between the two models that those composers put before us, and to be properly sceptical towards the dogma that tells us to throw away tonality and to defy the musical ear. For this dogma is rooted in the theory of music rather than the sound of music, and is addressed to the task of justifying avant-garde music in the way that Mark Twain jokingly justified the music of Wagner, by arguing that it was better than it sounds.

BIBLIOGRAPHY:

Beckerman, Michael *Janáček as Theorist*, Stuyvesant, New York, 1994.

Holloway, Robin 'Expressive sources and resources in Janáček's musical language,' in Wingfield, Paul ed., *Janáček Studies*, Cambridge, 1999.

Janáček, Leos *Úplná nauka o harmonii*, in *Hudebné teoretické dílo*, ed. Zdeněk Blazek, Prague, 1974, vol. 2. This volume also contains the important text, '*Můj názor o sčasování*', in which the composer gives his theory of rhythm as a multilayered structure.

Schoenberg, Arnold *Harmonielehre*, 3rd Edn., Vienna, 1922.

Tyrrell, John 'Janáček'in the New Grove Dictionary of Music.

Štědroň, Bohumír *Janáček ve vzpomínkách a dopisech*, Prague, 1946.

Trkanová, Marie *U Janáčku*, Prague, 1959.

2

Schopenhauer and Music: a musician's approach

Menno Boogaard

'The Wild Years of Philosophy' is the title of a book about the philosopher, Arthur Schopenhauer, written by the German writer Rüdiger Safranski. It is a surprising title, for 'wild' is not the word that first comes to mind when we mention the names Hegel, Fichte, Schelling and Schopenhauer; the philosophers of the so-called transcendental idealistic movement. But Safranski did not choose this title merely because it would be a good way to make philosophy interesting for the MTV-generation. The ideas of these men thoroughly turned over the ground of philosophy.

Those 'wild years of philosophy' were also golden years of music. Schopenhauer, for instance, lived from 1788, three years before the death of Mozart, to 1860, when Wagner had already completed *Tristan und Isolde.* The stylistic developments, as well as the sheer quality and quantity of the musical masterworks produced in this era defy the imagination. Also, the stature, which music had come to occupy in the general culture of the period, was quite unprecedented. Beethoven's confession to Bettina Brentano, that 'music is a greater revelation than the whole of wisdom and philosophy', gives us a clear impression of the transformation.

Music as revelation, the composer as sage; that was a long way from music being the serf of secular and ecclesiastical powers, as it still was in Haydn and Mozart's day.

Despite this tremendous upsurge in creativity in both music and philosophy, and despite Beethoven's claim, their worlds remained quite separate. Kant considered music to be the lowest art-form, 'playing merely with sensations', and Beethoven, although he was prone to ruminate extensively about intellectual matters, probably had no clear grasp of Kant. Among philosophers, however, there is one exception to this mutual ignorance; Arthur Schopenhauer did not merely take a great interest in music, but also considered it the highest art-form. For him, music was clearly in the same league as philosophy. 'Music is an unconscious exercise in metaphysics in which the mind doesn't know it is philosophising,' to quote his famous paraphrase of Leibniz. He even made a claim similar to Beethoven:

> If it would be possible to succeed in giving a perfectly accurate and complete explanation of music, which goes into detail, and thus a detailed articulation in concepts of what music expresses, this would be at the same time an adequate articulation and explanation of the world, and hence the true philosophy.
>
> (*The World as Will and Representation, vol. 1,* p.264)

From this, it can be easily imagined that any practising musician interested in philosophy (and the writer of the present article is one) is bound to be drawn to the work of Schopenhauer.

German transcendental idealism took its cue from Kant. It was a highly diverse movement, and the thoughts of Fichte, Hegel and Schopenhauer show such enormous differences that they (especially Schopenhauer) would certainly not have approved of my mentioning them in one sentence. It is not the aim of this article, nor the specialism of its author to provide a clear exposition of all these ideas, so I will limit myself to describing the element of interpretation of Kant's work, which was taken up and developed by Schopenhauer.

This idea can be presented as follows: the world which we perceive, cannot exist independently from the forms or laws of our understanding. Schopenhauer states it emphatically in the first sentence of his main opus, '*Die Welt ist meine Vorstellung*'; the world is my representation. This is Schopenhauer's version of what he considered to be the main insight of Kant. Anyone who only reads this first sentence might feel that some kind of rationalistic solipsism is being articulated. But then Schopenhauer continues: the inner resistance we feel, when we hear such a claim, leads us to suppose that the world must be something more than just that. It must also be something 'in itself', as distinguished from what it is for us or how it appears to us. In Kantian terms, there must also be a 'noumenal' or metaphysical side to reality, apart from its phenomenal, representational side. This metaphysical aspect of the world Schopenhauer identifies as 'will'. This may be the most concise and even simplistic explanation of Schopenhauer one can possibly give, but it is also comprehensive. One can say that the whole of Schopenhauer's philosophy resembles one gigantic set of variations on this theme, which is also the title of his great work of 1818, *Die Welt als Wille und Vorstellung — The World as Will and Representation*.

Let me expand upon the elements that make up this basic theme. When one says: the world is will, it begs the question: whose will? Schopenhauer seems to say, it is nobody's or, if it is anybody's, we cannot possibly know to whom or what it belongs. For Schopenhauer the will is a blind, indiscriminate, eternal (or timeless) and undivided force. It is the underlying, essential nature, the 'in-itself' of every phenomenon, from inorganic matter up to and including human existence. At the most fundamental level, everything in the world is essentially the same thing, that is 'will'. It is important to note that a human being's own 'willing' is not identical with the world-will, but is one of its many phenomena. (The confusion that can arise from the neglect of this last point can be illustrated by what Roberto Benigni says to his son to give him courage in the movie, *La vita è bella*: 'Schopenhauer...willpower!') However, Schopenhauer considers our experience of our own willing to be the most immediate experience of the world 'in-itself' that we can have; which is also why he identifies this as 'will'in the first place.

Then there is the other element of Schopenhauer's basic theme: *Vorstellung* or representation. What creates for us the world as representation are the laws of our understanding. For Schopenhauer these are: time, space and causality. These are not phenomena we observe in the outer world, but they are the tools with which we observe it. Time, space and causality make up the 'principle of individuation', or to use Schopenhauer's favourite term for it, the 'veil of Maya', a term borrowed from Hindu philosophy. This principle lets us experience the world of phenomena or presents to us, differentiated into phenomena, what is in its essence un-differentiated: namely the 'will'.

A crucial element of Schopenhauer's philosophy is implied in how he sees or values the will and all the suffering, for which it is responsible. It is, of course, his notorious pessimism. Schopenhauer did not regard *la condition humaine* as something to rejoice in, to say the least. In another paraphrase of Leibniz, he even proposes that we could be living in 'the worst of all possible worlds'. The eloquence with which Schopenhauer expresses his pessimism borders on the provocative:

> ...were the evil of the world even a hundred times less than it is, its mere existence would still be sufficient to establish a truth,...namely that we have not to be pleased but rather sorry about the existence of the world; that its non-existence would be preferable to its existence; that it is something, which at bottom ought not to be;
>
> (*WWR I* p.576)

Many of Schopenhauer's ideas, especially about aesthetics and ethics, derive from this bleak and despairing world-view, but it is my personal conviction that many of his greatest insights do not arise from this pessimism.

As I said before, what Schopenhauer says about music can

hardly fail to attract a musician with philosophical interests. His belief that music is somehow 'true philosophy' is already enough to achieve that. If musicians without these inclinations would also read Schopenhauer (if only!), they would find themselves flattered: '...such a great and exceedingly delightful art...the most powerful of all the arts...this wonderful art...'. He even calls music, '...a cure for all our suffering...' and '...a paradise so familiar and yet eternally remote...'. Schopenhauer's account of music is surely the most positive review any musician or composer is ever likely to receive.

But what precisely *is* music's special status for Schopenhauer? The answer is as short as it is far-reaching. Music expresses in the most direct way the 'will' itself, the essence of the world and of ourselves. In Schopenhauer's own words:

> Music expresses, in an exceedingly universal language, in a homogeneous material, that is to say, in nothing but tones, and with the greatest distinctness and truth, the inner being, the in-itself, of the world.
>
> (*WWR I* p.264)

This sounds wonderful, but it may need some explanation. In Schopenhauer's aesthetic, music is the only art that is in no way concerned with the expression of what he calls the 'Ideas'. These 'Ideas' could be denoted as being the eternal entities that underlie the world of appearances. As is well known, this concept derives from Plato. Schopenhauer calls these 'Ideas' 'the first objectification of the will'. All the arts, except music, from architecture to drama, in one way or another express these 'Ideas', and therefore do not express the will 'immediately'. Music, not being concerned with the world of appearances, is the one art that directly speaks of the reality behind these 'Ideas'. It bypasses them, so to speak. In Schopenhauer's words:

> ...music is therefore not, as the other arts do, representing the ideas, but is an image of the will itself...: therefore the effect

of music is so much more powerful and penetrating than the other arts; for these others only speak of the shadow, but music of the essence.

(*WWR I* p.257)

That is, then, how music is, 'completely and profoundly understood by man in his innermost being as an entirely universal language, whose distinctness surpasses even that of the world of perception itself'. This insight, i.e. that music combines the greatest generality of import with the utmost clarity of expression, is also stated in the following:

...[music] does not express this or that particular and definite pleasure, this or that affliction, pain, sorrow, horror, gaiety, merriment, or peace of mind, but joy, pain, sorrow, horror, merriment, peace of mind as such, to a certain extent in the abstract, yet their essential nature, without any accessories, and so also without the motives for them. Yet we understand it, in this quintessence, completely.

(*WWR I* p.261)

It is important to note that such a passage also shows us that for Schopenhauer music expresses the will as it is experienced by the human individual, and not as some abstract concept behind or transcending reality. He is very articulate in saying that music expresses human feeling, as opposed to abstract concepts:

...melody relates the story of the intellectually enlightened will...[it]...says more; it relates the most secret history of the intellectually enlightened will, portrays every agitation, every effort, every movement of the will, everything which the faculty of reason summarises under the wide and negative concept of 'feeling', and which cannot further be taken up into the abstractions of reason.

(*WWR I* p.259)

Schopenhauer, therefore, considers music to be inherently opposed to abstraction; a consideration worth bearing in mind, when we come to discuss twentieth-century music.

It may be appropriate to mention that Schopenhauer's chapters about music, more than anything in his work, have more or less the character of a meditation and not an irrefutable line of argument. The idea of a direct relationship between music and the will, or even music's identifying with the will is, he says, unproven, but it is an opinion that 'is wholly satisfying for myself and for my philosophy, but may be equally enlightening for those, who will have followed me thus far and agreed with my view of the world.'

As a matter of fact, a question might have been raised by the same reader, whom Schopenhauer here addresses so confidently. It is a frequent question in the mind of many readers, and it is sometimes referred to as the 'Schopenhauer-paradox'. Even someone who has read nothing about Schopenhauer, but this short introduction, might ask himself: how is it possible that Schopenhauer, who calls this world 'the worst of all possible worlds', at the same time *celebrates* the very art that immediately expresses the innermost essence of that world. In his *The Philosophy of Schopenhauer*, Bryan Magee writes: '...as it is, his theory is so starkly self-contradictory that one is at a loss to understand how he could have failed to notice'. Magee also believes that any reconciliation of these conflicting arguments can only be found in repudiating either Schopenhauer's claim that the world is 'the worst of all possible worlds', or the one that states that music is the most wonderful and elevating of all art-forms. What Magee writes may well be the case, however, Schopenhauer's philosophy has a built-in defence against such a conclusion, in what Schopenhauer calls the 'pure subject of knowing'. This concept plays a vital role (if 'vital'is the right word in this context) in both Schopenhauer's aesthetic theories and his ethics.

For Schopenhauer, the basic, original function of the human intellect is as a tool for the preservation of the individual; a mechanism for survival. This idea arises naturally from his philosophy of the 'will'. That we ourselves are, in our fundamental essence, 'will', implies that our intellect does not produce willing, but serves our organism, which *is* will, in its one aim: to be. It is possible, however, Schopenhauer contends, for the human intellect to transcend its immediate purpose. In that case, the intellect can function to make the individual know things as they really are and not just see them as they exist to serve or frustrate his urge to survive. There are instances in which the understanding can detach itself, as it were, from its original, 'will-directed'function. In those instances, it can become a 'pure subject of knowing', a means for true insight into the real nature of things, i.e. the underlying unity beneath the world of appearances; an insight unhampered by and detached from the will's needs. In such an instance, the 'veil of Maya' is lifted, and we transcend the 'principle of individuation'. We recognise that what we observe is, in its essential nature, the same thing as we ourselves. In extraordinary instances, moreover, which means in those cases where the human intellect is unusually highly developed, this ability to see things totally objectively can achieve a marked predominance. The artist or philosopher of 'genius'(Schopenhauer always writes from his own experience) is thus able to recognise and to communicate in his works, the timelessness and generality of those things which, in everyday life, we mostly see only in their particular will — and individual-bound appearance.

In principle, however, this ability to look at things totally objectively is, to a lesser or greater extent, present in most people. The contemplation of art is, for Schopenhauer, something in which we can use that ability and, thereby, transcend our individuality. Observing or creating a work of art is not something we do to further our own interests or serve our egoism (or, at least, it is not meant to be that). Its aim is exactly the opposite: this contemplation is something that can free us from our own willing, and thereby from our suffering, because it makes us look at things totally disinterestedly and objectively. We become 'subjects of pure, will-less knowing'.

It is not difficult to see how such a line of thought serves the pessimist, as it leads him to consider art the one thing that is truly consoling in a disconsolate world. The idea of will-less contemplation in art is inseparably bound up with Schopenhauer's pessimism, because for him, in an important sense, this contemplation serves as a temporary escape from life. Here also the link can be felt between Schopenhauer's aesthetics and his ethics, between the artist and the saint. Although this is not the place to explore Schopenhauer's ethical theories in the depth that would do them justice, it has to be said that there is an unmistakable tendency in his aesthetics to regard the contemplation of art as a kind of 'preparation' for what is achieved by the saint, namely the 'renunciation of the will' through the total abnegation of everything that binds us to the world. This may be best understood from the following quotation:

> That pure, true and profound knowledge of the inner nature of the world now becomes for him [the artist] an end in itself; at it he stops. Therefore it does not become for him a quieter of the will, as...in the case of the Saint, who has attained resignation; it does not deliver him from life for ever, but only for a few moments. For him it is not the way out of life, but only an occasional consolation in it, until his power, enhanced by this contemplation, finally becomes tired of the spectacle and seizes the serious side of things.
>
> (*WWR I* p.267)

In the view of art that is implied here, the consolation and, in a sense, also the beauty of art do not seem to lie *per se* in what art expresses, but in the act of contemplation itself. Schopenhauer writes, 'Everything is beautiful only so long as it doesn't concern us. Life is *never* beautiful, but only the pictures of it, namely in the transfiguring mirror of art'. If we look back now at our paradox regarding Schopenhauer's statements about music, this may help us to understand how his total and exclusive focus on 'pure contemplation' in artistic experience, including musical experience, could be thought to resolve the contradiction. Although music directly expresses the will, the cause of all suffering, music is also the means for the detached contemplation of the will, and thereby, somehow, manages to make beautiful in contemplation what is painful in actual experience. And yet, we have to ask ourselves, can such a line of thought be altogether convincing, if compared to our actual experience of music?

The role that is played by the 'pure subject of knowing' or 'understanding' in artistic experience is most explicitly expressed by Schopenhauer, where he deals with the arts that, according to him, express the Platonic Ideas, that is all the arts except music. Bryan Magee suggests that Schopenhauer develops two aesthetics: one for music and one for the rest of the arts. However, there is at least one thing that strongly unites these two aesthetics, if there are indeed two. It cannot be denied that even in the case of music, Schopenhauer maintains his stress on 'will-less contemplation'. This is most apparent in his later work, where, in a way that once again reminds us of Plato, he actually seems to advocate a certain sobriety in music:

> Therefore the affections of the will itself, and hence actual pain and actual pleasure, must not be excited [by music], but only their substitutes, that is in conformity with the intellect as a picture or image of the will's satisfaction, and that which more or less opposes it as a picture or image of greater or lesser pain. Only in this way does music never cause us actual suffering, but still remains pleasant even in its most painful chords, and we like to hear in its language the secret history of our will,...even in the most painful melodies.
>
> (*WWR II* p.451)

This concludes a passage in which Schopenhauer argues that, although music deals with human emotions, it can and must do that in a way that speaks foremost to the 'pure subject of understanding'. This is made possible by the fact that the 'images' of human emotion, experienced in music as consonance and dissonance, can also be perceived as the relationships between tones, and thus the emotional content is objectified.

One cannot avoid the impression that Schopenhauer by putting so much stress on the role of the purely intellectual understanding of music, tries to adapt his musical theory to his whole system of aesthetics and ethics, with its stress on contemplation and denial of the will. This leads to a forced result. He produces a verdict about what music *should not* do: one of the rare instances in which Schopenhauer speaks *ex cathedra*. It is one of those passages, where the wish of the pessimist seems to be the father of the thought. If one wants to claim, as Schopenhauer does, that music 'must not affect the will', one is compelled to neglect some of the basic attributes of musical experience. Schopenhauer even acknowledges this, and in the very same chapter from which the last quotation stems, he writes:

> Because music does not, like all the other arts, exhibit the ideas or grades of the will's objectification, but directly the will itself, we can also explain that it acts directly on the will, i.e., the feelings, passions, and emotions of the hearer, so that it quickly raises these or even alters them.
>
> (*WWR II* p.448)

If we compare this to the remark I quoted earlier, we cannot help concluding that Schopenhauer has put himself in a fix. He admits that music simply cannot avoid doing something that according to him it 'should not' do. The need for passivity and emotional neutrality, which Schopenhauer proclaims with regard to perceiving art, clashes headlong with the very nature of music itself. Approaching music in such an intellectual way, objectifying it, so that it transcends its direct emotional appeal, means ignoring what may be its most defining characteristic: its ability to affect our will.

Furthermore, there are a number of factors related to this direct impact of music, that are thus swept under the carpet. First of all, there is the role of the performing musician. It needs no explanation that, for the musician, total passivity with regard to

music is an impossibility. Making music is an act of will. That is
true, of course, for all art-production, but for music it applies in a
much more fundamental way. Movements of the will are the very
stuff from which music is made, as Schopenhauer himself states.
For the musician, who has to communicate these movements of the
will, emotional involvement is an absolute necessity. The process
of playing an instrument or singing is, in a very deep sense, also a
process of willing. This unavoidable element of involvement in
musical performance would therefore, if we adhere to
Schopenhauer's point of view, necessarily leave the player with a
perception of music which is further removed from its inner truth
than that of the 'purely contemplating'listener; a conclusion which
is difficult to accept. A musician, who tries to remain detached
from his emotions, may communicate a kind of Schopenhauerian
'pure understanding', but in performance that is bound to result in
bloodlessness and boredom. The musician does not project an
image or concept of emotion to the mind of the listener, but communicates emotion directly as an experience. In attending a
concert, we achieve a congruence of feeling with the players and
the rest of the audience, far more than we transcend our
individuality by becoming 'pure subjects of knowing'.

In our own day, we have an excellent opportunity to become
aware of that, because we can compare the impact of a 'live' performance to that of a recording. I doubt anyone would contradict
me, if I claimed that attending a performance, compared to listening to a recording, is a considerably more involving experience.
Schopenhauer himself was not in the position to compare these
two ways of listening, but sometimes he leads us to suspect that he
might have owned the first hi-fi stereo-system. In any case, he
gives the impression of someone who would prefer to listen to
music in detached isolation.

The indefinable sense of something extra, of a direct
experience, which we have when we attend a concert, compared to
listening to a recording, is strongly related to another aspect of
musical performance that Schopenhauer seems to ignore: the
element of ritual. (To avoid misunderstanding, I use this word in its

broadest sense, which means implying the social as well as the religious). In this case, Schopenhauer's aloofness comes as no surprise, since ritual usually implies a gathering of people, something this great misanthrope among philosophers abhorred. He regarded the social gathering as arising from the wish of the average man to escape his own mediocrity by seeking out the company of other mediocrities. The fact that, at a concert, he was compelled to be in the company of others, must have diminished rather than enhanced his enjoyment of music. Therefore I presume that, although he was an anglophile through and through, he would have been ill at ease with, for instance, a *Proms* concert. The Last Night would have been too much for him, of that we can be certain.

Schopenhauer gives short shrift to all those forms of music which are, in one way or another, meant for an occasion, or non-musical purpose. This covers quite a lot of ground; he mentions church-music, opera and dance-music. In the case of church-music, the reason for his reserve is not hard to find. Being one of the first self-confessed atheists among modern philosophers, and being especially impatient with organised religion, his neglect is understandable. Yet the religious ritual has been a factor in the production of some of history's greatest music, and ignoring this function gives us, at the very least, an incomplete picture of music. In the case of dance-music, Schopenhauer makes himself very clear. Someone who states that, '...every bodily sensation is in itself excitement of the will' and that '...the affections of the will itself must not be excited by music...' does not consider dance-music worthy of much serious thought. What should not be forgotten, however, is that most of the music Schopenhauer himself revered (Mozart and Rossini were his favourites) had strong historical roots in dance-music.

In all these instances, according to Schopenhauer, the real 'aesthetical effect' of music, and therefore, of course, the objective perception of music by the 'pure subject of understanding', is violated, when music is forced into the straitjacket of an external purpose, something that is more or less alien to its true nature; a purpose therefore, that essentially discourages detachment, or 'will-lessness'. The only place where music can move absolutely freely, he writes, is in the concerto, the sonata, and especially the symphony. It can be assumed therefore, that Schopenhauer would certainly not have applauded the development of symphonic music in the romantic era, in which the sense of social or religious occasion became an ever more important element in the performance of great works; a development which started with Beethoven's Ninth Symphony and reached its culmination in works like Berlioz's *Roméo et Juliette* or Mahler's Eighth Symphony. Be that as it may, the element of ritual, especially in opera and church-music, but also in regular concert-life, is not something that diminishes the effect of the music, but something that greatly enhances it and is an integral part of it. To ignore this element of 'occasion' in music, as Schopenhauer does, somehow throws out the baby with the bath-water.

All this shows the asceticism with which Schopenhauer wishes us to contemplate music has an uneasy relationship with the emotional directness, which is its primary characteristic. Schopenhauer himself acknowledges music's power to impinge directly on our will, our own emotional life. Our involvement with it is something we cannot avoid. Music has an inescapable immediacy, which is why complete emotional detachment from it is not a matter of simple choice for us.

Of course, the kind of music we listen to is an important factor in this. The fact that Schopenhauer vigorously maintained his preference for the music of Rossini and Mozart, also in his later life — the age of Berlioz and early Wagner — betrays that these composers somehow gave him a chance to listen to music in the way he preferred: remaining at a safe distance from any violent musical emotion and maintaining the possibility of an objective, emotionally uninvolved response; one that left his treasured 'pure subject of knowing' with all its rights untouched. Although that seems somewhat hard to believe, considering the irresistible nature of so many of Rossini and Mozart's works.

But this defender of will-less contemplation was, as we look at the further development of the musical language in the nineteenth century, in for a hard time. Music's power to impinge on our will and its ability to affect or even alter our feelings, became ever stronger in the music of the composers of the romantic school. In the works of one of this movement's strongest exponents, Richard Wagner, this tendency reached an impressive climax, which remains unsurpassed to this day. One of the most defining characteristics of Wagner's music-dramas, something that any musical person who has attended them will acknowledge, is that it leaves its spectators with very little opportunity for will-less contemplation. Those who defend the view, as Schopenhauer did, that music should not become too much of a real emotional experience, do not feel at home in the *Festspielhaus* at Bayreuth, and those who are sceptical about the ritual aspect of music feel equally alienated in the Wagnerian milieu.

The range of human feeling heard in the music of Wagner and his followers was inconceivable throughout most of Schopenhauer's life. Music became capable of expressing some of the strongest human emotions with great nuance and psychological accuracy, especially those associated with sexuality and spirituality. It also became possible to evoke with added power the darker side of human nature; such as neurotic anxiety and barbaric cruelty. This kind of music did not portray these feelings in a way that would leave an audience in a state of 'detachment'. Some places in Wagner and Mahler could even be described as consisting of musical 'shock-effects' — and it is likely that the near-hysteria of Act III of *Tristan und Isolde* or the devastating hammer blows of Mahler's Sixth Symphony would not have received Schopenhauer's approval.

As is well known, Wagner's reading of Schopenhauer was one of the most important factors in the genesis of *Tristan*. We can safely assume that Schopenhauer's doctrine of will-lessness in artistic contemplation did not much interest Wagner, judging from what kind of work *Tristan* eventually became. Wagner's awareness of the overpowering effect of his music is well documented. He wrote to Mathilde Wesendonck:

This Tristan is turning into something frightful! — nothing
but mediocre performances can save me. Completely good
ones are bound to drive people crazy — I cannot imagine
what else would happen...

It may be worth following the course of music-history a little
further, while keeping Schopenhauer in the back of our minds. In
the first half of the twentieth century, the vehement emotions that
music had become able to express in the work of Wagner, became,
in late Mahler and early Schoenberg, such a predominant aspect of
music, that it acquired the label 'expressionist'. In a work like
Schoenberg's *Erwartung*, we are confronted with a dramatic
extrapolation of Tristanesque despair, which makes the music
assume an unrelenting sense of pure horror: no detachment here, to
be sure. But then we come to those developments that have put
their indelible mark on music in the rest of the twentieth century:
the advent of twelve-tone technique in Schoenberg and his pupils,
which later found its continuation in the integral serialism of
Boulez and Stockhausen. The overheated and neurotic atmosphere
of expressionism had, even in the same composers that developed
it, provoked a drastic reaction: a type of music in which human
emotion was denied direct expression, and in which the guiding
principles were exclusively intellectual and quasi-mathematical.
The rules of logic were preferred to the laws of the human heart.

If we observe the phenomenon of twentieth-century modernist
music in the light of Schopenhauer's aesthetics, we are almost
tempted to conclude that here the concept of the 'pure subject of
knowing' has found unprecedented illustration. Whereas in
Schopenhauer the transcendence of the subjective self into a state
of pure objectivity was achieved through an ideal state of detached
artistic contemplation, in much of the music of the twentieth
century, this same rationalistic attempt at transcendence invaded
the realm of artistic production itself. If such music expresses anything, individual human experience is certainly not included. The
best example, in this context, is Anton Webern, for in his later
music, we encounter total will-less objectivity; a complete ban on

the expression of human emotion. This is music that attempts to find a way to free itself from 'all-too human' limitations by taking the escape-route of the intellect. This has a remarkable parallel with Schopenhauer's ideas about the 'pure subject of understanding.' Webern is indeed known to have been influenced by German idealist aesthetics, and arguably the theory that total disinterestedness and objectivity can make us 'know' the 'thing-in-itself', is central to what this music tries to evoke. Of the composers of the second Viennese school, Webern was the key model for later developments in serialism, and we can conclude that idealist aesthetics influenced music far into the twentieth century.

This parallel between Schopenhauer's aesthetics and the objectivism of the modernists goes even deeper. This element of Schopenhauer's aesthetics is inseparably bound with his pessimism. The link is so important that it deserves recapitulation. In the wider context of Schopenhauer's philosophy, the 'principle of individuation' is regarded as being, along with the inherently unquenchable 'will', the essential factor that makes this world the desperate place he considers it to be. The fact that we are individuals, at all, is something to be overcome, rather than something with which we should be content. The supreme consolation of the human being is twofold: the contemplation of art and, more drastically, the renunciation of the will. This last, drastic step is presented by Schopenhauer as the ultimate consequence of what art teaches us: the separation of our knowing from our willing, and thereby from ourselves.

The philosophical background of twentieth-century music offer us many parallels. The radical objectivism of serial music was accompanied by an equally radical pessimism or even nihilism. Music that sought to exclude human emotion had powerful allies in philosophies that provided a vehement critique of individual human existence. The fact that the twentieth century witnessed two world-wars of unprecedented devastation and human misery made it a fertile breeding-ground for the development of such philosophies. French existentialism, personified in Jean Paul Sartre, defined human individual existence as a state of total isolation, creating a sense of *néant* or nothingness, boredom and nausea. Sartre's modish musings on the human condition were later joined by theories like the 'deconstruction' of Derrida, and the anti-bourgeois nihilism of Foucault. The human 'self' is subjected to an 'historical-critical' analysis; unmasked as merely a construction of the mind to be removed from the centre of objective philosophical investigation. Although these philosophies, because they were linked with an historical trauma, were markedly more nihilistic than Schopenhauer could have imagined, it is impossible to deny that he may have contributed to the modern situation. His estimation of individual human existence indeed smacks of existentialism, and his theories about the 'pure subject of knowing' have more than a whiff of deconstruction. In his book about Wagner, Michael Tanner puts it like this:

> ...we find, then, that long before Nietzsche, Barthes, Derrida, Foucault and their innumerable progeny came along, Schopenhauer had 'decentred' the self with a vengeance.

Are we to conclude that Schopenhauer would have felt perfectly at home in the company of the philosophers Tanner mentions here? I am quite sure that we are not. If we imagine Schopenhauer making a triumphant entry into the ranks of the deconstructionists, we run the danger of overlooking a very important element of his philosophy, which is found in his treatment of self-awareness. For Schopenhauer, self-awareness is the other side of the coin of human consciousness, the first side being our, now familiar, 'pure knowing' of the intellect. This is how he himself explains it:

> I remind the reader that our consciousness has two sides; in part it is consciousness of our own selves, which is the will, and in part consciousness of other things, and as such primarily knowledge of the external world through perception, apprehension of objects. Now the more one side of the whole consciousness comes to the front, the more does the

other withdraw.

(*WWR II* p.367)

The phrase, 'our own selves, which is the will', already indicates that for Schopenhauer self-awareness is of great significance in his whole philosophy, especially regarding the central place which the concept of 'will' occupies. This significance of self-awareness, or awareness of our own will, lies in the fact that it is a phenomenon which grants us knowledge of the nature of something, namely our own being, from the inside. For Schopenhauer, this consciousness of our own will, as the true nature of our being, leads us to the apprehension of the true nature of what is around us, and therefore of the world; which is also how he comes to make the step of choosing the word 'will' to denote this true nature of the world.

What we encounter in Schopenhauer is a love-hate relationship with the phenomenon of interior knowledge or 'intimate sense'. On the one hand, he says it does not grant us 'complete'knowledge of the will as 'thing-in-itself', because this self-awareness is still very much subjective, whereas, as already observed, real insight for Schopenhauer comes with extreme objectivity. In his view, pure understanding comes with the objective intellect. Subjectivity only grants us apprehension or intuitive knowledge. But, despite these reservations, his remarks about self-awareness often sound conspicuously enthusiastic:

> In fact, our willing is the only opportunity we have of under-
> standing simultaneously from within any event that
> outwardly manifests itself; consequently, it is the one thing
> known to us immediately and not given to us merely in the
> representation, as all else is. Here, therefore, lies the datum
> alone capable of becoming the key to everything else, the
> only narrow gateway to the truth.
>
> (*WWR II* p.196)

What should be observed is that these are the words of the same philosopher, who elsewhere declares complete detachment from

ourselves as the road to salvation. It is quite peculiar that, for
Schopenhauer, the road to deliverance from the world, by way of
'pure knowing' and selfless contemplation, necessarily entails a
turning away from the very thing he calls 'the gateway to the
truth', namely the awareness of ourselves. This is a strong example
of how Schopenhauer's pessimism, which is responsible for his
whole stress on pure objectivity, damages the recognition of one of
the most important elements in his whole thinking: the value of
self-awareness and interiority.

But what has all of this to do with music, one might ask? When
Schopenhauer deals primarily with the concept of self-awareness
or interiority, he never establishes a direct connection with music
or any other art. Where he deals with them, they are mostly accompanied by reflections on the 'pure subject of knowing', because
that is very much at the centre of his whole aesthetic. This does not
mean, however, that Schopenhauer never invites us to make the
association with music in his ruminations about self-awareness. If
the self is proclaimed as being the thing that grants us the most
immediate *apprehension* of the will, that should remind us that
Schopenhauer singles out music as the one art that is the will's
most direct *expression*. Let me take, for example, a passage in
which he describes what distinguishes self-awareness from the
other phenomena in our consciousness:

> ...the inner knowledge is free from two things belonging to
> outer knowledge, the form of space and the form of causal-
> ity, which bring about all sense-perception. On the other
> hand, there still remains the form of time,...Accordingly, in
> this inner knowledge the thing-in-itself has indeed to a great
> extent cast off its veils, but still does not appear quite naked.
> In consequence of the form of time which still adheres to it,
> everyone knows his will only in its successive individual
> acts, not as a whole...Yet the apprehension in which we
> know the stirrings and acts of our own will is far more
> immediate than is any other.
>
> (*WWR II* p.197)

What distinguishes the awareness of ourselves from the aware-ness of other phenomena appears to be exactly what distinguishes music from the other arts: namely, it is expressed in the parameter of time and known in its successive acts. Because our awareness of it is purely internal (free from space and causality), music is experienced in the most immediate way. The immediacy of our sense of self therefore has a strong similarity with the immediacy with which we experience music. The special status of music, as we have seen, is its ability to express our will, our true being, most directly. The special status of self-awareness is that it grants us a similar closeness to exactly the same thing which music expresses. Schopenhauer uses a beautiful simile to illustrate this function of self-awareness:

> ...a way from within stands open for us to that real inner nature of things to which we cannot penetrate from without. It is, so to speak, a subterranean passage, a secret alliance, which places us all at once in the fortress that could not be taken from without...
>
> (*WWR II* p.195)

This also strikes me as a beautiful description of what music does. The non-conceptual communication, which music provides, offers a unique passageway, an intuition of the true identity and inner-most nature of different individuals, in a way that makes them feel the same thing at the same time. Music makes them apprehend that they *are* the same thing.

In his reflections on self-awareness, Schopenhauer does not establish an obvious connection with music in the way I propose here, but this should not make us forget that in his chapters on music, the self receives a real place of honour. Illustrating just how important Schopenhauer considers the self to be in what music expresses (as distinguished from his ideas on the objectivity with which we have to contemplate art), would entail quoting his remarks on music almost in their entirety. He gives us no hint that music could express anything which is not related to our sense of self, our 'intimate sense'. Michael Tanner, in another of his essays on Wagner, even puts it like this:

> The nature of music and the nature of the self: it was Schopenhauer's distinction to link them in a crucial way, and it is this linking which alone puts him in the first rank of philosophers.

This associating of music with the self is precisely what makes Schopenhauer's stress on pure, objective contemplation in art so problematic, when we try to translate it to his account of music. The very immediate impact which music has, and its similarity with the immediacy of self-awareness, is the reason *par exellence* that music remains a subjective art. It can only very reluctantly, if at all, adapt itself to the demands of pure objectivity: a compromise inherently against its true nature as a subjective and internal experience.

Although I have pointed out the parallel between idealist aesthetics and the music of Schoenberg, Webern and the later serialists, I would like to stress once more that this is not music which Schopenhauer would have endorsed. For him, music must always express 'everything that reason classifies under the concept of feeling':

> ...for only the passions, the movements of the will, exist for it, and, like God, it sees only the heart.
>
> (WWR II p.449)

If we try to make music seem otherwise, we are trying the impossible, because we are turning it away from itself and rendering it meaningless.

Finally, let me draw attention once more to the influence of Schopenhauer on Wagner, especially concerning the genesis of *Tristan und Isolde*. It is clear that the concept of the 'pure subject of understanding', while it influenced 'objectivist' music, had no profound influence upon Wagner. To understand what

Schopenhauer meant for Wagner, we have to consider the philosopher's ideas about our interior awareness of the will. These ideas contributed a great deal to make the music of *Tristan* achieve its powerful sense of 'inwardness'. In his essay, *Zukunftsmusik — The Music of the Future*, written not long after the completion of *Tristan*, Wagner writes:

> With complete confidence, I immersed myself, while composing Tristan, only in the depths of the soul's inner movements, and from this intimate centre of the world unhesitatingly created its outer form.

I believe that such a passage should give the lie to anyone who states that Wagner is the great precursor of musical modernism, especially considering the extent to which modernism had its background in philosophies that 'decentred' the self. The frequently held view that Wagner, in *Tristan*, prepared the way for Boulez, the champion of serialism, is as questionable as placing Schopenhauer shoulder to shoulder with Foucault. *Tristan* may even be the least abstract or objectivist music ever written. Of course, *Tristan's* modernity is, time and time again, linked with its alleged atonality, or at least the work is understood as a preparation for that phenomenon. Since atonality later became the common feature of especially the 'de-subjectified' music of the serialists, we should really ask ourselves if it is right to assess *Tristan* in such a way. The heightened state of inwardness and subjectivity Wagner achieved in *Tristan*, would not have been possible without the stable background of tonality as a point of reference; indeed, from a psychological standpoint, tonality might even be claimed to be the very precondition for the evocation of subjectivity in music. Emotional expression in music needs tonality as a point of reference, just as the human being needs a sense of 'self' to define his inner experience, and this is something Schopenhauer acknowledges, both implicitly and explicitly, in his chapters on music.

In the twentieth century, the idea that music portrays inner emotional experience was often considered old-fashioned or regressive. Nothing could be further from the truth. By being aware of our own will, we have the most immediate apprehension of what Schopenhauer considered to be 'the inner, true, and indestructable nature of man'. Music, that succeeds in making us experience this, is as imperishable as Schopenhauer's 'world-will' itself.

BIBLIOGRAPHY:

Golther, W. *Richard Wagner an Mathildem Wesendonck: Tagebuchblätter und Briefe*, 1853-71, Leipzig 1904, rev. 1906 (English trans. by W. A. Ellis, London, 1905)

Magee, Bryan *The Philosophy of Schopenhauer*, OUP, rev. 1997.

Satranski, Rüdiger *Schopenhauer and the Wild Years of Philosophy*, Harvard University Press, 1991

Schopenhauer, Arthur, *The World as Will and Representation*, Vols. I and II (English trans. E. F. J. Payne, Dover Publications, New York, 1966)

Scruton, Roger *Kant*, Oxford University Press, 1982

Tanner, Michael *Wagner*, Flamingo, London, 1997

Wagner, Richard *Zukunftsmusik, Vorwort zu einer Prosa-Übersetzung meiner Operndichtungen*, 1860

3

'. . . the madness that is believed . . .' a re-evaluation of the life and work of Arnold Schoenberg

Peter Davison

'And from the burning back to the ice...'
(*Dr. Faustus*, Thomas Mann, 1947)

The great break with tradition in European music is commonly understood to be the abandonment of the established hierarchy of tonality. Tonality, which has its origins in the natural phenomenon of the harmonic series, was replaced by artificially selected hierarchies and relationships in the organisation of pitch. This change reputedly took place in 1921 with Arnold Schoenberg's first claim that he had invented the technique of twelve-tone serialism, and the first examples of the rigorous use of the technique can be found in the piano pieces, Opus 25. This innovation is not to be confused with the free use of dissonance or polytonality, which came about through an evolutionary process. The extension of tonal means, and thereby the expressive palette, was a continuing strand in European music and rooted in the common aural experience of composers, performers and audiences. For Schoenberg, the invention of twelve-tone serial technique was a solution to the problems of composing in a fully chromatic idiom without the structural support of tonality. It was also for him a threshold in the history of music; a paradoxical moment of liberation, a critical development towards the new. Total chromaticism and the breaking down of tonality were an irrevocable, if reluctant step; there could be no going back. Thus, the irreversible momentum of history drove Schoenberg to a revolutionary act, abandoning a basic tenet of Western music in the name of progress.

Despite his break with the past, tradition tyrannised Schoenberg. He, like everybody else, felt the need for appreciation, to belong to the group, to be part of a mainstream of cultural practice and to live up to the example of his heroes. So why was such a revolutionary step necessary? Schoenberg was, after all, a master technician in the post-Wagnerian idiom and an innovator extending that language into astonishing new territory without dismantling the fundamentals of the style. Schoenberg was better equipped than anyone to inherit the Austro-German tradition and to make it grow. Encouraged by Zemlinsky, Schoenberg initially strove to reunite a tradition divided by the Brahms-Wagner polemic. In his *Verklärte Nacht* (1899), Wagner's harmonic language was fused with the dense motivic and contrapuntal style of Brahms to powerful and beautiful effect.

The tradition was threatened not just by splits within, but also by the success of imitators and rivals from other countries, for instance, symphonists from France, Russia, Czechoslovakia and Scandinavia. The supremacy of German music could only be maintained if the Brahms-Wagner schism were healed, and if a revolutionary gesture of newness, exceeding even the overwhelming example of Wagner, placed German music firmly in the avant-garde. A tension inevitably arose between the desire to preserve the essentials of the German tradition and the need to break away from those elements that had already fruitfully been dispersed across Europe. The element of that musical tradition which could justify a radical change in Schoenberg's view, was the logic of counterpoint. This was the most ingenious and rationalistic feature of music; a logic of correspondence that could generate its own momentum. Most importantly, through counterpoint could be achieved total thematic or motivic integration, as in a Bach fugue for example, while the horizontal momentum of the voice-part also had the capacity to justify and generate extreme dissonances.

A paradox and a personal dilemma surrounded the advent of serial technique. A break with the past, while it could achieve preeminence for German music, also risked rejection by the general public and the accusation of disloyalty to that tradition. Thus, although the idea of an artificially generated set of note relationships was revolutionary, Schoenberg in his writings went to great pains to show that his method was merely an extension of existing practices that could be traced back to the earliest counterpoint. This justified the notion that the horizontal and the vertical were equivalent, and that a dissonance no longer needed to be resolved. Thus serialism's main link with the past was forged by the argument that German music was founded on the contrapuntal tradition of Bach, Beethoven and Brahms. Indeed, even the endless melodist, Wagner could be accepted into the fold as a secret contrapuntist. Schoenberg played a perverse game with his pupils to spot inner voices in *Tristan*. The shocking aesthetics and emotional impact of this opera became secondary to its ingenious structure. Schoenberg had an obsessive desire to justify the sensual in music by intellectual means. After he had composed works such as the *Five Orchestral Pieces* (1909) and *Erwartung* (1909), which burst out of his subconscious with great speed and force, he was terrified by the extent to which this music could not be analysed rationally. Their forms were entirely intuitive. This threatened his notion of the German tradition, as being founded upon strict counterpoint and rational processes. The motive or thematic fragment, in Schoenberg's view, was an entity open to endless combination, transposition, inversion and retrogression. It could never be simply a lyric impulse or expressive gesture. Every note had to have a rational justification. Harmony for Schoenberg was only the outcome of the logic of counterpoint, expression the result of the coherence and economy of the idea. All these assumptions made the step to serialism seem natural and inevitable. The twelve-tone theory could be understood as the intellect's response to the sudden release of irrational forces in expressionist scores such as *Erwartung*. The theory was an overreaction on Schoenberg's part; a mistrust of his own psyche. Ironically, what was motivated by the desire to shore-up a particular and personal view of tradition, became a revolutionary rupture with it.

What other factors led Schoenberg to abandon the path of evolution for revolution? The explanations lie deep within the contradictions of Schoenberg's character and the problems of his own psychological development. The reasons were as much personal as historical. Around the time of his break with tonality, Schoenberg's wife, Mathilde, ran off with his friend, the painter, Richard Gerstl. Webern was able to act as an intermediary to persuade Mathilde to go back to her husband. This caused Gerstl to commit suicide; a shattering blow to both of the Schoenbergs. Out of this experience came the second string quartet of 1908 and its vocal Finale, which self-consciously liberates itself from its tonal bondage with the words, 'I feel the air from other planets'. Breaking free of tonality was synonymous with the resolution of his emotional crisis, but this was a temporary catharsis and may have been achieved by a psychic rupture that brought further trouble in its wake. To add to this personal anxiety, not long afterwards, Europe descended into the turmoil of the First World War, and the disintegration of the Austro-Hungarian empire with Vienna at its hub. One cannot underestimate the impact of the carnage of the Great War on such a sensitive and analytical being as Schoenberg. It was a moment of existential crisis for him; a fundamental collapse of value and meaning, a loss of trust in sense and intuition. Schoenberg confessed that it was 'the overturning of everything I believe in'. The war years brought national service, illness and anti-Semitic victimisation. Composing all but stopped and the immediate post-war period was also not productive, as if some spark of spontaneous creativity had been extinguished.

Confronted by emotional disturbance and general social upheaval, Schoenberg had entered a wilderness. What was there to believe in any more? There was only the madness of a civilisation self-destructing. People react to crisis in different ways. Some find in human suffering a catalyst for compassion and insight into the human condition. Others feel profoundly betrayed, become cynical and pull up the shutters of their emotional being. Negative feelings of revenge, victimisation and resentment replace the flow of positive energies that permits creativity to flourish. Europe and Schoenberg were in trauma. Schoenberg reacted to the collective catastrophe by turning in on himself and blaming errant human emotions and hostile Nature, which had given man an inclination to barbarity and conflict. The conventional, pleasing surface of music represented the deceptive facade of bourgeois culture. It was a facade that concealed the corruption and decadence of a failing empire and social system. Austere, unadorned art was the only way to establish integrity as an artist. Was Schoenberg perhaps right to believe that, in a world capable of the Great War and then the holocaust, artists had a duty to provide a harsh critique of social norms and to be suspicious of the mannered traditions and social structures that had led to a collapse of civilised values? Music had to rebel against the perceived banalities and comfortable aesthetics of figures like Richard Strauss and the more conservative factions, who represented the old order. Serialism was born of the need to reconstruct culture by means of an unprecedented artifice, where the past, the established order and even Nature itself could not be trusted. In a world, where established culture hid the darkness within, someone had to express the reality of the wilderness behind the facade.

The historical facts, however, suggest reasons other than flaws in human nature for the collapse of European culture. It was a failure of leadership in times of difficult change. The cause stemmed from the cultural hegemony among nation states and the ethnic groups within them. There were vain rivalries among the corrupt ruling elites with their futile and destructive adventures meddling in other cultures around the world. The internal pressures of urbanisation and industrialisation and growth of mass political movements among the increasing number of working class people created polarisation within society. A huge pot was boiling over with repressed anger and frustration. Far from human nature or

Nature itself being to blame, it was the constraining of the human spirit in the arid wilderness of the urban and industrial lifestyle that brought moral decline. When people are treated as economic units in a vast impersonal machine, when the injustices of wealth and poverty are too clearly visible, when expectations are raised but cannot be fulfilled, when leaders are oblivious to this and instead indulge their fantasies of power and domination, chaos is bound to ensue. If the problem is badly diagnosed, and Nature is blamed, then the cure will also be wrong. The break with Nature was part of the problem, so the invention of man-made Utopian constructs as solutions merely compounded the difficulties. Fascism and communism thrived on the chaos. People became slaves to demeaning ideologies and to the totalitarian parties that enforced them.

> *'The genius learns from himself, the man of talent mainly from others.'*
> (Arnold Schoenberg, *Problems of Teaching Art*, 1911)

Schoenberg's reaction to personal and social upheaval was also to influence his two principal disciples, Alban Berg and Anton Webern, who both had to solve the same problem of composing with all twelve tones of the chromatic scale without the framework of functional tonality and associated forms. The relationship between Schoenberg and his two supporters was ambivalent in its fruitfulness and conflict. Schoenberg was undoubtedly the senior figure, but he was insecure to the point of needing to fend off any possible undermining of his dominance. Webern, for example, has been described by Christopher Hailey as a someone who 'came to Schoenberg a self-assured young man of considerable training and accomplishment. When he left Schoenberg, he was a bundle of nerves and insecurities...'. Towards the end of his life, Schoenberg was jealous of the attention Webern received from the younger generation. He revealed in an essay on *Klangfarbenmelodie* (1951) how suspicious he was, in the second decade of the century, of

Webern's acquisitiveness of his own compositional ideas:

> Webern immediately uses everything I do, plan or say, so
> that ... by now I haven't the slightest idea who I am.

The same essay makes it very clear that Schoenberg's concept of
Klangfarbenmelodie had not come from Webern, as is commonly
understood. Webern is painted as possessive and ungenerous by
comparison with his teacher. Schoenberg also wants us to realise
that he was secretly working on the twelve-tone method long
before he made it public, which gave him the opportunity to set his
own chronology against the pattern of innovation among the
second Viennese school. Schoenberg viewed innovative compositional technique as intellectual property, which others could only
inherit, once the historical fact had been firmly established that it
originated from him. Rivalry with other nationalities, rivalry with
his own peers and pupils within the German tradition drove
Schoenberg on: a victim of his own devilish insecurities as a
personality and his need to forge preemptively a unique place in
musical history.

The relationship with Berg was even more ambivalent.
Aesthetically, Berg was much more pragmatic and at ease with the
sensual aspects of music. He was in temperament akin to Mahler
and much more comfortable as an intuitive composer than
Schoenberg. There is considerable evidence that Schoenberg was
threatened by his gifted pupil, and sought to suppress his potential
for public acclaim, causing strain in their relationship at times. The
fatherless Berg was easily dominated by his teacher, but he was
well aware of his weakness in relation to Schoenberg. He
described it as 'a problem I've carried around with me for decades
without being able to solve it and which will be my downfall'
Schoenberg was not above bullying his talented follower, and, to
quote Hailey again, 'Berg's psyche was the frequent object of a
blistering assault', in which Berg was accused of every human
weakness imaginable, all justified by the absurd notion that it was
a provocation which was good for him. Berg responded most often

with helpless subservience and sycophancy, which was a great source of irritation to his wife, Helene.

History, in Schoenberg's eyes, could not accommodate more than one prophet to lead the way out of the wilderness. While dodecaphonic tendencies were a common part of the highly developed tonal ambiguities of music in the first decades of the twentieth century, there was nothing systematic or dogmatic about these occurrences. The final song of Alban Berg's *Altenberg Lieder* of 1912 contains the earliest-known example of a twelve-tone row. For Berg this kind of chromatic saturation was an expressive and symbolic device, not the outcome of a theory. Its appearance was therefore not a self-conscious act of historical daring, rather the outcome of a creative process that drew upon a variety of self-imposed limits to the infinite range of choices available in an idiom free from the established laws of consonance and dissonance. There is no strictness of procedure here, merely a richer palette of expressive devices.

In 1912, Schoenberg himself began work on an opera or oratorio based on Balzac's novel, *Seraphita*, which never progressed beyond an outline sketch. However, his preoccupation with the Balzac text is a significant indicator of what issues may have been in his mind at that juncture of his development. In an essay of 1941, *Composition with Twelve Tones*, Schoenberg tried to explain and justify the idea that a twelve-tone row does not change its essential nature, if it is rearranged by transposition, inversion, in retrograde or retrograde inversion. He illustrated this by citing the description of Swedenborg's heaven, in Balzac's *Seraphita*, as a space in which, 'there is no absolute down, no right or left, forward or backward.' This is the principal theoretical assumption that makes twelve-tone theory possible. The idea that the variants of a tone row can be perceived as the same object in musical time-space means that an unprecedented musical unity can be achieved. A serial work, by this definition, can only be understood as a direct manifestation of a metaphysical world, where there is no dimensionality and, by implication, no time. Schoenberg's compositional technique originated from an ideal reality, and was not born of practical musical experience.

It was because Berg insisted on developing his fully-chromatic compositional method with reference to musical experience (which inclines to tonality), while Schoenberg insisted on an uncompromising metaphysical theory, that teacher and pupil began to fall out. During 1915, Berg and Schoenberg had a strong disagreement about Berg's Four Pieces for clarinet and piano, Opus 5. A serious rupture lasted for a year, and relations were not fully restored until 1918, when Schoenberg permitted Berg to use the familiar '*du*' form, once again. It is not entirely clear what lay behind this rift, but evidence suggests that it was indeed connected with Berg's tight, yet undogmatic organisation of pitch in these works. Relations appear to have been restored only when Schoenberg had gone some way towards developing his own more rigorous organisational systems. As Adorno has written, 'Schoenberg envied Berg his successes', and in order to keep the historical record straight, Schoenberg was always eager to show that he was at least as advanced as his colleagues in solving the compositional problems of using the twelve-tones. Schoenberg himself made much of the fact that he had drafted a scherzo as part of an incomplete symphonic work, (which became the torso known as *Die Jakobsleiter* of 1914-15, which main theme contained the twelve chromatic tones without repetition.) Yet despite the uniqueness of Schoenberg's movement, this is yet another incomplete work, and by comparison with Berg's songs and clarinet pieces, is impractical to perform. Schoenberg stumbled in his work at the simple level of deciding what note to write next, as intuition and creativity deserted him. He needed a means to avoid the agony of infinite freedom without a guiding inner voice. That Berg was ahead of Schoenberg both in the technical handling of the dodeca-phonic idiom and in the creative instincts needed to bring it to life, must have irritated his teacher. Schoenberg tried to conceal that the evolution of ideas about composing with twelve-tones was much more an equal dialogue between himself, Berg and Webern. The ideas of the eccentric theorist Hauer were also stimulating debate at that time (even as late as 1923, Schoenberg was in a dialogue of

equals with Hauer on the subject), and one should also not forget
the road upon which Mahler had embarked in his late music. The
first movement of the tenth symphony, for example, is one of the
most remarkable achievements in the use of the full expressive
range of the twelve chromatic tones. It was Schoenberg's
compulsive desire to be the principal historic figure, at a time when
his own inspiration was failing, and others were making fast
technical progress, that led Schoenberg to what Boulez describes
as a 'premature attempt at codification'.

In the years after the Great War, Schoenberg tried to discourage
Berg from writing his opera *Wozzeck*, and one can speculate that
the teacher must have felt once again threatened that his gifted
pupil would surpass him. In Berg's extraordinary work of 1921,
traditional forms are often used as inaudible constructivist devices
giving coherent form to an idiom, as in the *Altenberg Lieder*,
unfettered by the traditional laws of consonance and dissonance.
Wozzeck achieved an enviable success in its time, of which
Schoenberg also disapproved. It is the only expressionist opera of
the period that has established itself in the regular repertoire of the
major opera houses. The work is characterised not by its
abandonment of tonality, but by the way in which tonality emerges
at crucial points to articulate the drama. The dénouement of the
opera, after Wozzeck's suicide, is a moving orchestral interlude in
D minor, climaxing with a huge and obvious perfect cadence.
Tonality is symbolic of immutable fate, that which can be no other
way. It is Nature, against which there can be no meaningful
rebellion.

Schoenberg's dominant personality made it inevitable that Berg
should be influenced by his theories relating to twelve-tone
composition techniques. He was, at the same time, not instinctively
inclined to such a 'scientific' approach to creativity. If the debate
about twelve-tone compositional technique was going on from as
early as 1912, it may be that Berg was moving in the direction of
an intuitive solution in defiance of his teacher, who inclined to a
more analytical approach. It seems hard to believe that Schoenberg
would not voice his concern for the need to impose intellectual

order upon free atonality, even if he did not codify it as a theory. It is known, for example, that Schoenberg and Webern exchanged letters discussing the exciting possibilities of the *Jakobsleiter* scherzo. Did Berg in fact feel a deep scepticism for the motivation of Schoenberg's domineering theories? The approach to twelve-tone composition in *Wozzeck* might suggest that this is so.

In the opera, the crazed doctor treats Wozzeck as an anatomical specimen for experiments. There is no compassion here for a fellow human being, just the bullying of a victim whose vulnerabilities deprive him of the freedom to choose for his own well-being. Ultimately, in Büchner's play, but not in the opera, Wozzeck ends up on the anatomist's table, dissected for science in total denial of his humanity. Scientific research, in the doctor's sadistic hands, assumes a neurotic edge; the pursuit of knowledge to gain fame at any cost. It is the egoistic drive of an obsessive personality struggling for an identity. He can find it only in the gratification of his own self-importance and a delusion of the perfectibility of man through science. Berg weaves a highly complex Passacaglia with 21 variations throughout the Doctor's exchanges with Wozzeck. It is a web of sound depicting Wozzeck's disorientation and the Doctor's nervous excitement, punctuated by fleeting moments of tonal lucidity, as Wozzeck explains to the Doctor that Nature's force is inescapable:

> When Nature has vanished and the world becomes so dark
> that you have to grope around with your hands, and one
> thinks that it dissolves like a spider's web … what is there
> to hold on to?

It is almost inevitable that the Passacaglia figure itself is a strict twelve-tone row with an obvious allusion to Schoenberg's developing theories. The tone-row technique, Berg seems to suggest (maybe unwittingly) is the product of disorientation brought about by the withdrawal of Nature and the neurotic desire to restore identity by artificial and, by definition, unnatural means.

In this context Schoenberg's peculiar utterance, that he had 'discovered something that would secure the supremacy of German music for the next hundred years', takes on a potentially different meaning. It was the outburst of a supreme egotist; a remark which acknowledged the overpowering presence of a German, Beethoven, as the standard-bearer of greatness in European music in the previous century, while insinuating his own right to carry the flag for the next. The sentiments of German nationalism betrayed his insecurity as an Austrian Jew in relation to the thoroughly German lineage of Bach, Beethoven, Wagner and Brahms. This was not the proud assertion of a man destined to restore Austro-German music as the model for high art in the new age, but the desperate feigned confidence of a man uncertain of himself and the world around him. There was also an overbearing wish to retain the ideological initiative, to fulfil his very personal sense of historical destiny, which did not permit the limelight to be shared by those close to him or from other nations.

Schoenberg embodied the Doctor/Wozzek conjunction in real life: the tormentor and the tormented, the recklessly ambitious experimenter and the victim of fate. Everywhere are the shadows of unnamed opponents: the public, other composers, critics, academics, other cultures and nations. Then suddenly like the doctor, he could declare 'Oh my theory, Oh my theory, Oh my fame, I shall be immortal, immortal, immortal', all his antagonists and competitors could be damned, because he could now become the great composer, the historic figure. Thomas Mann found in Schoenberg a resonance for his character Adrian Leverkühn, in his novel *Dr. Faustus*. Indeed, the Faustian archetype, one who through a diabolical pact achieves knowledge, fame and dominion over Nature, is easily observed in Schoenberg's ambitions.

Thus a role model for the twentieth-century composer was born: the overcompensation for a profound sense of victimisation, born of being misunderstood, of being a prophet in evil times. An egocentric historicism demands that all creative actions must be justified in relation to the past, while also being self-consciously and daringly new. Composing becomes a form of architectural construction. No longer intuitive, composition becomes a matter of manipulating concrete ideas rather than realising the aesthetic inner vision. Idiom and form are historically determined, and every musical process must be analysable. The composer becomes a scientist in search of the objectively provable and excluding the random or subjective. Yet, through the supremacy of the intellect, complex webs replace the void where Nature has withdrawn. The problem with such webs is that they are spun to entangle their victims and disable them. There is an echo here of Stravinsky's *Poetics of Music* (1942):

> Modern man is progressively losing his understanding of values and his sense of proportions. The failure to understand essential realities is extremely serious. It leads us infallibly to the violation of the fundamental laws of human equilibrium.

> *'There arose not a prophet since in Israel like unto Moses, whom the Lord knew, face to face...'*
>
> (Deuteronomy 34, verse 10)

Schoenberg's identification with the misunderstood prophet found its ultimate expression in the unfinished opera, *Moses und Aron* of 1932. The paradox of the one chosen by God, only to be rejected by the people, is a consistent characteristic of Schoenberg's creative personality, and it is embedded in the very aesthetic assumptions of his musical language after Opus 25. What do we hear in these early serial pieces? Music in neoclassical forms that grew out of tonality, but with notes decided by an artificial hierarchy that has no basis in the physical laws of sound or the psychological laws of musical experience. The effect is like hearing something familiar through the distortion of a mistuned radio signal. At best, there is an obscure 'wrong-note'irony, as the familiar is parodied through denial, with the added pathos of a tragic struggle to communicate, like someone frantically using sign language to explain the theory of relativity. The ambition is admirable, the means ingenious, but the possibility of success negligible. At worst, there is a delusional neurosis, which denies the intent to provoke rejection and gain identity through being a famous victim and cultivating a puritan's sense of moral superiority. *Moses und Aron* is about this very syndrome.

Moses brings the holy law in tablets of stone from God. These are the rules: absolute, inviolable, the will of God. It is a provocative gnosticism, which isolates the prophet from the people and their ordinary, worldly weaknesses, hopes and fears. The irony is that to worship the Word is as blasphemous as to worship the golden calf, maybe its inevitable antithesis. In the polemical exchanges of Moses and Aron is the epitome of our contemporary cultural confusion. Of course, Moses is right that people need the law as a manifestation of the higher spiritual order that God wishes for men, and yes, Aron is right too, men need more than pedantic law. They feel, have desires, are instruments of Nature. Schoenberg more or less confesses his failure to transcend the polemic in the text of his opera. Aron accuses Moses of making the word of the law unintelligible to the people because of its austerity and unattractive form:

> But your word was denied image and marvel, which are
> detested by you.

Moses later admits that the Word alone is not enough. Abstract intellectual concepts cannot express the nature of God. Words always fall short, and it is a delusion to believe that the mind alone can grasp truth:

> Thus am I defeated. Thus all was but madness that I
> believed before and can and must not be given voice.
> O word, thou word that I lack!

With such an open confession, it is not surprising that in the years that followed *Moses und Aron*, Schoenberg had a general rapprochement with tonality. While he never publicly abandoned his twelve-tone theory, he did compose several exclusively tonal works, which are worth listing, because they are not well-known and their chronology is surprising in the light of Schoenberg's own statements about serial technique and his artistic development. The works are:

Cello concerto in D Minor *after Monn* (1933)
Concerto Grosso in B-flat *after Handel* (1933)
The Suite for strings in G Minor (1934)
Brahms, Piano Quartet No.1 in G Minor, arr. for orchestra (1937)
The second Chamber Symphony in E-flat minor (1939)
Variations on a recitative in D minor for organ (1941)
Theme and Variations in G Minor for Wind Band (1943)

Schoenberg's Moses is not found in the biblical story, for in the Old Testament Moses breaks the tablets of stone not in frustration and failure, but in anger. God wreaks a terrible vengeance on the Israelites for their weakness in worshipping the golden calf, and He eventually provides new tablets as a reminder that the law remains inviolable. If the biblical Moses makes a mistake, it is that his people are lost without him, and while he is on Mount Sinai receiving the Word of God, they go astray. The bible tells the story of a great leader empowered by God to lead his people out of slavery and to elevate them as His chosen people, not the tale of a misunderstood prophet. Being a prophet is indeed lonely and difficult, but Moses largely succeeds in carrying out the will of God. Moses did pay a price for his intercession on behalf of the doubting Hebrews in the wilderness, for which God rather unkindly denies him the right to enter the promised land. The lesson here is that without faith, paradise cannot be regained, and Moses is punished for sharing the doubts of his followers. It is Joshua who is appointed as his successor and triumphantly reaches the end of the journey. (Perhaps Schoenberg feared this part of the story, which he suppressed. He did not want to pass on the glory of the German tradition to a worthy successor or let someone else lead the people into the promised land. Did his suppression of Berg and Webern reflect this fear? Did he deliberately stay in the wilderness to preserve his sense of persecution and to deny himself and his pupils the chance to make their own escape?) It is a projection of Schoenberg's own victim identity that makes Moses a much more tragic figure in the opera; punished for his relationship with God and bearing an unintelligible Word to an unwilling people.

> '...if it is true that we are intellectuals, we are called upon not to cogitate, but to perform.'
>
> (Stravinsky, *Poetics of Music*)

Schoenberg had the proud quality of total intellectual rigour. Had he been less concerned with theoretical consistency and taken a less analytical view of himself and the traditions to which he was born, life might have been easier for him. The immensely impressive tool of his mind was applied to problems where it should just have surrendered. Not every creative issue is open to rational analysis. The danger of turning music into a highly complex jigsaw-puzzle of abstract ideas, parameters and techniques is that the intuitive aspect is removed. The technical process becomes more and more the *raison d'être*, and the composer begins to see the surface of the music only, which inevitably reflects his own thought processes. There may be a demonstrable rationale behind every detail of a great piece of music, but the composer does not make his compositional decisions at the conscious level. What of intuition, inspiration, the capacity to eliminate thousands of alternative solutions in an instant? Like the conservative theorist, Heinrich Schenker, Schoenberg analysed great music to discover what was great about it, and drew some remarkable conclusions about invention, form, syntax and historical development. It does not follow that, if one self-consciously extends the complexity of these dimensions, great music will be the result. Nor can one assume the mantle of greatness by devising a theory that will be of equal fascination to analysts in future generations, as one is fascinated by the music of the past.

On so many occasions Schoenberg claimed that the manipulation of the row and its very identity were not conscious processes open to analysis. This seems unlikely. The nature of the technique demands intervalic rigour and its radical newness would mean that creating structures would be a painstaking affair, because there were no precedents to create a syntax that could be learnt to a state of fluency. It would be unthinkable to improvise in the twelve-tone technique, for example. It is most probable that Schoenberg had an acute sensitivity about his composing methods and guarded them as a secret to create the illusion of spontaneity, and also to protect himself from harsh criticism. One has to remember that this was a man who inclined to an obsessional analytic approach to the smallest task. He even redrafted the tram timetable for the City of Berlin in an effort to improve its efficiency.

As a composer, Schoenberg's problem was an excessive awareness of the supposed historical significance of his actions. One cannot contrive historical significance. True, Schoenberg was highly gifted, and he knew it, but he could not analyse his way to understanding the next historic step. That step must always be a leap of faith taken in total humility as to its historical meaning. To quote Pierre Boulez, 'the desire to make history is incompatible with actually being historically important.' Brash claims make one immediately suspicious about the motive and substance of such a claim. History and tradition are simply a body of knowledge and experience that exists and has accumulated through time. To see tradition or historical significance as being handed to one individual to perpetuate, destroy or revolt against, is to misunderstand the process and the role individuals play in it.

Why did a man of Schoenberg's musical credentials do something so unmusical and unnatural as to invent a composing method out of the ether as a self-conscious historical act? It seems unintelligible that a man could write music that is divorced from aural reality and also compose *Verklärte Nacht* and *Pierrot Lunaire* (1912). But one has to understand what a distorting neurosis can do to a person. Schoenberg was utterly convinced that the inner logic of his music transcended the sound, that as an idea the music had substance beyond its aural reality. What he heard when he listened was coloured by his awareness of his own thought processes. He needed to believe that the conscious mind, which practised the constructive elements of musical invention, could overcome its dependency on the unconscious for the mystery of inspiration. The lack of a sensual surface to his music and any sense of natural flow were both the consequence and the point of this effort. The listener is left in a state of cold alienation that means it is only possible to engage cerebrally, if it all. The problem is in the assumption that the average listener has the will for such an exercise; not only to crack the new musical code, but also to suspend his own instinct for making tonal relationships. The human mind or, at least, most human minds cannot do that. Furthermore, the avoidance by the composer of inadvertent tonal gestures requires an immense labour that in the end is achieved only by a perverse logic of denial.

In the last song of the atonal *Pierrot Lunaire,* the crisis of the work is resolved when the vocalist breathes the 'ancient scent from the time of fairy-tales,'symbolised by the return of tonality, here E major. Until the invention of serialism, Schoenberg's intuition held onto the idea that tonality represented normality, the return to life. The sense of stable hierarchy, the assertion of consonance over dissonance remained the background against which all the expressionist devices had their effect. The tonal works of the mid and late years suggest that this basic truth was never abandoned by Schoenberg, the composer, even if Schoenberg the theorist and historical figure had to profess otherwise. This is the sad outcome of an unresolved psychological trauma. The natural tendency of the human psyche is towards integration and harmonisation, the return of stability in the wake of crisis. The alternative is a descent into madness. This healing process takes time and cannot be imposed artificially, and that transformation will be different for each person. Creativity will perhaps be therapeutic during the crisis, but may well dry up once the stimulus of crisis is removed. The creative powers will only return, when the wound has healed and some integration of the pre and post-critical conditions has been achieved. This can be a period of immense frustration for an artist, but often a greater maturity may emerge from such a barren time.

Schoenberg was too impatient and too insecure to overcome his trauma naturally. His wounded pride could not accept his vulnerability. Composing was the battlefield for resolving these difficulties. He could have remained a genuine creative genius, waiting for the return of inspiration, but driven by egoism and deluding himself with dreams of immortality, he took the short-cut of rationality and conscious control of the musical material. Thus the invention of serialism consolidated his pathological condition, which resulted in a disconnection from his natural creativity. Now he fully believed that the technical surface of his music was also its aesthetic substance. He reinforced this self-deception by projecting, through his metaphysical theories of form and pitch, extra-musical significances, which were literal rather than metaphorical in their realisation. So, for instance, by making the assumption that musical space does not unfold in real time, Schoenberg ignored an important limit to the human capacity for musical perception. Tonal music can express transcendence through the metaphor of a sublime, abstracted as though timeless, structure, but it is the audible relationships between keys and thematic repetitions which are the means of building that structure, which can only exist in real time. Intuition governs the complex relationships in such a temporal structure, and these cannot be theoretically precise. What is right to the ear may not coincide with what is logically right to the mind alone, which cannot analyse every subtle interconnection and contextual variable. Tonality, which is a system derived from the interrelation of tones in real time, is the means by which the illusion can be created that the ordinary passage of time is suspended in music. The music thus takes on a spatial dimension, understood as form. Schoenberg's aesthetic theories originated in Swedenborg's account of heaven, where there is no gulf between thought and reality, time and space. By abandoning tonality, Schoenberg made music into a sequence of notes without the tonal framework that provides audible interrelation, and thus his music fails ironically to achieve its stated ambition for transcendence. In Schoenberg's distorted view, the metaphor of tonality was no longer needed, because the intellect, not the senses, is perceived as the best means by which to enter the spiritual realm. He wanted to liberate himself from time and space, by composing simply as though they do not exist. Sadly, reality does not comply with Schoenberg's idealism. Indeed, if one wished to express the idea of Swedenborg's heaven in the terms of our temporal world, the sublime metaphor of tonal music would be the best way to achieve it. Ironically, Swedenborg's heaven does not abandon space, merely gives it new meaning, and it also does not lack hierarchy. Indeed, Swedenborg makes the point that what is close has 'likeness' and what is far away has 'un-likeness', so that, for example, hell is very far from heaven. So, in Swedenborg's heaven, spatial awareness has a moral dimension, which would confirm to an even greater degree that tonality offers a better metaphor of this higher reality than Schoenberg's theories, where each note of the scale has equal status.

The reason for Schoenberg's identification with Moses is clear. He felt like the prophet touched by God and thus condemned, in this world, to loneliness and misunderstanding. Yet, if one were really able to bring something of heaven into the material world, it simply would not belong here. The spiritual can only realise itself on earth through allusion and metaphor. The limits of time and space make certain of that. Schoenberg tried to be a warrior on the battleground between two mutually exclusive worlds, but perhaps his problem can be explained even more simply than this. He was, after all, also human, subject to the same limitations as his per-plexed audience. He just failed to realise that on earth, unlike in a Swedenborgian heaven, something does not become true, because one would like it to be so. Human intelligence and perceptual pow-ers are finite. We cannot grasp essential forms or know the totality of truth or God. Schoenberg's aesthetic position, despite the high-minded, almost religious principles, which characterised it, was a gnosticism doomed to incomprehension. As a consequence of this aesthetic flaw, Schoenberg had to adopt a defensive position. He thus became a brilliant and brutal polemicist. He dazzled himself with the virtuosity of his own thought processes. His razor-sharp ability for finding the weakness in a common sense critique pushed the merely sceptical into an extreme position, while he could retreat into the wounded pride of his much vaunted integrity.

'When I hear music...I feel quite clearly that there are no questions at all.'
(Gustav Mahler, 1909)

What are the implications of all this for today's composers? Historical awareness should never be such a tyrant. It should not compel every composer to aspire to be a Beethoven, Wagner or a Schoenberg, nor should they be the benchmarks of greatness against which posterity judges others. If a composer believes that, he will most likely betray himself in pursuit of an unachievable goal. For some composers, it suits the essential qualities of their personalities to be ambitious and highly innovative. For others, greatness might lie in subtlety, intimacy and economy of expression. The history of music is not about technical processes after all, but aesthetic responses to certain fundamental truths for a specific time and context. Technical innovation as an end in itself is pointless, if it does not enhance the expressive means. Technical virtuosity can so easily become a substitute for invention. Musical development is not about increasing ingenuity and complexity, but about the enhancement of the human capacity for meaningful expression through sound. Good music is about people interacting with ideas and experiences to produce an art that is listened to and appreciated. It can never simply impose a set of technical norms and claim its superior validity. Technique is a means to an end, not an end in itself. A work should be judged by its effectiveness as an aesthetic object, as the refined expression of a unique compositional personality that has something substantial to say.

Why, should a contemporary composer want to alienate his audience? What does that achieve except to give music-making a bad name? When we hear music, it should move us inwardly. It is remarkable to see how music can stir people, when it is played well and stems from the deepest human instinct for expression and communicating with others. It is only relevant that such an impact can, under the right circumstances be genuinely achieved, not how it is achieved. This is the only benchmark of quality. Aesthetic judgement is never easy, but let us not abandon common sense in our appreciation. There is a difference between that which yields its full richness and depth only after repeated hearing to an averagely intelligent listener and that which remains impenetrable and obscure after countless hearings.

It may be possible to justify Schoenberg's aesthetic purpose in the way suggested by the philosopher, Theodor Adorno. The serial method created music aggressively independent of the prevailing culture and its conventions, acting as a mode of critique in corrupt times. Adorno considered Schoenberg's choice as the only moral action in a culture that had become decadent through capitalist excesses; the pollution of what we now call consumerism, but which was at that time characterised in terms of the 'class struggle' against the bourgeoisie. Tonality, which was perceived as the status quo, became synonymous with the brutality of fascism, the sentimentality of the masses and the sins of an imperial past. It was considered thus to be emblematic of a declining and immoral civilisation. This analysis is of course questionable. To deny the core of a culture because it has been abused is not a path towards saving it. Schoenberg's position, and Adorno's justification of it were nihilistic and defeatist, identifying only the most negative forces of the culture. By so doing, they denied the possibility that an artist could any longer express his inner reality, that an individual could rescue the meaning of his experience from the wilderness of the cultural context and then share it with another. In their view, resistance to the collective aberration could only be through protest, because the malaise infected the artist's inner world. But this was to give too much authority to the group, to let negative experience overwhelm the spirit and to deny the untouchable core of humanity that lies within each person even *in extremis*.

Hegel's theory of autonomous historical process, which justified Schoenberg's progress to serialism, cannot be successfully applied to music. The conventions of music carry no meaning in themselves. Music needs the conventions of its time, because they are the only means available. The unconventionality of much great music still needs convention as the background against which its idiosyncrasy can be measured. By the expression of that idiosyncrasy, the conventions are transgressed, but also subtly transformed. Self-consciously to deconstruct conventions as a way of expressing individuality is to treat them too literally and too absolutely. By contrast, Stravinsky's *Rite of Spring* is genuinely idiosyncratic in expression, because it transcends the conventions of its time without fully rejecting them. It may depict, as Adorno suggests, the barbaric abandonment of the individual to the collective, but to believe that it advocates or expresses that as an ideology would be to assume that the audience, even today's audience, are primitive pagans likely to react to primitive stimuli. In actual fact, the audience for this work needs to be sophisticated and probably over-rational to appreciate how Stravinsky's music challenges the tradition to which it also belongs. Stravinsky incites us to acknowledge the barbarian within, but with the sophistication of highly civilised people. On the other hand, Schoenberg's dance around the golden calf, in *Moses und Aron*, incites us to the opposite. We are asked to condemn the barbarian with an act of psychic violence that wills him away. In the end, which music is psychologically more dangerous; Stravinsky's, which acknowledges a psychological reality, or Schoenberg's, whose angry prophet provokes decadence and resentment through prohibition?

History appears as an irreversible *telos* of cause and effect, but only viewed with hindsight. Music also develops, but not in the same way. It is conceived in the mind, outside the cut and thrust of events. Indeed, its true value may be in that it lies outside the maelstrom of history, existing in the timeless territory of musical space, where experience can be reflected upon and integrated. Musical innovation is not about crossing irrevocable thresholds, rather the discovery of an ever increasing range of possibilities. A threshold of possibility may be crossed, but it does not then become a dividing line between what is and what is not possible. Schoenberg made a plausible case for the irrevocable step, and this set the pattern for the development of twentieth century music thereafter. Constant revolution has been the norm ever since, Schoenberg set the example, but did not reach the promised land, so he is perceived by many as a transitional figure. Webern was the first total decontructivist. Thence Boulez, inspired in some part by Adorno, and the post-war generation sought the Nirvana of a new and totally artificial musical language of the future. Music, it seemed, at this juncture, could only progress through the most radical questioning of tradition to excise the damage of a corrupt culture. The symbolism of this crossroads is historically appealing, but it does not reflect the actuality. Even the example of Schoenberg's own development was not as linear as he would have us believe, and this should lead us to question the Hegelian paradigm. His tonal works of the 30's and early 40's indicate that even he ultimately found a path to the reintegration of tonal elements. The rhetoric of the serial revolution and its justification as the product of irresistible historical forces are unconvincing.

Stravinsky offers us a much more balanced view of the whole aesthetic territory of liberation from diatonic tonality and the dangers of a break with the past. In his simplicity, clarity and humility, the prospects appear much less apocalyptic. The composer of *The Rite of Spring* did not consider himself a revolutionary. He writes:

> Art is by essence constructive. Revolution implies a disruption of equilibrium ... so I confess that I am completely insensitive to the prestige of revolution. All the noise it may make will not call forth the slightest echo in me. For revolution is one thing, innovation another.

His relationship with tradition is one of respect and lacks in any sense of personal dilemma or historical inhibition:

> A real tradition is not the relic of a past that is irretrievably gone; it is a living force that animates and informs the

present...Far from implying the repetition of what has been, tradition presupposes the reality of what endures.

Most striking of all, he has no difficulty in a broad definition of tonality, because he accepts that tones have a natural gravitational pull that generates and releases tension according to a given natural law. This is what makes expression possible. He merely reminds us that diatonic tonality of the late eighteenth century is not the historical norm, but that the ebb and flow of pitches as something with its own innate dynamics was as alive in Gregorian Chant, as it is today. He calls this the 'polar attraction of sound'. It is not for him an arbitrary choice as to how these poles operate, but a matter of intuition, experience and natural law. Intervals generate tensions, tensions which demand resolution, but in an infinite variety of possible ways. Tonality sets the limits, based upon experience, as to what is intelligible by a listener. Audiences are furthermore familiar with its laws and conventions. The clarity and non-polemical position of Stravinsky's aesthetics comes from his ego-less understanding of the phenomenon of music. He is a vehicle for the idea. His mind potentially can corrupt the creative spirit, and this must be resisted. Craftsmanship and the intellect are skills in the service of the higher purpose, which is art. As Stravinsky himself says, 'music comes to reveal itself, as a form of communion with our fellow man — and with the Supreme Being.'

In conclusion, what can be said of Arnold Schoenberg by way of a more realistic evaluation of his historical significance? The answer is not entirely negative. In the works of his before 1921 is a well of untapped creative possibilities. The *First Chamber Symphony* (1906) is one of the finest examples of an infinitely supple and rich musical language that is at once tonal, but free from restrictive diatonic norms. Equally, the expressionist masterpieces of *Pierrot Lunaire* and the *Five Orchestral Pieces* are exceptional works, extending the expressive boundaries with remarkable surety. Serialism was a mistake; an unnecessary and premature theorisation of a process that would naturally have emerged alongside more traditional types of harmonic and melodic practice. This self-conscious act was brought about by complex historical and psychological circumstances. The tortuous polemic that was then necessary to justify his actions was the outpouring of a bitter man, whose alienation from the past was self-inflicted, and a tragic error of judgment for his own development as an artist. From then on, Schoenberg's creativity was in a strait-jacket with paradoxical results. The consequence for musical life has been to polarise it, to normalise extremism, and this has been a sad diversion from real creativity for many composers. Schoenberg had the talent to take music into new territories and to salvage much from the wreckage of European culture. Instead, his obsession with his own historical significance and his alienation from aural reality squandered this potential.

It would be wrong to blame Schoenberg's personal flaws for all the problems that have followed in the music of the last century. Schoenberg was a mirror on a crazy world, trying to resolve the contradictions of a collapsing civilisation. Composers of our own times, like Webern and Berg before them, have been receptive to his example because they want to be, and the alienation of serious artists from the mainstream of society has been and continues to be a fact of life. So we should not judge Schoenberg too harshly. Anyone exploring his music and ideas will come to the heart of the twentieth century and its tragic absurdities. Schoenberg suffered greatly for his cause, and the tragic truth of his inner struggles cannot be questioned. As a critique of all that is shallow and thoughtless in art, Schoenberg's music and life are a testament. He was in many respects a victim of his apocalyptic times, which cultivated in him a destructive egoism driven by paranoia. He shows us the danger of fanatical self-belief, as well as the perverse capacity of human consciousness to distort reality. One man's musical invention does not and can never fully embody the historical moment. To identify with history is an absurd egoism, but one which appeals to the vanity of anyone with too much ambition. The consequent polarisation of twentieth century musical life into the 'traditional' and the 'new', should be exposed as arbitrary and as having diminished music's much needed power to transcend the questions of the restless intellect. Schoenberg wanted to embody the paradox of his age, which imposed an immense inhibition upon his musical invention. His elevation to cult status has not served our culture well, and only when he takes his proper place in the history of European music, as an exception rather than a rule, will an important misunderstanding be resolved.

BIBLIOGRAPHY:

Adorno, Theodor W. *Philosophy of Modern Music*, 1941-48 (English trans. Anne G. Mitchell, Wesley M. Blomster Seabury, New York 1973, Sheed and Ward, London, 1994)

Boulez, Pierre *Orientations, Collected Writings*, ed. Nattiez, Paris 1981 (English trans. by Martin Cooper, Faber and Faber, London, 1986)

Hailey, Christopher *Berg's Vienna* from *The Cambridge Companion to Berg,* ed. Anthony Pople, Cambridge University Press, 1997

MacDonald, Malcolm *Schoenberg*, Dent, London, 1976

Mann, Thomas *Doctor Faustus*, Bermann-Fischer Verlag, Stockholm 1947 (English trans. by H.T. Lowe-Porter Secker and Warburg, London 1949, Penguin, London, 1968)

Stravinsky, Igor *The Poetics of Music,* (English trans. by Arthur Knodel and Ingolf Dahl, Harvard University Press, Cambridge, Mass. 1942)

Schoenberg, Arnold *Style and Idea*, *selected writings,* ed. Leonard
    Stein (English trans. by Leo Black Faber and Faber, London,
    1975)

Walter, Bruno *Gustav Mahler,* (English trans. Lotte Walter Lindt,
    1958 Quartet Books, London, 1990)

4

Chromatic Engineering: 'unnatural' musical intervals and the fate of the hexachordal modes

Robert Walker

Thirty years ago, an office somewhere off Soho Square put out a series of recordings under the all-embracing title 'Music for Pleasure'. I was always struck by this title. Did the record company executives who dreamt this up imagine there was music other than 'for pleasure'? What kind of music could that be? Music for dental drilling perhaps? The inference of this seemingly innocuous title was obvious; the implication serious: those recording executives had hit upon an unspoken reality. There did indeed exist in the world a type of music which might be called 'Music for Displeasure'— music so unpalatable that it was unpleasurable. It exists with us still, and many composers who desire street credibility are still writing it.

'Music for Pleasure' was thirty years ago, when the juggernaut of post-Webernian composition was at full steam. No one — especially not a timorous undergraduate like myself — could question the validity of that system of composition called 'serial technique', which was put before us. The whole panoply of arguments was succinctly laid out in front of us: Wagner's *Tristan und Isolde* was the sunset and the dawn; Schoenberg, then Webern were the way to a brighter future. Their tree of serial knowledge was groaning with fruitful possibilities. (Alban Berg was too pleasurable to be part of the pantheon.) Their dodecaphonic system of composition, said the futuristic pundits, was the only real future we had. Boulez carried the torch ever onward; Stockhausen followed hard on his heels. Having no computers to make their great leap forward easier, everyone from Elizabeth Lutyens to Justin Connolly brandished their slide rules with ever-increasing fervour to light up the sky. Yet one immutable fact could not be erased from the minds of us undergraduates. The music was unpleasurable. It was so disliked that the overwhelming majority of musically literate people gave it a wide berth.

The argument put forward in defence of atonal music — that Beethoven's music was horrible to his contemporaries, that Wagner was considered a madman when he produced *Tristan,* that there was a riot at the first performance of *The Rite of Spring*, that it was only a matter of time before concert-goers would grow to love this new music — was so specious that no one with any knowledge of history seriously paid any attention to it. Beethoven, in twenty years of writing the last quartets, was the composer to whom every other composer aspired. Wagner's music dramas became standard repertoire throughout the opera houses of Europe and the United States, almost as soon as they were written. As for *The Rite of Spring*: it was conveniently forgotten that the first performance took place at a charity gala night at the *Théâtre des Champs Elysées* full to the rafters with Parisian high society — not a collection of people renowned for their open minds. Had Harrison Birtwistle first shown *The Second Mrs. Kong* to the corporate members of *Country Life*, he would probably have got the same response. Nor must it be forgotten that, at the second performance of *The Rite*, Stravinsky was carried shoulder-high through the streets. But it has been eighty years since Schoenberg's first experiments with atonality, and still this method of composition is given the cold shoulder by most of the concert-going public.

There were, it is true, even thirty years ago, some still, small voices in the wilderness: Ligeti still, quietly looking at his clocks and clouds. Tippet occasionally pulling out from his rag-bag of a mind an adventitious nugget of pleasure, and from the East Coast of the United States even fainter voices were beamed across the ether to show us there was indeed at least one other way forward, if only we would take it seriously.

I knew that there was something wrong with the intellectual argument for atonal serial technique, but couldn't put my finger on it. I even wrote music using that technique, fearing that I must be missing out on something. But there was circumstantial evidence that this music was going nowhere. At no time in the history of world music was a movement, a school of thought, so intensely disliked by so many people for so long. (This was not some trivial rejection of 'modern'music; of all works by Stravinsky, for example, or Messiaen, it was noticeable that the atonal, serial ones were among those least likely to be performed.) Thirty years later, I think I have the answer. It is not an answer that everyone will agree with. But I put it forward as a counterpoint to the propaganda which has beset the music student too aggressively and for too long.

And I begin with Bach's *Wohltemperierte Clavier*. It is not clear whether this monumental work is built on the premiss — then but recently in the ascendant — that the octave is best divided into twelve parts, and, more significantly that each of those twelve parts should be equidistant from its neighbours. But by writing twenty-four preludes and fugues in all the keys, major and minor — not once, but twice — Bach opened up a Pandora's box. He showed that any piece of music could have as its fundamental base any note of the chromatic scale of the keyboard. Even he, as we now know, found this awkward, and first composed some of the preludes and fugues in more familiar keys, and then had to transpose them into the more outlandish ones. Bach was by no means the only composer to write such a work, but its popularity has subsequently given it a seminal influence. Not only did the popularity of the *Wohltemperierte Clavier* confirm to the musicians of Western Europe that it was feasible — desirable — to write music in any key, not only did Bach sow the seeds of the discord which would eventually plague the music of twentieth-century Western Europe, but he sounded the death-knell of the very foundation of music up to that point: the hexachordal mode.

Let us get a few definitions out of the way. A mode is any invariable sequence of notes which forms the basis of a musical construction. A scale is a mode, but a mode is not necessarily a scale. Play some music using only the black notes on a piano, and you are using a mode, but it is obviously not a scale (there are some bits missing). Diatonic ('twice toned') scales are a stepwise ('scala' — steps) sequence of notes using only whole tones and semitones within an octave. There are no bits missing. Our much hated practice of scales is based on the three commonest versions: the major scale, the minor and the chromatic. A hexachord is the first (or last) six notes culled from any diatonic scale: C to A (or E to C) on the white notes of a piano, put at its simplest. The vast majority of music before the middle of the eighteenth century was written using the transposable hexachordal mode as its primary building block of notes.

It can be no accident that at the very time atonal music — the ultimate expression of Bach's experiment — reached its zenith in the twentieth century, so there began to appear a renewed interest in music of pre-Bach eras; that is, music based on simple, singular hexachordal relationships. It is as though a Jungian collective unconscious was at work, repulsed by the enormity of the aurally chaotic but stringently logical position music had got itself into, in search of a Rousseau — like past of sweet airs and inevitability. The proof is in the pudding; for every concert given by the *International Society for Contemporary Music* or the *Park Lane Group*, fifty are given by the *Academy of Ancient Music* and *Les Arts Florissants*.

Another strand in this tangled web is a simple truth which any fiddle player or singer will acknowledge: the hexachordal mode is the product of natural phenomena and the natural inclinations of the ear. The relationship between any note and the note a fifth above it (or a fourth below) is a small part of the universal laws of acoustics. I shall expand on this a little later, but pause briefly to point out that this 'natural'interval of a fifth is not the one you usually hear (if your piano has been tuned recently). Equal-tempered chromaticism — the notion that all the semitones in the octave are the same distance apart from their neighbours — is a fabrication developed by harpsichord and organ-tuners of the early eighteenth century. I do not deny its legitimacy; clearly equal temperament had to be concocted to satisfy the needs of composers who were drifting further and further away from the confines of closely related keys. But fabrication or concoction it is none the less, and we should bear that in mind. We should also bear in mind that this move to equal temperament — that all the semitones are the same distance apart — was a slow and halting one. When Beethoven, in the *Waldstein Sonata*, shifted from his original C major to a new idea in E major, it would not have sounded the same to his audience as to us. The E major passages would have had a different feel, because the spacing of the notes was different to the spacing in the original C major. Beethoven was making a virtue out of necessity; but if we were to hear the *Waldstein Sonata* as Beethoven imagined it, we would hear it out of tune, because we are conditioned only to hear equal-tempered scales.

It should be remembered — and stressed — that nowhere on the globe, save Western Europe and its satellites, is the octave divided into twelve equal parts. In Asia, with the notable exception of India, modes are almost always based on a hexachord, and most frequently are pentatonic (using only five notes) within the hexachord. I could take any number of examples from Japan, China, Tibet, Korea, Thailand — even, if I move out of Asia, Ireland, South America and Central Africa — but it is only proper for me to use as examples for my argument the music with which I am most familiar: that of the Indonesian archipelago.

It says something for their durability and infinite subtlety that, from northern Sumatra to Papua New Guinea, there are only two significant modes on these 13,000 occupied islands. They are *slendro*, a pentatonic mode extracted from the hexachord C-A (CDEGA), and *pelog,* a pentatonic mode extracted from the hexachord E-C (EFGBC). My discovery, which I have not seen written in any musicological treatise, is that if you superimpose these two modes within one octave, you get our common diatonic scale of C major, though of course not in equal temperament. The tuning of *slendro* and *pelog* is much subtler than that. Now musicians in the Indonesian archipelago are not stupid. They have stringed instruments and bamboo flutes over-blowing at the octave and fifth; and they can sing. Blow across the top of a bottle to get a note; blow it harder, and the note changes to either an octave or a fifth above. This is a natural phenomenon. *Slendro* is quite clearly a redistribution of the first five notes of this natural cycle of rising fifths (CGdae becomes cdega). The ancient Babylonians knew of this; and so did the Chinese in the first millennium BC, as Laurence Picken has demonstrated in his recreation of the Zhou dynasty melody *Longevities without boundaries*, which uses the first four notes of the cycle of fifths (gaCD) eschewing the last E, which redistributed becomes the third of the mode, in the first five notes of a diatonic scale. And *slendro* is, by other names, perhaps the most common hexachordal pentatonic mode to be found throughout the world. It is our black notes on the piano. The Scots and the Irish have it, the Indians have it, the Chinese and Koreans have it, the Aztecs have it and so do the Malays. Even Debussy gives it prominence in many of his works. I am still recovering from the shock of hearing an old Balinese *suling* player piping out *Auld Lang Syne* to attract tourists to buy his bamboo flutes. Any day now, a *slendro* gamelan group will discover they can play *Amazing Grace*, and then we are all doomed.

Slendro is common throughout the world, because it is derived from natural laws; the overblowing of flutes and the halving of string lengths follow the same acoustic precepts. It is not, then, a confection of man. Man has learned of it, much as he learned of the hybridization of plants or the breeding of livestock. The first bow-men plucking bowstrings learned empirically about the position of acoustic nodes along a stretched string. We have ancient mouth-bows and tromps (what used to be called 'Jew's harps' — the *genggong* still in use in Bali); they all made their contribution to the empirical understanding of harmonics and pitch relations. This understanding was achieved in relative isolation. Can it be possible that an Aztec flute player had an ancient, common point of reference with a Javanese gamelan? Certainly, we can imagine the Greeks learning from the Egyptians, who learned from the ancient Babylonians of the third Millennium BCthe properties of the hexachord through their own empirical knowledge of the cycle of fifths.

Pelog (efgbc) is a harder nut to crack. It is a pentatonic mode, but formed, as, I demonstrated before, out of the hexachord at the upper end of the diatonic scale. But how was it formed? It has no direct link with the natural harmonic series. There is a simple explanation, which involves its relationship with *slendro,* but this simple relationship with its more common cousin has ramifications, which will make every protagonist of atonal music blanch. If you transpose *slendro* up a third within a notional diatonic scale, you get *pelog*. It is as simple and as complicated as that. Moreover, if you extract from that notional diatonic scale the notes which are common to both s*lendro* and *pelog*, they form that sweetest of chords — the major triad. If you reverse the process and transpose *pelog* up a third within a notional diatonic scale, you get *slendro*. And this diatonic scale is the Phrygian mode, or — to put it more pointedly — an early version of the modern minor scale; and again, the notes common to both modes form a minor triad. This is quite startling. It means that, in the Malay archipelago, there must have been previous knowledge of the diatonic major and minor scales which preceded the abstractions of these two modes. It is too much of a coincidence to suppose the superimposition of these two modes on each other 'accidentally' creates the very same diatonic scales we have in the West. Western Europe is always considered to be the birthplace of the major and minor scales — and a latecomer to them at that. But I am convinced that the properties of these comparatively modern scales were known by peoples much older, much more scattered than has previously been thought possible. *Pelog* and *slendro* are not the confections of man. The diatonic scales, major and minor, are not the confections of man. I would go so far as to say that all indigenous modes throughout the

world, with the singular exception of the equal-tempered chromatic scale of Western Europe, are products of a slow, sometimes
cautious discovery of what may reasonably be called 'natural phenomena'. All over the world, men have for millennia discovered
sections of, or entire, diatonic major and minor scales and their triads without the benefits of communication, or the aid of notation.

Had Bach arranged his two books of twenty-four preludes and
fugues in the more natural way — as a cycle of rising or falling
fifths — he would have done us a great service. He would have
shown the marvellous and magical phenomenon of the unending
circle of relationships of fifths which is unique to the dodecaphonic, equal-tempered scale. At the same time, he never allowed
individual preludes and fugues to fluctuate from intrinsic hexachordal key relationships. Instead, perhaps deliberately or perhaps
without thinking, he arranged them chromatically; and by doing so
set off a train of events from which we in Western Europe have yet
to recover.

Nevertheless, progress — if that is what it is — towards full
chromaticism, which propounds that all twelve semitones have an
equal intervallic relationship with every other semitone, was very
slow. I need not lay out the history of the rise of chromaticism here;
whole libraries are devoted to it. But all through the nineteenth
century and even as late as Richard Strauss, there is an intrinsic
acknowledgment that hexachordal relationships, discovered and
elaborated on long before equal-tempered scales were theorized
sufficiently to become the standard, are the fundamental building
block of music. Consider the waltz from *Der Rosenkavalier*; it
lurches wittily from one 'unrelated key' to another, but in each
phrase the melody and the harmony remain firmly within the hexachord — indeed, the waltz-tune itself blossoms into a series of
hexachords. Richard Strauss, like every other composer before
him, instinctively holds to all hexachordal truths; they are, after all,
incontrovertible natural phenomena.

Schoenberg, blinded by the possibilities of unconfined chromaticism, forgot where this chromaticism had come from. He
assumed, wrongly in my view, that because all the twelve semi-

tones were now tuned equidistantly, they possessed intrinsically an equal relationship with every other semitone. However much apologists for his theories protest to the contrary, he confused 'note' with 'interval'. But the ear of the listener intuitively knows otherwise. The natural affinity of the diatonic intervals within a hexachord outweighs by far the theoretical notion of an affinity between any or all semitones which are tuned equidistantly. Thus the perfect fifth or even the augmented fourth (notwithstanding that old medieval law) have 'natural characteristics' which the minor ninth or the major seventh or any other non-hexachordal interval cannot possibly possess. Moreover, our ears tend to grasp hold of these 'natural characteristics' as they flash by. In any random cluster of notes, the ear will still pick out from the aurally chaotic mess those intervals which adhere to the principles discovered by our bow-plucking ancestors. As we receive cluster after cluster into our brains, we cannot help but force their seeming atonality into a personal kind of tonality. And if these clusters are too difficult or too fast for the brain to accommodate, or to sort out into their component, hexachordal parts, we become confused. The aural experience, the music, is no longer 'for pleasure'. This repulsive reaction is nothing to do with our subjective responses to 'new' music; it is not a qualitative judgment born out of ignorance, as the protagonists for atonal serialism would like to believe, which we can correct by education. We are children of the universe, and the universe stays loyal to its hexachord. There is, even now, research abroad which seems to show there is a mathematical relationship between the diatonic scales and the formations in the cochlea.

Equal temperament and the consequent aural acceptance of complete atonality are, if you like, the 'genetic engineering' of music. This genetic engineering of sound may produce something wonderful, just as biochemical genetic engineering might produce the perfect potato; but equally it may produce a monster. My contention is that Schoenberg and his followers did not think carefully enough about what they were doing when they ignored so much of, and tinkered with, the natural characteristics of the hexachord.

Their genetically engineered baby, serial atonality, is a Frankenstein's monster: 'Music for Displeasure'.

[first published in the *Times Literary Supplement,* 8 September 2000 and reprinted by kind permission]

5

Modernism and After

Robin Holloway

[This essay was written and first published in *The Cambridge Review* in 1989. I have not attempted to update the main text, but rather, have added some further reflections after 10 years of progress. It is worth saying at the start that my use of the catch-phrase 'postmodern' does not invoke any so-called theory or philosophy, which seems to me on the whole shallow and insubstantial, when not downright trumpery.]

Before exploring musical postmodernism, it would be well to try a condensed amount of modernism itself. Modern music as a whole consists of the entire spread of the post-Wagnerian century, a release of energies from the impact, whether direct, oblique, or in vehement rejection of the most influential composer there has ever been. Modernism itself is, strictly speaking, a disparate mixture of particular attitudes within this whole. But for present purposes, general and particular will be taken together. Their focus remains the first twenty years or so of this century. Though this period is still rightly termed the heroic, pioneering phase of modern music, and still best characterised by images of revolution and explosion, its multifarious manifestations also include the music of composers long-since widely accepted. Its unacceptable face — a residuum fraught with problems that continue to hang heavily over much that has followed — still receives colloquially the term 'nasty'. 'Nasty modern music', i.e. incomprehensible and unattractive, has not yet been assimilated, many decades after it was written, and perhaps never will be. Postmodernism has inherited this split and is an attempt to put it right.

The heroic pioneering phase is above all a time of liberations — emancipation of the dissonance in the atonality of Schoenberg, Berg and Webern, which seeks to register an unprecedented intensity and ramification in expressionist 'onomatopoeia of the emotions'; emancipation of the consonance, in the rebirth of modality and the uses of tonal chords unattached to tonal function, whose origin lies in Debussy (and behind him Satie), though it ramified quickly into such widely different figures as Stravinsky, Bartók, Vaughan-Williams and Puccini. (These two views of harmony can overlap and complement each other, as also the contemporaneous ways in which rhythm is emancipated. The Viennese version tends towards extremes of fluidity and fluctuation, the Franco-Russian towards a strict mechanisation of metre and pulse heard, at its most drastic in Stravinsky's *Rite of Spring* and *Les Noces*); emancipation of form to fit programmes, evoke pictures, or symbolise inner states of feeling; emancipation of musical material (following the example of Beethoven in the finale of his *Choral Symphony*), whereby cheap strains from barracks, café, dance-palace and gutter penetrate the concert hall and opera-house. This can be bitter and tragic, as in Mahler and thence Berg, festive in the crowd-scenes from Stravinsky's *Petrushka*, ironic and pathetic to characterise the life of its puppets indoors, or all these things at once. Ives makes the musical foreground of a work like the *Holidays Symphony* out of vulgar Americana, the purpose being at once communally transcendent and nostalgically personal.

In all this, music timbre takes on a new importance; the vast orchestra is a complex machine of individual effects for evoking the magical, the erotic, the primeval etc. by outer depiction or inner exploration, in turn heralding the emancipation of sonority itself; Varèse, combining the influence of Debussy and Stravinsky, plus an admixture from expressionist Schoenberg and the modernistic Strauss of *Elektra*, with sounds evoking heavy industry, can render equally the exuberance of the city, the emptiness of the desert, the organisms of nature, and processes inspired by physics and chemistry.

Alongside all this rises the birth of a specifically modern form of imitation. In France Debussy's early flirtation with the Watteau period à la Verlaine (*Suite Bergamasque; Fêtes galantes*) develops via the more explicit *Pour le piano* and *Hommage à Rameau* to its final sublimation in the last sonatas (three completed from a projected set of six, published with a pastiche eighteenth century title-page, as the response to the first world war of a *musicien français*). Ravel's *Sonatine*, Piano Trio, and *Le Tombeau de Couperin* are clearly comparable. In Germany, there is the voluminous neo-Bach of Reger, who also wrote a *Concerto in Olden Style*. The *ne plus ultra* remains Strauss' *Der Rosenkavalier* (1910): this work, with its apparently blatant *volte face*, after his recent expressionist excesses, to a rococo setting with pastiche-Mozart (albeit very Ritzy to later ears) infused with strains from Italian opera into a post-Wagnerian leitmotivic texture, the whole swathed in a luscious recreation of the mid-nineteenth-century Viennese waltzes of Johann Strauss (no relation), can epitomise the tendency already present amidst the pioneers themselves towards the postmodern aesthetic of nowadays, where historical accuracy goes for nothing and appetite reigns supreme.

None the less the prevailing aim was deliberate innovation, and it is hardly surprising, after such radical and rapid change, that retrenchment should have set in; for the problem of how to follow on from it must have been acute. Schoenberg, having reached the stage where expressionist freedom could be lightened, broadened, 'normalised', falls silent and then (aged 47 in 1921) comes up with an artificial language hierarchising the twelve semitones, with which he proceeds to build gigues, waltzes and other old dance forms, soon moving to variation-sets and sonata-works whose internal contradiction between form and technique proved incapable of resolution. Bartók, after the astonishing flowering of stage-works, songs, and chamber-works c.1911-22, turns (aged 42 in 1923) to increasingly formulaic treatment of rhythmic, melodic and structural symmetries, which for some listeners dry the life from the greater part of his admirably single-minded inter-war development, until the works of his exile (America 1940-45) mitigate the rigour.

Stravinsky (aged 38 in 1920) makes the oddest rebound from his own modernism (which had been succeeded by a few years of apparently fragmentary explorations of many incompatible directions). Diaghilev's request to arrange some standard early eighteenth-century material attributed to Pergolesi produces *Pulcinella* (1919-20), an 'epiphany' (as Stravinsky described it later) that opens up a previously latent aesthetic of creative 'kleptomania' (again his own term), rifling given areas of the past for raw cliché material that he then recomposes and makes his own. Another ostensibly hack-job from the same time — orchestrating a couple of extra numbers needed for the 1921 revival of Tchaikovsky's *Sleeping Beauty* — proved to be equally fruitful. Not immediately, since this influence only surfaces in *Apollo* (1927); but his next ballet, *The Fairy's Kiss* (1928), is entirely made out of Tchaikovsky's material, moulded by a creative identification, at once affectionate and detached, that transcends arrangement or pastiche. So the way lies open for another quarter-century or so of transformational theft, culminating in a full-length neo-Mozartean opera (*The Rake's Progress* 1948-51). Such a procedure would be a recipe for disaster in lesser hands; Stravinsky does it with such geometric rigour, and such a strong personal profile, that what seemed to cultivated musicians of the time mere jerry-built footling, shows by now every sign of permanence.

All these are in the obvious sense 'postmodern'reactions by the principal modernists themselves. Radical innovation that had been largely intuitive is followed either by laborious rationalisation or brilliant evasion. Even when viewed with sympathy and affection, a sense persists in all three composers, by common consent the principal figures in twentieth-century music, that an astonishing youthful achievement brings forth occasional mature masterpieces — rather than a sustained harvest.

The next wave of modernists was far from sympathetic. For their spokesman Boulez (aged 20 in 1945) this broadly speaking neoclassical turn on the part of the great pioneers was not so much a retrenchment as a betrayal. Boulez's notoriously unforgiving attacks are the negative aspect of a new, fighting hard-line that takes as its starting-point the late work of Webern in conjunction with the first primitive experiments by Boulez'teacher Messiaen in the serialisation of durations, dynamics and modes of attack. These composers (including Stockhausen and Nono, with Boulez the erstwhile 'Holy Trinity' of the European avant-garde) set up as heirs to the revolution, returning to the strait and narrow in 'correction' of the great pioneers' 'backsliding'. The only permissible past is an invented trajectory of perpetual progress, arrogantly prescribing that every work must be a completely new start.

Such drastic restriction of music's freedom of speech could not last long. Yet while it did it exercised an influence out of all proportion to its actual interest or efficacy. For the general music-lover, the late 1940s through to the mid-60s are, so far as contemporary music goes, the years of Britten and Shostakovich. But for those within the ivory tower, the compulsion to be utterly 'modern' was strong. The sense of an inquisition sniffing out sins of style, a police-force vigilant for crimes against historical inevitability, chimed all too easily with internal self-censorship to cripple the spontaneous musical faculty of a whole generation of composers. It is still around, albeit driven to ground in a few Italian and West German radio stations, American universities and alchemical ghettoes of acoustical research.

The first sign of a thaw came from within the citadel itself, Ligeti's orchestral works *Atmosphères* (1961) and *Lontano* (1967) recognise the unreality of the unbelievably complicated schematics of total serialisation, using them instead for what the ear *can* apprehend, in slow moving wedges and clouds of sound almost impressionistic in effect, though ultra-precisely notated and monitored by an exquisite untheoretical ear. Between these two pieces came the *dada* hilarity of the *Aventures* and *Nouvelles Aventures*, and the massive application of the same world of sound-effects in the marvellous *Requiem*. After this, Ligeti was free to reinterpret, in his own highly idiosyncratic way, the basic terms of music (*Melodien; San Francisco Polyphony*), evolving for such moments as the closing duet of his first opera a 'non-tonal consonance' whose transparent beauty arouses highest hopes for his long-awaited second, a version of *The Tempest*. Ligeti, a figure of the highest importance, is only postmodernist in being a refugee from the prohibitive extremes of the avant-garde. He has not abandoned their aesthetic stance; calling his masterly Horn Trio (1982) a *hommage à Brahms* does not mean that he quotes or imitates — indeed his published interviews deplore such practices (though the work is none the less built upon a characteristic 'bending' of the archetypal horn-call that runs through all Western music since the eighteenth century). [It is now sadly apparent that Ligeti has not achieved his *Tempest*, but the harvest has yielded plentiful minor works of high compositional elegance, and the major series of *Etudes* for piano continues to expand and astound.]

The other thaw came from without the citadel in the impish personality of John Cage. Under his mind-softening influence, the avant-garde changed overnight from total rigour to total anarchy, in a happy chaos of multimedia 'happenings', fast-food Zen Buddhism and games of chance, whose spiritual value could be assured by evoking the *I-Ching*, and whose intellectual respectability was provided by Mallarmé's *Un coup de dès*. But it takes a stronger artistic personality than any composer involved here to turn either strict serialism or aleatoric freedom into a means of genuine expression; both straitjacket and infinite liberty produced for the most part an anonymous predictability of gesture and greyness of sound. The survivors from this second thaw are the less pretentious pieces by its more musical exponents, above all the delightful Berio, once dubbed 'a kind of avant-garde Rossini'. His *Sinfonia,* with its multi-lingual layers of inter-textual song and speech, and the famous central movement, where the entire course of the scherzo from Mahler's second symphony underpins a surface of inventive, suggestive, and sometimes profound puns upon quotations from and allusions to a range of music from Bach to Berio's own coevals, remains a key work of the 1960s, a period-piece that has, as Stravinsky said, 'dated in the right way'.

The later course of the 'Holy Trinity' themselves has been almost uniformly disappointing. Nono, lost for more than a decade in the slogan-screaming wastes of radical chic, has more recently surfaced in a series of gentle, introspective works of definite, if pallid, beauty. Boulez now runs the European avant-garde Establishment from the IRCAM bunker alongside the Pompidou Centre, and occasionally tinkers with an old piece or adds a few more centimetres to *Répons*, a big work-in-progress for orchestra and technology. Stockhausen works with megalomaniac confidence at *Licht*, his seven-day cycle of operas that expands, with precious little musical content, his own life and experience into universal myth. A hard-line avant-garde continues with composers so different as Elliott Carter (aged 92), Shapey (80), Xenakis (78), Birtwistle (67), Ferneyhough (57) and Finnissy (55), just as it had during the 20s and 30s, when they reacted against their own radical achievement. [This remains true, even if in the last decade some of these figures, whose ages have been updated, have assumed the mantle of the establishment or begun in their own way a conspicuous rapprochement with a wider range of musical expression. I would specifically draw attention to Carter's recent *Symphonia*.] And now we seem to be entering an epoch of neo-avant-garde, whose young composers are, by their ignorance of history, in danger of rewriting what has already been written twice this century, while spouting the familiar rhetoric of obligatory perpetual innovation.

Meanwhile the wider musical world remained indifferent or hostile. Apart from mainstream figures, distinguished or mediocre, who simply carried on regardless, there have been many individual reactions against official modernism. They show by now every sign of coalescing into some sort of counterculture, however incoherent, which for aesthetic and stylistic, as well as the obvious chronological reasons, can be termed post-modernist. The main difference from the earlier phase of reaction in the inter-war decades is that it is not an affair of the principal figures 'reneging' upon their own earlier advances.

One of the first was the self-transformation of a run-of-the-mill avant-gardist, out of sheer desperation at the poverty of his language, into a 'born-again' traditionalist. George Rochberg's Third String Quartet (1972) attracted considerable attention at the time; but its *ersatz* Mahler and late-Beethoven do not survive familiarity, and the 'dialogue' placing these transfusions from the beloved past next door to standard twentieth-century quartet sounds of Bartók, Schoenberg and Stravinsky sounds more than a bit jejune. A rather different exactly contemporary endeavour, my own attempt in three works from the early 1970's to get inside favourite Schumann songs and expand them in different directions (gathering up *en route* a medley of references to later romantics, impressionists, and early moderns) was born equally out of a sense of the prohibition by the *Zeitgeist* of music's natural expressive possibilities. Clearly one can't spend the rest of one's life recomposing Schumann! This was a steppingstone from the arid to the fertile, an 'open sesame' to riches that, once gained, could be spread and spent in many different ways: a personal answer to a widely-felt need that now seems very much of its time.

But by far the best-known anti-modernist reaction of the last two decades is that of the American minimalists. Born in the golden glow of 1960s California, Terry Riley's *In C*, Philip Glass's *Einstein on the Beach* and the process-pieces of Steve Reich still retain a quality of delightful simplicity: a return, not exactly to fundamentals, but to something unpretentious and refreshing in its play of pattern. This 'answer' to the tortuous complexities of the avant-garde is mainly in deed, not word. Glass's much-quoted opinion of the modernist music he encountered during his years in Paris (as one of the last of a long line of American composers who came to study with Nadia Boulanger) is no doubt symptomatic. In finding Paris a 'wasteland'and its dominating musical taste 'crazy and creepy', he probably spoke for the unwitting millions who have subsequently flocked to minimalist events and bought their recorded albums. The huge international success of this movement in recent years is more akin to pop than classical mainstream and a far cry from the three-quarters-empty halls which confront contemporary composers of any other stylistic persuasion.

Yet Reich's more recent music for big symphony orchestra and Glass's adventures in the conventional opera house have manifestly forfeited the first attractive spontaneity: while younger successful composers in this vein tend to put their most fetching invention into their titles — e.g. John Adams (*Nixon in China; Harmonielehre; Shaker Loops*); Michael Torke (*Ecstatic Orange; Bright Blue Music; The Yellow Pages*). There is no neo-classicism or neo-romanticism in this music, but neither is there much to listen to. On present showing minimalism needs to be inter-fused much more closely with 'real music' for its considerable potential to be realised and released. [This was well under way at the original time of writing in the music of Louis Andriessen, whose more recent pieces fuse facets of Stravinsky with pop, rock and California day-glo. John Adams has also expanded, filling out the attractive surfaces of his earlier successes with something that sounds suspiciously like real content.]

Another American composer provides a quirky footnote here. David Del Tredici belongs to the same generation as the older minimalists and shares the same background of serialism under a balmy Californian sun. In discovering 'the power of the musical cliché' he did not relinquish the modernist techniques which had already produced some very individual and powerful work. So *Pop-Pourri* and other early pieces from the series inspired by Lewis Carroll's *Alice* books take the formulae of tonality at its most moribund, to explore and explode them with minute exactitude. The bizarre consequences reach their apogee in *Final Alice* (1976) where the process is applied to the full-blown romantic symphony orchestra of Strauss and Mahler. After this dangerously ambiguous success, the sharp edge has become increasingly blunted. Later *Alice* works are longer and squashier; the discrepancy between technical mastery and content that is trivial or absurd, at first part of the knife-edge joke, is now merely disconcerting. Again, as with the minimalists (different in everything else but comparable in making a little go a long way), one awaits with hope an upward turn towards more fruitful pursuits.

This account of its background has already overlapped with some of postmodernism's most important musical manifestations. I will now, more uncertainly, attempt to sketch the situation as it currently stands, and to indicate some aspects of a post-modernist aesthetic, its practice and its future.

The most striking positive is the extraordinary availability of musical sources, an embarrassment of largesse from world-culture embracing many centuries of the European tradition, and moving outwards to incorporate 'ethnic musics' from every known race and clime. Natural and quasi-natural sounds can be used — bird song, whale song, etc. — machines, bells, traffic — both raw and 'cooked', for a further immense extension is provided by the rapid advance of acoustic technology, either to transform what already exists or to bring into being what never existed before. This gigantic time-and-placeless supermarket affords unprecedented opportunity for Stravinsky's 'kleptomania'. It is his 'take, eat' attitude, (now mostly rampaging and indiscriminate) that has proved for the moment the most influential. In theory there should be no limits or prohibitions; nothing is impossible.

The negative is that such omni-availability conceals impoverishment. It is often said that while there has never been so much culture, this epoch has none of its own. We are all chameleons; everything is revival; and such superabundance of knowing allows any previous style to be made to order — here a classical job, here a romantic, here a modern. This skin-deep versatility recalls the happy promiscuity of interior decoration down the last two centuries or so: Gothic, Chinese, Pompeian, Indian, Elizabethan, Romanesque, Moorish, Greek, Queen Anne, etc. (all in heavy inverted commas). It is one of the most obvious features of recent architecture that this facility with décor now garnishes the outsides of buildings as well. Behind the musical version of this lies, rather than Stravinsky's transformation of borrowed material, the aesthetic stance of Ravel who, in recommending that composers should find models to imitate, claimed that their originality, if any, would be shown in their 'unwitting deviation'. Another angle on this stance comes with a remark made by his son about Prokofiev — 'first my father composes music like everyone else, then he Prokofievizes it'.

Obviously practitioners in all the arts have always imitated both deliberately and inadvertently, and working directly from models used to be a principal method of instruction. Direct imitation leads to replica-art á la Quinlan Terry, whereas in Rochberg's 'late Beethoven' the modern version reveals incomplete mastery of the old rules, and an 'unwitting deviation' that is shown only in feeble insipidity. The playful replica streets, colonial mansions etc. of Disneyland are more spirited and skilful. Each is vulnerable when compared to the real thing. The Prokofiev-Ravel-Stravinsky stance was different. And what they did for themselves with assured particularity has broadened now into latter-day 'cubism', whereby the elements of any style can be redeployed, through dislocation and re-assemblage, to make new configurations that contain new meanings.

Imitation could be something different again, neither slavish nor subversive, but more casual and unselfconscious. A composer exploring the possibilities of his material can find himself upon an old track which seems to draw him forward with irresistible magnetic force. This Roman road was once the only track across the terrain; everyone knew it, understood it, used it. By now overgrown, it is still the most direct way to get from here to there; it took this course because it was the best way to go. The thrill of rediscovery transcends the temporal and personal. A composer need not be excluded from a communal experience of great accumulated richness. Fundamentals of technique and expression are impersonal, timeless and there for the asking. It is like plugging into an electricity grid that stretches far back in time and place.

Then there is the particular thrill of personal affinity for an era, a genre or form, above all a specific composer. Close relationships can now be established with figures remote in time and culture, relationships that formerly could only exist within a tradition. If I want Bruckner (say) for my compositional father, I can have him. A tradition-based descent would be a matter of inheritance and continuity in which the original is perpetuated and transformed (Bruckner into Mahler, Schmidt, Sibelius, Stenhammar). This presupposes an 'essence'beneath the 'veneer' of stylistic surface. The 'elective affinity' goes rather for what it *can* go for: the music's manifest surface of sonority, procedure, gesture, manner, physiognomy; in a word, its style.

There are two possibilities here. The first is archeological — the resolution of what Bruckner couldn't choose for himself — a sympathetic reconciliation of, for instance, the many self-contradictory versions of his third symphony or a fusion and completion of his successive drafts of a finale for his ninth. For the second there is no adequate term — it would involve, somehow, a realisation of the symphonies that Bruckner didn't write, where 'unwitting deviation' could produce something of independent value that manifested the imitator's own original creativity. Between the two comes *Menardisme* where, as in Borges's well-known fable of the re-author of *Don Quixote*, the aspirant is so absorbed in the model as actually to compose it identically again; but this is really only a conceit and not so deep as it at first seems. [A recent analogue is provided by Anthony Payne's 'elaboration' of Elgar's sketches for his Third Symphony, where Payne has stepped boldly, yet respectfully, into the master's skin to realise what failing powers could not achieve. While not the popular success of Elgar's actual First Symphony, which received 100 performances in its first year, Elgar's Third has been played worldwide to enormous effect.]

This is not prohibited by law; so why, in practice, does it turn out to be so impossible? Compare the manifest influence among contemporaries (which if taken too close actually could infringe copyright!). In the early 1980s, most of the student composers in this country were doing their own Peter Maxwell Davies, in the mid-80s the wind veered towards Birtwistle, [who is once again in fashion], and after a flurry of minimalism, the principal aims became Ferneyhough and Finnissy. To make Bruckner the goal is in theory the same, save only for the time-and-culture gap. Should I want to wear his clothes, wield his weapons, drive his locomotive — or, more soberly, use his forms, procedures, sonorities — there would be nothing to prevent such a consummation except censors within and without whom it ought to be easy to outwit.

So why the guilt; and where exactly is it located? The old law said, 'Thou shalt not steal', but after Stravinsky the new order is 'Steal away'. It is pointless and stupid to replicate what has already been achieved. Yes: but why shouldn't there be more of it, if possible? The criterion, as always, is *quality*. If the result is good enough, it is justified — a computer could do it, if a computer could do it *well* enough. Creative impetus would be demoted to the perpetuation of genres; personal expression would be lost in craftsmanship, like the replicating phases of Egyptian and Chinese civilisation.

There is a certain hollowness to all this! The dream of complete stylistic transparency is an illusion or a projection into the future, and it is hard to imagine that we will ever cease to value the 'unwitting deviation', whereby human error becomes original creation. More manifestly fruitful is a somewhat different return to the past. History and hindsight tend to make factitious inevitability out of what must in fact have been completely fluid. The choices made, the paths taken, were not the only possibilities. This, true for particular works from all periods, also applies to broader questions of style and language. Especially in transitional periods — the epoch of Monteverdi, the overlap of late baroque with early classical, the open-endedness of the early romantics, above all the vast pregnancy of the area where deliquescent romanticism overlaps with pioneer modernism — the past is full of roads not taken, branches that didn't flower, latent and nascent alternatives that a composer can return to, develop and bring into being 'what might have been'.

This is certainly retrospective (at least to begin with) but by no
means a dead exercise in replica or a narcotic nostalgia-bath. At the
most modest level it might be quite functional, a 'house-in-order'
aesthetic tidying up loose ends, rescuing and realising potential
that might otherwise be wasted — very much the spirit of the age
in politics and economics. While its higher flights are of course
unpredictable, and could lead to some very interesting places.

Another more complex related tendency is the stylistic and pro-
cedural cross-copulation that arises as a matter of course out of
a-historical omni-availability. For in practice undivided devotion
to one model is unlikely; everyone likes many different things in
their own unique way. Cross-pollination to a programme would
once have seemed absurd (suppose Strauss had decided before-
hand to mix Mozart, Wagner, and Viennese waltzes in making *Der
Rosenkavalier*, or that Stravinsky deliberately planned for *Oedipus
Rex* its amalgam of Bach, Verdi, Offenbach, Russian sacred and
secular). It just happened anyway as a result of strong individual
predilection. But now its possibilities are endless, it might even
reconcile ingredients that are on the face of it mutually incompatible and antagonistic. One can not only imagine a cubist
fragmentation of the stylistic constituents of a Machaut,
Mendelssohn, Mahler and Messiaen, but foresee cross-fertilisation
between aspects of any two, three or all four. [Even back in the
early 60s, I was thinking along these lines, as my notebooks testify,
where I listed together a range of diverse musics that included,
among many others, plainsong, Hindu rhythms, the Can-Can,
Semprini and The Rolling Stones. I had made the comment at the
time that the old obligations of choice, dexterity, control and
organising material, invention, taste, conscious artistry are not
lessened by this freedom. Indeed, I sensed that new and more complex ways of imposing order on increasingly diverse and far-flung
material would have effortfully to be discovered.]

Real substance can begin in just such playful games. For music
is fluid, by its nature a perpetual recycling of the same constituents.
A fifth is always a fifth; a clarinet is always a clarinet. Music could
be compared to the water in a fountain or, more organically, to a

life-cycle of growth, decay and rebirth. Far more than in the other arts, the same fundamental sonorous facts are at work. They are of course always evolving and being extended, reinterpreted, revived and renewed; but very little is actually added. Implicit in the immemorial 3 against 2 is the 17 against 31 (or whatever) of the 'new complexity'. Implicit in the earliest emotive dissonance is the grimace at the start of the *Choral Symphony* finale, Kundry's demonic laughter, Salome's death's-head kiss, the apocalyptic chord of Mahler's tenth symphony and so on. Implicit in exact tuning, all the subtle shades and nuances of micro-intervals. Most radical innovations down the decades have remained outside the mainstream of the art. Composers and performers agree in theory, but carry on as before. Even nowadays one feels that, in almost every instance, the spectacular new technologies either remain special effects or are only resorted to by composers short on good musical ideas.

Because, therefore, of its inherent malleability, music lends itself naturally to all the 'replicatory' possibilities I have been discussing. It remains astonishing that such apparent limitations should be capable of as many new twists and turns as there are composers of calibre.

Modernism meant an avidity for newness to carry music forward into realms of sensibility, organisation, sound itself, that had not existed before. The prevailing feeling is now that everything is complete, all that can be discovered has been, the elements can only be recycled in different alignments and juxtapositions. There is a sense that the great pioneers went too far, too fast — this excess being the very essence of their boldness — and in doing so a certain straightforward reciprocity between composer and audience was warped. The famous scandals of early modernism showed that this reciprocity was still intact; but in the decades since, after too much provocation and disappointment, too much exhortation to understand the incomprehensible and love the unlovesome, the audience has grown first fed up, then indifferent;

they vote with their feet and find their principal new thrills along the frontiers of the authentic performance movement [or in the simplistic wallpaper of 'holy minimalism'á la Tavener, Pärt and Górecki.

So postmodernism in music is tidying up after the orgy, putting the pieces together again, restoring the gaps and attempting to set up an establishment that will attract and satisfy a clientele. Hence the backward-looking, whether evasive or frank, of so much contemporary music. It is saying: 'Come in and hear our pieces. You'll like them, you'll understand them — music is music again !'

Neo-tonality, particularly neo-romanticism, is explicit in its appeal to old times when music went 'from the heart to the heart' to be understood and enjoyed without problems. Less obvious is the nostalgia of the avant-garde itself to revert to and perpetuate a time of innovatory revolution — the attitude, if not the music, aches with longing for every work to be a new start. The cold war between the two versions of nostalgia seems to be becoming a thing of the past. To use my own experience for its typical value, I remember, as a dissatisfied child of the 1950s-60s avant-garde, how difficult psychologically, as well as technically, it was to break away. The first shy efforts seemed to work — players liked it, audiences were pleased; so I went further along the same lines. What had begun speculatively, born of desperation and loss, became rapidly more natural. One waxes bolder, even provocative, in the face of a critical climate largely out of touch with what audiences actually want. One casts the net ever-wider, assimilating everything it catches to one's own native speech. Thus the spell is broken; one is admitted into the happy pluralism already described, where the avant-garde idiom, which had once been a stranglehold, becomes simply another available option.

So the immediate function of nostalgia is that it provides a starting-point in the familiar and loved: a way of reaching again the alienated audience for an age which once more places communication above the abstract goal of advancing the language. The great moderns were fervent to *say* something; all their innovations were directed towards utterance at the highest level of intensity. This fervour has been transferred into the now-prevailing nostalgia, giving to an ostensibly escapist attitude an urgency in which its principal function resides.

For the appeal of nostalgia is actually very strong. It is a general reaction to a century which has consisted of uniquely terrible series of disasters on the large scale and a mess of everything on the social and human scale. As it raved to its end (a constantly growing list of nuclear weapons, ruination of the environment and the institutions, degradation of all standards, AIDS, more cars, planes *etc.*), the call in the tiny microcosm of the arts to go on making it new became meaningless. Make it sweet, make it smile are better injunctions; even warnings of doom have got to be attractive and comprehensible, otherwise they will fall upon empty concert-halls. The awareness of what we have lost is so painful, where we find ourselves is so uncongenial, that the past becomes not so much a cosy retreat as a last-ditch shelter, a repository of all the values that really matter. It is where things are good — undestroyed, unpolluted, unabused. 'Nostalgia' is a burning emotion, fierce rather than enervating, purposeful rather than lazy. Its purpose is of course to enable composers once again to say what has always been said, and permit music to touch anew on what its listeners feel in ways that they will understand and enjoy.

Everything I have ventured here has inclined towards toying with or evading altogether musical history and rendering meaningless musical tradition as normally understood. What happens if a present-day composer, indifferent to time-travelling over the ocean of stylistic bric-à-brac, should seek to re-establish direct lineage with the great masters of the past? When Alexander Goehr, echoing Brahms, says that 'they knew something, which we have forgotten', he reflects a wide yearning for lost musical syntax and expression and the unified culture to which they belonged. If 'what the masters knew' is a sort of Philosopher's Stone, then it will prove impossible to locate. If, rather, it is the realisation that for them the musical usage was in accord with individual artistic imagination, then it becomes for us not an impossible Grail, but a realisable goal. We might know what the masters knew, as we might learn to write Latin and ancient Greek: what we ourselves possess is within our grasp, can be put to practice and constantly added to. Its location above all is our memory, mother of the muses; an obedient and productive Erda.

There has been a drastic break in continuity; the modern epoch grew out of a musical language that had been used very hard, and was for the moment spent (except for the occasional Rachmaninov, Nielsen, Schoeck or Franz Schmidt); an enormous shock was needed to liberate the freshness latent in the exhaustion, to show that there was, in fact, still matter and energy in plenty. But the familial link between past and present was broken. Talk of tradition nowadays makes one think wryly of Stravinsky's image of refitting old ships or Eliot's of cut flowers stuck into sand in the hope that they'll grow. For it was these two and their peers who snapped the chain; after them tradition can only be wooed and won obliquely, by such tactics as I have described. Even the most wide-eyed return to the past has to be aware of this. To employ its basic commonplaces, let alone the complex procedures of its maturity, is to wield a dangerous weapon, even if it is only used for the moment to trim the hedge and mow the lawn. And whether the attempt is for continuity, replication, fragmentation and re-assembly, or takes the form of yet another start from the blank page, it will have modernism behind it. Modernism is everyone's immediate past, and any remoter past can only be reached through it. Meanwhile we have the present: infinite possibility, dislocated like a wrecked mosaic that has been incorrectly restored.

But as time passes, there is a strong sense that the fragments want to join up again to form a coherent face. Stylistic schism is always slow to heal. The twentieth century's, the worst and most prolonged in the history of the art, will be correspondingly harder and longer to mend. But the general mood now tends towards integration and synthesis. Out of unprecedented multiplicity and eclecticism a new common practice in the handling of equal temperament is slowly emerging. The new possibilities of rhythmic fluidity and rigidity can be harnessed again to the internal and external movements of the human body. The discoveries of atonal, serial and post-serial pitch organisation can be integrated into the unchangeable verities of the harmonic series and the perceptual powers and pleasures of the human ear. The task now is to take up the most fertile possibilities released by the radical experiments of the pioneer moderns and their avant-garde followers in order to plough them back into good brown earth.

6

Form and Meaning:
the inner life of music

Robin Walker

'Lenzes Gebot, die süße Not, die legt' es ihm in die Brust,
nun sang er, wie er mußt!'
'Spring's law, from sweet necessity, placed it in his breast,
then he sang, as indeed he must!'

Die Meistersinger von Nürnberg, Act II, scene iii

Form is a musical shape perceived in its totality after its unfolding
in real time. This is not to be confused with structure, which is a
describable pattern or design. We recognise a person subjectively
as a personality, and physical characteristics play a part in this.
However, ultimately we sense them as a form; the sum total of all
our reactions and stimulated feelings. We may also define a person
objectively as a structure in terms of limbs and vital organs, but
this would not be their form, merely a description. The experience
of form goes beyond words and beyond conventional analysis.

A successful musical form is expressive because it is laden with
meaning beyond words. We respond emotionally because the
sounds as a whole awaken our deepest sense of self and value.

Such music affirms identity while also being a significant extension of it, adding to experience and unlocking potential for growth. Inherent in any convincing form is the idea that the familiar is made new. It affirms what already is and permits growth by showing what may yet be. The resonance of meaning comes from our recognition of the formal archetype, which originates from the universal and primordial structures found in Nature. This gives us a feeling of clarification and validation of belief, creating the feeling that we have stepped closer towards a goal. Our sense of truth is deepened by being nearer to it than before. Great music offers us a paradigm of a dynamic and ideal way of being.

In the contemporary context, the prevailing culture of iconoclasm, scepticism and relativism mean that the traditional archetypes that govern our sense of value have been eroded. The reference points that are the fundaments of the healthy psyche and provide the goals of growth are no longer directly available to us. The composer has to find these absent archetypes in himself and in opposition to the culture around him.

Despite the prevailing poverty of modernism, humanity is still naturally inclined to develop towards its flowering in classical civilisation; an adaptation of Nature which is, at the same time, harmonious with it. It is the existence of archetypes in the psyche that make this evolution possible. As such good art, and especially good music, bring forth civilised value through the expression of the model of the integrated psyche, which is both the evidence of and the path towards classical culture.

The contemporary composer is faced with an immense challenge, if he is to rediscover the expressive power of form, which is the desired object of all musical endeavor. In the mind of such a creative artist, the achievement of form is intimately bound up with his desire for meaning, and meaning is elusive in modern culture. For the successful creator of such forms, and for his authentic listeners, the reward should be a sustained and imperishable sense of meaning; a rich and lasting impression on those who experience it. This is rarely achieved now, and it is worth investigating why this is so.

Formal incompleteness reduces meaning. In fact, a work that is without formal expression is strictly speaking not worthy of serious consideration, measured against the criterion of bringing forth civilized value. If a work is no greater than the sum of its parts, it is a failure in terms of form. Unfortunately, the ambition of the artist to express himself is often far in advance of his ability to achieve that expression. So, while the desire for expression may drive an artist's creativity, there is often a misunderstanding as to how to make an objective or autonomous artefact out of that desire, with a consequent failure to achieve form. Without the psychological depth and musical technique to make coherent this desire for expression, the creative effort will most likely stall at a level below that of a successful form. This results in a reduction of expressive power and potential, which exists then only at the structural level. It may even produce no more than an uneasy series of dislocated gestures, vitiating expressive power entirely.

The desire for meaning, which motivates the artist to create forms, is bound up with the need for integration of the Self. One of the distinguishing features of the artist is that he recognizes that to take the path to integration is to accept a universal invitation, one which requires that all obstacles are removed from the determined path. The path to integration is no less than the great spiritual quest, which, above all things, can only be conducted at a pace not determined by the individual, but by the nature of the process itself. It is necessary to surrender to the unpredictable and probably slow pace of this journey, however severe the psychological discomfort. The painstaking creation of a space in which 'to be' is essential groundwork for the artist who wishes to create expressive form, and any attempt to hurry this process is bound to bring it down at an early stage. We have to remind ourselves that while structures are constructed, forms only grow, and that structures are made in response to a formal vision, not the other way round.

It can be appreciated how important it is to reject any timesaving intellectual interventions that suggest themselves in the process of formal contemplation. Such interventions, ideas often of a non-musical origin, however plausibly they may present themselves, do not operate at a level above that of structural know-how or manipulation. When constructing in response to formal require-ments, such ideas may well make a contribution at the problem-solving level of labour, but cannot be used as shortcuts to formal completeness. One can have intellectual ideas about growth, but they do not themselves ensure that it happens. The strong tempta-tion presented by deadlines, the external pressures of career and peer pressure have to be fiercely resisted.

The composer is concerned both with the motivation for making forms and with finding guarantees for their successful making. The spiritual quest, which is the engine of form-making, is an archetypal experience recorded down the ages in song and story. Clearly, Man is made for such a journey. That is not to say he is automatically equipped to undertake it. Before the artist can contemplate the success of such a journey, and of the things he might produce on the way, he must perceive what is necessary to aid him. He needs respect for materials, passivity, practical train-ing, stamina, and a host of other things besides. Above all, he must suppress the postulating intellect in favour of intuiting the unfold-ing of his material, through its latent, almost physical, properties. He must be, in fact, a contemplative craftsman.

For the composer, the integration of self, driven by the desire to find meaning, stimulates a creative response which produces sym-phonic music. This is a field where the sounding together of disparate elements creates a harmonious unity. It was Debussy who said that every composer seeks to write the symphonic music of his time, and the composing mind that seeks to fashion unity finds that best represented in symphonic terms. It is an arena where long-term processes can be initiated and then work themselves out over an extended period. The unity that is sought comes to the artist, and then to the listener, as an archetypal experience of form, and this is the outcome of the integration process, so satisfyingly experienced in symphonic forms. As he works towards this goal, the composer experiences something of a paradox.

The expressive shape that he senses and moves towards has to be worked out over a long period, at the same time the musical scores of the masters tell him that the archetype of expression he seeks, at least at the macro-level, is going to be one of a limited number of coherent forms that exist in music. While the success of the outcome is in doubt until the very end, the composer's aim remains constantly to identify with and aspire to join the many already existing examples of form that express archetypal experience. Familiarity with these models may be his greatest incentive to integration and musical form, but these models will also be a measure of his inadequacy to achieve either of these conditions.

It is partly the frustration of this paradox which misleads many composers into making intellectual decisions to model their works on the success of previously acknowledged masters. Formal archetypes are never intellectually summoned or manipulated into existence, they are rather brought into being by contemplation and by craftsmanship. This suggests an introverted state of mind. Furthermore, the potentially successful practitioner, in Jungian terms, places Feeling over Thinking in the valuation of experience; he is likely to be a slow-chewing and slow-moving beast, who is not tempted by the seductions of a mercurial intelligence. While such a person by nature appreciates there are only two or three formal moulds and their derived variants, he recognises that this narrowing of the field does not reduce the labour necessary for the achievement of formal expression. Furthermore, it is accepted that the challenge to achieve archetypal experience through form is renewed for each composition. One never learns a simple formula, and nowhere is such a formula written down. While examples of the successful following of formal procedure are all around, the route to achieving them remains mysteriously inimitable. The rich abundance of the life of the mind, shaped and presented over a period of time, does not survive that time as a living and analysable thing, rather it has to be made continually anew.

In the course of making expressive form the composer submits to the life of Sense, in the outer world and in himself, and attempts to harmonise the two. The process involves the time-honoured crafting of this experience into meaning; a meaning that is guaranteed by using a language rooted in common experience, tried and tested by tradition. The process of making forms is also one of constant discovery, the incessant birth of material. This material unfolds in accordance with the laws of its own autonomous nature. The true artefact must stand eventually independent of its creator. At the same time, such an artefact should communicate in a reverberative style, echoing its forbears and inviting development by future generations.

Why should a vast territory of common experience, which is the basis of any language or means of communication, have to be reaffirmed as the means to making expressive form? We all recognise 'the language of music' when we hear it, and immediately sense whether or not we have had a musical experience when we listen. There are many composers of recent times who, no doubt, understand the language of music, but in their own work do not offer it back to us. This affliction, feeling one thing and producing another, is at the present time in its fifth generation of operation; from the early twentieth century until the present day. The encroachment of intellectual ideas of an amusical origin onto the traditional processes of crafting material results inevitably in the mis-shaping of form. The making of things that have no archetypal validity reduces their powers of expression and thus the meaning that we take from them.

So how is an appropriate language discovered and used to assist the desired outcome of expressive form? The chief effect of an experience of form is completeness. The achievement of completeness implies the overcoming of turbulence, the sanitising and healing of an erstwhile unstable state of affairs through a powerful sense of unity, balance and strength. This process has a language and a treatment of that language implicit within it. It has been practised since the Middle Ages, and can best be defined as modal chromaticism. Within this denomination can be housed a disparate fraternity. Haydn Wood and Paul McCartney, just as much as William Byrd and Claude Debussy, find a place there. The test of belonging to this broad church is simple: is what the composer has to say, and the way that he says it, one and the same thing? Do the musical idea and the manner of its presentation make a match?

Looking back at the five generations, where these two expressive factors have too often failed to match, it is clear enough that many composing theories and practices are found wanting. These include serialism and the so-called 'new complexity'. They are all linguistically inferior in their capacity to make intelligible forms, and offer evidence that the broad territory occupied by the language of music has shrunk to a small hinterland of extremes. The posture created by the musical manner of such composers is self-consciously adopted, rather than arising intuitively from the well of tradition and related to the deepest need for personal integration.

It is only in the common ground of tradition that the healing power of music can do its work, making well the unwell and completing the incomplete. Clearly the language of such a music must have mobility, the means of conveying one state into another and changing it for the better. Music itself tells us that such mobility is the result of development. It also tells us that potentially the richest development, producing the most expressive form, is to be generated from acoustic experience systematically expressed in a natural hierarchy, namely the scale. This is because only the scale guarantees the ability to generate and resolve tensions at many levels. A modal scale, with locally expressive chromaticism, is the foundation on which stable forms are made, and that has grown up over generations through the experience of our common humanity and its needs.

Musical action along these lines depends on the perceptions of Feeling and Sense, and the making of form arises from the processing of such perceptions in a non-intellectual way. The composer must work as a reflective craftsman, with the tools and the thought-processes appropriate to his craft, if he is to do justice to his material. This simply means making the artefact that the material itself suggests should be made.

Ultimately we are all obliged to seek reality, which is most often a question of facing up to physical truth; the indisputable reality of Nature itself. As such, reality obeys physical and aesthetic laws, which, if broken, separate us from truth and the successful meeting of our inner needs. If Man is 'a vibration in the

universe', he needs to be a good vibration. This means understanding vibrations before working with them and making sure that
Man, the composer, ends up with a more unified collection of
vibrations than those with which he began. If Man adjusts himself
in certain ways, as he receives and treats experience, he will make
meaning for himself by achieving archetypal forms. This is the
moral task, which propels us all towards inner integration, and
which — against substantial odds — makes possible the creation
of human civilisation.

7

Reviving the Muse

Peter Davison

This essay explores the impact of modernism upon European classical music and what might follow its demise. Evidence now suggests that the modernist revolution has lost its way, and that a vacuum exists in musical life. How and why did the modernist revolution take place? What did we lose, and can and should that loss be recovered? What kind of music does our complex and ambiguous culture now need? Through an understanding of modernism's historical origins and psychological motives, it may be possible to find a way forward from the current impasse.

The term 'modernism' describes both an artistic movement and the philosophical position, from which it is derived. It implies something self-consciously new, defined by its separateness from the past. It is an attitude to the world; a *Weltanschauung* that can be carried into every sphere of life. There are indeed causal links between the rationalist and materialist attitudes of modernism and many of the social phenomena of our times; the decline of religion, permissive morality, the prestige of science and technology. A network of subtle, but crucial, relationships exists that makes our beliefs, personal morality, social norms and creative culture interdependent. In this sense, the precepts of modernism influence our sense of selfhood and also our sense of society. Modernity's most convincing claim upon us is that it has delivered unprecedented material well-being. It has liberated us through science and the breaking of taboos from our weakness before Nature and from the moral constraints which formerly prevented us from fulfilling our deepest desires.

The truth of these claims is not entirely disputed, but the price of this liberation is not often raised. Our liberation as individuals has been achieved at the expense of our awareness of mutual dependence, that is our regard for others. More importantly, this weakening of our sense of kinship with our fellow man has a heavy cost for the human psyche. This is an insidious and rarely considered impact of modern living. The assumption is made in this essay that the collective is bound by a common well of the unconscious, which is, as the great Swiss psychologist, C.G. Jung, described it, the source of our spiritual lives and through which we gain our deepest sense of identity. We discover, in that secret realm, what we share as essentially human, but also what makes each of us unique. This profound interconnectedness of humanity makes artistic creation an ethical concern. Creativity is not a private matter, but one that defines an individual's relation to the collective. If art by definition has a purpose beyond both itself and the individual that makes it, it must therefore possess the potential to add to or subtract from the common good.

Anyone brought up in the European classical music tradition will recognise that it has specific characteristics of compositional and performance practice. It demands, in its greatest manifestations, an inner or spiritual way of listening, which is made possible by the system of hierarchical tone relationships commonly described as tonality. It is debatable whether the ideals of modernism are compatible with this way of listening and the dialogue about inner identity which it permits. Art music has always played an important role in shaping our individual and collective identities by acting as a gateway to a hidden world of meaning and possibility. This function of music has been largely forgotten by contemporary composers, yet the living artist continues to carry an immense responsibility in the affirmation or denial of identity.

Art and civilisation

Culture, in its broadest sense, is about identity. It helps to define who we are, where we think we have come from and what our destiny might be. It can do this for us as individuals or as a group. Culture is most often simply functional and taken for granted by the majority of members of any such group, until they meet something alien to that culture. It is then that cultural emblems become significant in deciding whether one is in or outside of the group. Possessing such emblems becomes a source of pride, inspires feelings of superiority, security and comfort. They are a symbolic rallying point, something to defend and even for which to die. In order to demand such fierce loyalty, the instincts of men obviously consider such symbols of fundamental significance in forging identity. An attack upon them is interpreted as an attack upon the self or the group. Such deep-rooted instincts are the essential building blocks of social identity, but their presence is also potentially threatening to the civilised or highly developed society, where the icons of group identity can justify the blind venting of primitive feelings. Religious persecution is a typical example, where one religious group will defend its belief in tolerance and love with terrible acts of cruelty against a rival group. Evil is always projected outside the group upon any easy scapegoat. A strong and even highly developed culture is thus no guarantee of civilisation, for the complexity and sophistication of that culture might merely become the mask that conceals its barbarities.

High art is a special area of culture, since it belongs outside the field of everyday function. In this it can be distinguished from folk art, which is a part of the routine narrative of people's lives, and serves the purpose of defining common experience, origin and characteristic. It does not have within it the capacity to set out a potential for future cultural or individual development. It is not a civilising influence. Moral growth has traditionally been the province of religion, which contains the sense of that which lies beyond the routine narrative. High art is the flowering of the spiritual, and is therefore potentially transcendent of time and place. It deals with the common elements that bind men together; love, birth, growth, death, good and evil, but in terms of their meaning as metaphors of the spiritual realm. High art, be it sacred or secular, deals with the universals of human experience, and must have its roots in the deepest layers of the artist's unconscious. Here the traditional archetypes of religious feeling, sexuality and group identity are to be found untainted by the corruption of the material world. For a society to remain civilised, it must constantly renew its contact with these archetypes in a way which makes them relevant and meaningful. This is why artists are important and necessary to society.

The Marxist cultural historian and philosopher, Ernst Fischer, in his *The Necessity of Art* (1959) described art as a magic aid towards mastering a real, but unexplored world. He concluded that art fulfils the need to make a man whole, by allowing him to be, for a while, what he is not, and thus putting him in touch with the collective. He writes:

> Evidently man wants to be more than just himself. He wants to be a whole man. He is not satisfied with being a separate individual. Art is the indispensable means for this merging of the individual with the whole. It reflects his infinite capacity for association, for sharing experiences and ideas.

Critical to his idea of art is that it is not just a reflection of the 'here and now', but that it should have visionary qualities that stake out man's potential for growth:

> All art is conditioned by time, and represents humanity in so far as it corresponds to the ideas and aspirations, the needs and hopes of a particular historical situation...it also creates a moment of humanity...

Art must affirm and enhance the sense an individual has of his own identity in relation to a coherent collective, if it is to have value as a contribution to culture. Affirmation means dispelling the negative effect upon identity created by misfortune and fear, the dark side of human experience, thus adding to the well-being and productivity of the individual or social group. Art must make us more human, more aware of our own and others' humanity by evoking fellow-feeling and joy on the one hand, self-knowledge and catharsis on the other. In this we must distinguish high art, which seeks to stimulate psychological development by increasing knowledge of ourselves and our true relation to the world, from popular art, which may at best only confirm a status quo. Good popular art tells us what we are at a given moment and makes a pleasure of it. It cannot tell us what we might be. Its purpose is not in the first place to make us probe beneath the surface or to ask questions about ourselves. It is important that there is no blurring of this distinction, for profundity is a hard-won characteristic of high art, which can be easily cheapened by popularism, pandering to fashion or empty pretension. So, while high art may have mass appeal or a popular form be absorbed into high art, cultural achievement can only be measured in terms of quality and spiritual function. When popular art becomes cynical and commercialised, it becomes an empty fantasy that tries to tell us what we are not by a process of subtle falsification. This characterises much of the so-called 'pop'culture of our own times. These differences between high art, popular or folk art and 'pop'art are increasingly denied, because it serves the commercial interest of those selling 'pop'that critical standards are not encouraged.

One can conclude that contemporary art is currently failing in its purpose, as Fischer defines it. It is not mitigating the attack on identity made by modern life or helping us to grow. It seems more to reflect and compound our lack of collective identity. Consequently, people take refuge in alternative and often spurious ways of finding identity, such as indulging fanaticisms and escaping into addictive behaviour of various kinds. These, along with religious fundamentalism and nationalism, show the need for people to belong, to share something with others and to explore realms beyond themselves. In the twentieth century, European culture was unable to find a stable relationship between the individual and the collective. There remains much instinctive spiritual yearning, but the institutions and traditions that were previously a channel for these needs have largely broken down. In the vacuum, a myriad of false idols have replaced any sense of collective higher purpose.

The development of a high culture and advanced forms of human consciousness are painstakingly slow. Arguably, a degree of stasis, a stable framework provides the ideal environment for civilisation. A flourishing culture is at ease with itself, confident of its values and yet capable of adapting to change, when proven necessary. Stability can only arise from respect for both the physical limitations and the renewing power of Nature. Sustaining civilisation requires an instinctive caution. A culture must keep close to roots, for civilisation is like a well-maintained garden, in which humanity tames and checks the wildness of Nature, but cannot abandon its fundamental laws. It is a partnership between man and the creative forces of life, in which human consciousness makes a respectful and constructive intervention. This harmony with Nature is not easily achieved and it requires many generations of accumulated experience. Any unrealistic expectation or denial of Nature's power can invite the weeds of chaos to grow back, quickly strangling the fruits of a highly developed society. We have to acknowledge and manage our potential for primitivity, through a vigilance towards our fragile social order.

Civilised normality is the consensus of human values that endure within the constraints of Nature, in other words, that which is sustainable, because it is practical and successful. Normality is not necessarily the values espoused within our contemporary world, although these values may appear to have a consensus of approval. The contemporary consensus is often a sentimental illusion designed to conceal the unpalatable fact that society consists mainly of interest groups and segmented markets of consumers. Civilised normality would demand that our sense of community should be an actuality experienced through those upon whom we depend, and those that depend upon us. This common sense is generally suppressed, so that a confrontation with the disintegration of the collective can be avoided. We strive to be free of our obligations to our neighbours and they to us. The cacophony and obscurity of modern music tells us the truth of this sorry predicament, but in so doing it fails us. It appears as merely a symptom of the pervading malaise of our isolation, and offers no incentive to the rediscovery of our mutuality.

Modernism in music as a norm

We live in an era when contemporary music is expected to be difficult, if not incomprehensible. It is usually self-consciously new, therefore alien and provocative. While such music deviates markedly from our inherited sense of normality, it is given official approval, because the cultural climate encourages extreme individualism and the questioning of traditions. There is thus the paradox that it is normal for music to be in revolt against the past, when one of its important functions in the pre-modern period was to connect us to the past. But what is normality? What has modernism displaced, and is it possible for the abnormal to become a common currency? Our benchmark of normality is now historical rather than actual. Our sense of value has become a self-conscious memory. We are thus very concerned with the remnants of the past, as they tell us about a time when certain values could be taken for granted. The modernist sensibility allows consciousness to interfere in processes that were previously governed by intuition or else imposed by a higher authority, which was often tradition itself. By objectifying our values, they are consigned to memory, thus rendering powerless the moral imperative of past custom and practice.

Progressiveness has always been an ingredient in art music, since change and adaptation are part of human experience. Whether this constitutes progress in an absolute sense is less important than that a civilised society feels it should have a capacity for change. High art of this kind serves as a focus for reflection and self-knowledge. It is part of its *raison d'être*. Never, before now, has progress necessitated an attack upon an existing body of knowledge. Progress was rather seen as a gradual extension of boundaries; an evolution. Revolution is rarely justified, unless a culture has become stagnant and corrupt beyond redemption. There is a latent absurdity and destructiveness in the idea of endless revolution, as Mao Tse Tung practised in China, for example. How can an orthodoxy endorsed by the establishment be good and true on one day, then be declared as corrupt and dishonest on the next? This creates serious confusion of identity and can be used as the justification for barbarity and destruction. The evidence of Maoist revolution and counterrevolution is that such a context generates fear, atrocities of the group against the individual and the destruction of accumulated knowledge.

The collapse of civilised values, which can both produce and be the consequence of psychological imbalance and existential despair, is very much part of our twentieth century experience. We have a greater awareness than ever before that human life is full of impersonal, destructive forces. In this century, two world wars, the holocaust, totalitarianism and now cultural globalisation have overwhelmed the old Europe. Artists are as much victims of these forces as anyone else. The crisis has been made more acute, because without orthodox religion, largely destroyed by science, there has been nothing to relieve the sense of inner crisis. It should not be surprising therefore that, in the twentieth century, the abnormal has become the norm, and any historical investigation shows that the *topoi* of modernism have grown out of the standardisation of what were previously understood as extremes. A survey of the origins of modernist practices in music reveals that they are found in the expression of psychopathology and evil. Chromaticism, discontinuity, breaking-down of conventions and forms can be found in examples as varied as the mad scene of Handel's opera, *Orlando* (1733), and in the diabolism of the *Wolf's Glen scene* from Weber's *Der Freischütz* (1821). Wagner's opera, *Tristan und Isolde* (1859), the first real outbreak of aesthetic extremism, is about a socially disruptive and destructive love affair. Richard Strauss' most expressionist music, *Salomé* (1905) and *Elektra* (1908), are both operas about psychopathology and self-destruction. There is a tradition of such modes of expression, and the landmarks of the modernist revolution belong to it, even if the claim is of something historically unprecedented. The work which notoriously opened the door to atonality, Schoenberg's second string quartet (1907), was written in response to his marital crisis and the suicide of his wife's lover, the painter, Richard Gerstl. The expressionist works, which followed, *Erwartung* (1909) and *Pierrot Lunaire* (1912), are overtly about madness.

In subsequent years, through the codification of atonality in twelve-tone serialism, such extremes were rationalised as a norm. This eroded the sense that these techniques were extreme, which creates a paradox. The impact of an extreme requires an assumed background of normality and convention against which it can be measured. Simply put; dissonance has no effect without consonance. So the extremism of modernism undermines its own impact. For this reason, there is an inevitability about the failure of the modernist project. The claims by modernist composers that their innovations would one day be accepted as normal by the wider public have not been fulfilled. After the eighty years, since Schoenberg's invention of serial technique, which attempted to standardise the atonal idiom, there is no evidence that society as a whole has foregone its long-standing consensus about tonal music. Greater freedom of means is accepted, but a fundamental change of outlook has not occurred.

The general public's attitude has hardened against modernist music. The democratic liberal consensus, which now exists in Europe, considers that all forms of extremism and fundamentalism are threats to social stability and individual freedom. The public suspects that something unreasonable is being asked of them and they resist it. Less critical consumers enjoy new music and other forms of contemporary art, because it is titillating, scandalous or ridiculous. There is a still a sense of 'naughtiness' and adolescent rebellion among its standard bearers. Yet this rebelliousness pre-supposes an assumed consensus of old-fashioned values as the justification for the breaking of taboos. For the more informed musical audience, no amount of subsidy will bribe them, nor propaganda persuade them to become converts. It would seem unreasonable, after all, to expect an audience to surrender its sense of normality, especially at the state's behest. If an artist chooses to dismiss completely the prevailing consensus, opting for revolution rather than evolution, he cannot be surprised, if mainstream society does not come with him, although doubtless a few kindred spirits will always feel solidarity. In the longer term, even the 'shockingly' new must be assimilated into the mainstream within a generation or else it can be dismissed as mere posturing.

The bulk of art produced in any age conforms to the prevailing expectations and thereby lacks greatness, since it has no power to transform. If shock and revolution become the norm, then great artists will not be found among the shockers and revolutionaries, nor will great art prove itself by its shocking or revolutionary qualities. Furthermore, there is nothing inevitable about the antagonism between the artist and society, as Schoenberg and his followers would have us believe. Even in the modern era, a figure like Benjamin Britten became a living icon without being an empty conformist. If an artist articulates alienation, despair and madness, he cannot expect that this position should become customary, even if such a stance is, at that point in time, ethically and socially appropriate. Its function can only be as a corrective or voice of protest; not to establish unprecedented norms.

Much modernist art is claimed to be a critique of bad experiences, an expression of the atrophy which plagues us or even an idealistic breaking away from the destructiveness of the past. In this sense, it may make a valid contribution to our culture. Modernism is a reaction to terrifying historical circumstances and an awareness of the destructiveness of the human psyche. As such, it offers insights and warnings to us, which could potentially propel us to grow beyond that destructiveness. Critique, experiment and deconstruction may be appropriate for a period, but they must lead to some kind of reconstruction or reconciliation with the past. Stravinsky is such an example. What is *The Rite of Spring*, if it is not an attempt to reconnect with the creative forces latent in man? Is not the worship of Dionysus a necessary prelude to the worship of Apollo? Modernism's breaking the bonds of the past can only be justified as a temporary phase to reform or renew a tired tradition, and it can only succeed in this, if its exceptional nature is recognised. Real modernism shows us social fracture, a disintegrating collective consciousness and collapsing consensus. It can tell us how important identity, society and culture are, by expressing the pain of their absence. If that lack is accepted as a norm, becomes mannerist, it begins to threaten that which it is meant to protect. Modernism was born in the revolutionary white heat of idealism; a desire for renewal, to strip away the facade. Yet history tell us that most revolutions end in moral failure, as the revolutionaries assume the mantle of their former oppressors. The tyrannised become the tyrants of a new orthodoxy.

The psychological origins of modernism

If modernist idioms in music express psycho-pathological states, and the normalisation of these idioms has caused a rupture between the artist and society, why have artists attempted to do this? What ails the collective psyche that artists feel obliged to express such a narrow range of human experience? Jung has argued that art of any given period acts as a corrective for the prevailing consciousness, which is, at that time, the motor of social development:

> The creative process...consists in the unconscious activation of an archetypal image...By giving it shape, the artist translates it into the language of the present, and so makes it possible for us to find our way back to the deepest springs of life. Therein lies the social significance of art: it is constantly at work educating the spirit of the age, conjuring up forms in which the age is most lacking. The unsatisfied yearning of the artist reaches back to the primordial image in the unconscious, which is best fitted to compensate the inadequacy and one-sidedness of the present.
>
> *Psychology and Literature* (1950)

If Jung's premise is accepted, it is possible to explain apparently contradictory cultural phenomena. For example, one can show

how rationalism gave rise to Romanticism, as the unconscious balanced a heightened faith in reason. By the same law, the repressive facades and formality of the Habsburg Empire in the late nineteenth century gave rise to the unconscious explosion of expressionism. After the Great War, the old order of European culture lay in ruins. Jung himself argued that the modernism which then emerged was a valid expression of a fractured culture trying to reintegrate itself. Picasso's cubism or Joyce's ironical epic, *Ulysses*, he considered to be nihilistic, but also potentially transcendent, because they were so uncompromisingly true. Can the same be said of our own time? Is our art exposing and healing the cultural rifts, balancing our worst extremes as a society? It is hard to believe that this is so, for Jung's theory presupposes that there would be an inevitable, instinctive hunger for the ideas of contemporary artists, for people would just need this art in some way.

The reality is different. The majority consider modern art, especially modern music, irrelevant to them. They are much more interested in the art and music of the past. The obscurantism of the avant-garde, the lack of trust by the common man of contemporary music, would suggest a decisive break in communication. Modernism claims to attack the vulgar, the sentimental and the irrational. It does not take the materials of mass culture and try to elevate them. It rejects the primitive aspects of collective identity, and posits in their stead, a belief in the possibility of an autonomous human subject devoid of vulgarity and weakness. Thus modernism intentionally attacks those who remain bound to the collective and the traditions which make that possible, for it has, by its own definition, to destroy that which makes people contingent upon external phenomena for their identity.

Are primitive people and emotions really the root of our social difficulties? It is a complex problem, for while the sexual urge may lead a man to rape, it may also bring about the profoundest expression of erotic love. As Jung understood it, the problem for modern man is the suppression of his animal nature, which, left unintegrated, expresses itself in ugly and destructive ways. Modern man is divided against himself and thus unable to relate to others.

For this reason, Jung was concerned by the cubist distortions of Picasso's paintings, for example, which he considered to reflect a profound psychic disturbance in the artist's mind. He made an ambivalent prognosis for Picasso, whom he believed was exploring a schizoid reality. He pondered whether it might be a path to destruction:

> As to the future of Picasso, I would rather not try my hand at prophecy, for this inner adventure is a hazardous affair and can lead at any moment to standstill or to a catastrophic bursting asunder of the conjoined opposites. Harlequin is a tragically ambiguous figure. He is indeed the hero who must pass through the perils of Hades, but will he succeed...he is the greater personality who bursts the shell, and this shell is sometimes the brain.
>
> *Picasso* (1934)

Picasso's journey into schizoid fantasy can be viewed as a paradigm for the disintegration of European culture in the twentieth century. It is paralleled by Schoenberg's atomisation of musical processes, Webern's pointillism and the deconstructivism of late twentieth century modernism, which are all evidence of the fragmentation of the collective psyche. But is this the fault of artists themselves? Should not artists reflect the world as they see it, portray society as it is? If the prevailing climate is one of schizoid alienation, then surely artists should shout that as loud as possible in the hope that someone hears them. That would be fair, if it were the simple truth. A closer understanding of the schizoid condition reveals that being heard is not always what the damaged psyche wants. This is the tragic futility of modernism, for it fiercely resists the realisation of its own truth.

The philosophical ideas which underpin modernism are well-known, although these have never been elevated to a popular ideology or creed. They are best exemplified in the varied existentialist writings of Sartre and Heidegger. There are many shades within existentialist thought, but the common thread is that the phenomenon of being is assessed 'from inside out'. The subject is 'the self' made into an object of investigation, which must be defined in relation to the world. There is an implicit alienation from any sense of belonging to a greater whole in this process. To objectify the self through analysis is also to objectify 'the other'. There is even a tendency for the individual consciousness itself to split apart in this introspection, as the self observes itself and notices that there are conflicting forces at work in the psyche, that do not coalesce as something coherent. In other words, existentialism does not lead to a stronger sense of self, rather the opposite, because it wrongly pursues identity as something concrete, rather than fluid, and it does not acknowledge the extent to which identity is conferred by interaction with and responses from 'others'. If 'others' are crucial to identity, then the myth of the autonomous individual is a distortion of reality. If the knowable self is also a chimera, then the conclusions of this kind of enquiry will always be destructive and nihilistic. This may explain why Heidegger, despite his capacity for elevated discourse, possessed sympathies with National Socialism during World War II; a political philosophy that pandered to every base collectivism imaginable, and where respect for the individual was sacrificed to preserve a myth of racial superiority and strength.

In the work of Emmanuel Lévinas, a pupil of Heidegger, the ontological investigation is built upon the alternative premise that our sense of being, our identity, comes from what we know about ourselves from and through others. By acknowledging the vulnerability of our selfhood in relation to one another, we avoid the dehumanising effects of treating the self as an object or mechanism, and thus treating others as the focus of a projection of our own insecurities. This is a fundamentally different orientation from Sartre and Heidegger, and one that comes about in direct response to the tragedy of Nazism. Lévinas was appalled by the sympathies of his teacher and, as a Jew, suffered greatly at the hands of the Nazis.

It is necessary to explore in detail how the existentialist philosophical orientation translates in terms of the psychology and behaviour of people in practice. The psychiatrist R.D. Laing, influenced by phenomenological philosophy, defined the schizoid personality as resulting from profound ontological insecurity, which is comparable to the alienation of the existentialist. This, he proposed, leads to great difficulty in setting the boundaries of identity, particularly in the relationship between the individual and others. The schizoid personality is driven in two opposite directions. Such a person seeks affirmation from others to avoid loneliness and to gain identity, because without others, such a person doubts whether he exists at all. On the other hand, there is an acute anxiety about exposure to others about being known, for the schizoid personality is unsure how to maintain the boundaries of identity in an intimate situation. So, a game of 'hide and seek' develops between the self and others, the self and reality. The defences of the personality against reality create a false persona, an alternative self, that gradually assumes a degree of autonomy, ultimately crushing the real self and progressing to psychosis.

The alienation from reality that this process causes leads to a progressive emptying of the individual's creative energy, leading to feelings of deadness and despair. The hallmarks of such a personality can be categorised as follows:

- acute existential anxiety, alienation from the world
- creation of escapist fantasies
- petrification of the human into abstract processes or things
- paranoia, fear of real emotion and intimacy, of being known or understood
- delusions of omnipotence
- proclivity to manipulation, stealing of ideas and personas
- wearing masks to conceal identity
- lack of coherence and continuity
- nihilism and fatalism

Laing describes the schizoid fantasist's decline in drastic terms.

The person who does not act in reality and only acts in

fantasy becomes himself unreal. The actual world for that person becomes shrunken and impoverished. The reality of the physical world and other persons ceases to be used as a pabulum for the creative exercise of the imagination, and hence comes to have less and less significance in itself. Fantasy, without being in some measure embodied in reality, becomes more and more empty and volatilised.

The Divided Self (1959)

The schizoid personality can present a plausible exterior to the world, but at the price of real, consistent identity and with the strong risk that at some point the effort of will to present that facade will exhaust him. Thus the real damaged personality may emerge in a psychotic episode. It is a dangerous condition, born of defensiveness against a supposedly hostile world, but presented through a persona that wants to divert attention from that very state.

How much does modernist music demonstrate these schizoid characteristics, this unrecognised split between outer and inner identity? Some composers have even boasted of them. There is the determinism of John Cage, abandoning musical composition to chance, which is equivalent to denying the role of human person-ality in the creative process. There have been Boulez' early experiments with the total serialisation of musical processes, which tried to remove the human subject from the voice of musi-cal narrative. The British composer, Harrison Birtwistle, openly claims that his music is discontinuous. His music theatre piece, *Punch and Judy* (1967), explores the schizoid condition of Mr. Punch, as he carries out a series of brutal murders in pursuit of love. The autonomous self can justify any action in pursuit of its own gratification, if other persons are treated as objects. The text captures a mood of desperate existential trauma:

O Gods, this vile disfigured sight
Opens an abyss in my soul
The ears throb, the taste sours,

The eyes drown in a sunset of blood
The lights of the world go out
And I am alone with the beating of wings.
    'Lament', from *Punch and Judy*, Stephen Pruslin (1966)

The sincerity of this expression and the appropriateness of the
music that accompanies it cannot be denied, but the work is two
hours long, unrelenting in its intense concentration upon pathological states of mind. In music with text, the narrowness and
exceptional nature of the emotional territory is overt. In purely
instrumental music, all kinds of intellectual dissembling is used to
justify the emphasis on pathology. One thing is certain; we are not
meant to know anything of the true inner lives of such composers
through the music, nor can we say much about their cultural heritage. Identity is concealed from us by a wall of objectification and
obscurity. The Birtwistle at least does not pretend to be anything
more than it is, and one can argue that it tells us something we need
to know about the human potential for destruction. Unfortunately,
an excessive or exclusive focus upon these negative parts of the
human psyche can only lead to nihilism and despair: an
undermining of the potential of the human condition.

    Modernism relies upon a self-created myth of its own normal-
ity, and is thus vulnerable to more historically rooted concepts of
the normal. The past is not so easily denied and it poses a constant
threat. Many modernists demand the suppression of more traditional art, especially if it comes from a living artist. Yet, ironically
modernists are quick to validate themselves through historical lineage or from teacher to pupil, ignoring the inherent contradiction
of such a position. Modernity is meant to be a climax of history, an
irreversible moment of release from restrictive practices and hierarchies. That climax is explained by depersonalising the historical
development of style and technique. It makes it the outcome of
deterministic historical processes. Thus the claim is justified that
culture can be no other way. The alienation of the artist from society is explained as the consequence of the inevitability of change.
The paradox here is that true modernity should mean an artist has

total freedom of choice in relation to the past, not that he should become the victim of an arbitrary law of endless progress. There can be no renewal through such a dogmatic iconoclasm, yet since many have a vested interest in the stagnation of the status quo, the long-awaited renaissance is delayed.

It would be wrong to suggest that every modern artist is a latent or actual schizophrenic, for the schizoid experience is universal. For most people, however, it is a marginal realm of experience. The picture is in any case not universally gloomy, with many creative people struggling against the tide. In a climate of distorted value and delusion, even the most sincere artist will not be free from the prevailing fashions. On the other hand, even avowed modernists long for the freedom to express a wider range of feeling than their aesthetics permit. Behind a mask, many things become possible, which explains the success of Stravinsky's neo-classicism, but also why Schoenberg's later tonal works have to be excused as mere exercises and arrangements. Modernism is a totalitarian aesthetic, and its conventions are not easily dislodged. It is worth stating what these norms are, and considering them in relation to the previous list of schizoid characteristics:

- revolution as the norm, aesthetic extremism motivated by existential anxiety
- alienation from the mainstream of society and public taste in art
- creation of obscure, subjective worlds, private musical languages
- belief in the absolute autonomy of the individual
- cerebralism, ultra-rationalism, focusing upon abstract processes or things
- absence of direct emotional expression
- creation of a rigid aesthetic orthodoxy, fundamentalism
- lack of coherence and continuity
- denial of the past and tradition
- nihilism and historical determinism

Of course, extreme positions create contradictions, so that endless revolution, which attacks any established orthodoxy, itself becomes an inviolable orthodoxy worthy of attack. Furthermore ultra-rationalism ironically produces the effect of chaos or randomness, since it is based upon the false notion that the human mind is able to control consciously every detail of every process, no matter how complex. It is the danger of any ideological extreme that it pursues itself into paradox.

Despite these inherent absurdities, it would be unwise to dismiss modernism outright. The schizoid sensibility is a legitimate area for artistic endeavour, but it cannot be accepted as the mainstream or the goal of development. Only in its proper context can its significance be clearly understood, and its destructiveness prevented from holding sway. It has to be considered a corrective and symptomatic of the sickness of our European culture. The patient cannot recover until it is diagnosed. However, once the illness is understood, a cure cannot be effected by continuing in the same way. If contemporary norms have become destructive of civilisation, then a choice has to be made for a different direction, which begins to resolve the problem. Yet, like any neurotic individual, as a culture, we try to deny our predicament. This is born of a fear of a reality, that we cannot accept; a fear of meaningful contact with the 'other'; a fear of contingency. Thus, in our own time, mortality and evil are taboo, because confronting them would bring us immediately into the territory of what we find unacceptable in ourselves. We would be reminded of our mutual dependency and our need for spirituality, which were previously explored in more traditional art and religion. To fill the gap, sentimentality and banality pervade our popular culture, on the one hand, while, on the other, uncompromising austerity and confusion characterise our high art. The outcome in both cases is to avoid confrontation with the shadow of our collective psyche. To acknowledge that our weakness is at the core of our identity would be to jettison some treasured notions about ourselves as modern people. We try to delude ourselves that we can control our destiny and understand the human condition with scientific exactitude. We believe, against all evidence, that Nature can be manipulated, that everything can be explained, that man is good and potentially immortal.

Facing the legacy of modernism

The overwhelming prevalence of an idea can grant it a spurious validity in an act of collective denial that is symptomatic of an environment dominated by fear. No sane person wants to deny the obvious, but our culture does not help us to face truth, rather it helps us to cover it up.

Modernism thrives on the attractive but false assumption of individual human autonomy. To live under that delusion requires the denial of our mutuality and vulnerability. Thus, in Jungian terms, we surrender to our collective shadow, that dark part of us that we have hidden from ourselves, because it threatens our inflated self-image. This propels us deeper into the mire of psychic confusion and nihilism, rather than saving us from it. To cope with this predicament the population looks to the past for some splinters of an identity, clinging to the last vestiges of a lost cultural consensus. The absence of a relevant contemporary music drives educated people towards the museum culture of traditional concert life, to precisely that past which modern art strives to deny. There is no more devastating evidence that modernism has failed than this. The past is not only more alive than ever in the popular imagination, for many it is the only way of defining identity, the only way our sense of self and our sense of others can find any kind of stable relationship. If that clinging to the past seems exaggerated, it is an inevitable consequence of a fear of the pace of change and the intimidating nature of much modern music. In this sense, our culture reflects in practice Jung's diagnosis of art's corrective function. The past represents stability in a fast changing world, and the human psyche needs that point of reference the more to compensate for the pace of modernity.

If it is accepted that music should contribute to collective psychological growth, which also means the acknowledgement of the mutual humanity that exists between the artist and society, then the basis of modernist music is crucially undermined. Modernism can claim to provide a meaningful critique of many false ideas. It is a legitimate questioning of sentimentality, banality and dangerous irrational forces. Yet here we have another paradox: a critique that has no root in reality or the psychologically possible is destructive, for where can it lead? Equally, if an idealism is justified only by denying human weakness and vulnerability, then it may be philosophically attractive, but as a truth it is impractical. The full implementation of the modernist revolution would make us guilty of ignoring the limitations of human nature and avoiding the painfully slow pace of growth necessary for any human progress to have firm foundations. Part of that gradual process is the assimilation of the past as knowledge through tradition. This means the patient acquisition of crafts and techniques as well as an apparatus of evaluation, all inherited from previous generations, which set the benchmarks of quality in aesthetic judgement. By contrast modernism believes in the absolute validity of the individual's utterance, so that all creative endeavour, indeed any act deemed by its perpetrator as creative, has an equal claim to the name of art and any collection of sounds can become music.

The experience of modernism has insidious consequences, since its basic premise is to achieve uprootedness, and therefore a loss of identity. We know from Laing and Jung that the prognosis for the schizoid personality, with its identity problem, is poor: a progressive descent into unreality and madness. Modernism wants to persuade us that by severing our roots, we can be liberated from our past, from Nature, and enter a world of total freedom and autonomy, where identity is without contingency. But there is an essential denial of our humanity in this, since it panders to the view that we are ultimately highly sophisticated machines, which can be artificially engineered to any particular social or ethical goal. We may wish this to be true, but that does not make it true. Our human identity depends upon our interaction with the collective, with our past and upon defining the limits of the self in relation to others.

The social philosopher, Simone Weil, wrote in *The Need for Roots* (1943) of the dangers of this uprooting of identity brought about by modernism and its effect on the mass of people:

Uprootedness is by far the most dangerous malady to which human societies are exposed, for it is a self-propagating one. For people who are really uprooted there remain only two possible sorts of behaviour; either to fall into a spiritual lethargy resembling death...or to hurl themselves into some kind of activity necessarily designed to uproot, often by the most violent methods, those who are not yet uprooted, or only partly so.

Weil was no apologist for right wing political ideas, a crime of which traditionalists are often accused. She warned against the tide of totalitarianism, the political shortcuts that treated people as impersonal entities. Her plea was for respect of the individual's rights, including the right of that individual to belong, to be rooted, to have identity in the collective. The past is an emblem of that rootedness, an anchor of identity that is denied only with the most terrible consequences. The meaningful past is not something indiscriminate, however. The legacy is rare, and for that reason, precious. Her supposition is that the dialectic of past and future is destructive, because it denies that which is substantial and universal in human identity. A person who denies his past is left with nothing, including nothing with which to build a future or define an identity. After all, a man with amnesia does not know who he is:

It would be useless to turn one's back on the past in order to simply concentrate on the future. It is a dangerous illusion to believe that such a thing is possible. The opposition of future to past or past to future is absurd. The future brings us nothing, gives us nothing; it is we who in order to build it have to give it everything, our very life. But to be able to give, one has to possess; and we possess no other life, no other living sap, than the treasures stirred up from the past and digested, assimilated and created afresh by us. Of all the human soul's needs, none is more vital than this one of the past.

She makes a strong link with colonialism; the rape of other cultures. She sees the attack on our own past as essentially the same; an invasion of our own identity and humanity:

> The past destroyed never returns. The destruction of the past is perhaps the greatest of all crimes. Today the preservation of what little of it remains ought to become almost an obsession. We must put an end to this terrible uprootedness which European colonial methods always produce, even under their least cruel aspects.

Modernism as a general cultural phenomenon seeks to avoid contingency and so is fanatically intolerant of traditional cultures or any manifestation of an enduring past. It protects itself by claiming idealistic motives, when its goal can only be destruction. It posits an anti-culture, because in normalising the extreme, it must deny the existence of civilised normality: the environment in which people and societies can thrive.

While it is understandable that two world wars and the holocaust have traumatised the European psyche, nevertheless, trauma and neurosis must eventually be overcome. They otherwise inhibit growth, the capacity for evolution that is the hallmark of a healthy culture. The friction between what we are and what we think we are is all too obvious, but also vigorously denied. The gulf between modernist fantasy and the reality of life heightens the sense of alienation of the individual from the collective and makes him doubt the truth of his own experience. The schism between our actual experience of humanity, which is as a flawed creature, and the utopian myths of modernity, which preach that science has an answer for everything, has to be overcome, if we are to move on.

We now have a contemporary music that has become willingly alienated from mainstream society. It has become an isolated subculture, in which the tenets of modernism are the emblems of a minority group. Composers and artists generally have become one more social splinter, seeking identity without function, and unable to integrate fully with society. It is a self-fulfilling failure, however. Their goal is isolation, and the misunderstanding of the masses merely proves the rightness of their approach. Such art is intended as an attack on ordinary people, so it is unlikely that they will ever be grateful. To win public funding, this tortured group must address the formalities of democratic accountability, so the unpalatable is presented to the public as something good for them, which they time and time reject. The excuse for this consistent lack of public enthusiasm is discretely explained as due to the stupidity of the general population, who are thereby excluded from high culture.

There is even a yawning gulf between the more educated echelons of society and contemporary art music, since the anti-culture of modernism is not understood any better for having a good education, and it requires no need for a grounding in the principles of the music of the past. Music-consumers cannot acquire a critical apparatus for the purpose of evaluation, since there are no universally accepted points of reference. Many are just too puzzled and embarrassed to admit that they find no sense in modernist music, but are convinced by the authority of those they deem should know better. Modernist music and art in general cannot be evaluated or comprehended, and so it cannot accumulate as a well for cultural identity. This creates a climate in which art becomes a lower and lower social priority. At best, art becomes an historical phenomenon, at worst an exaggerated commercial commodity dictated by fashion. The vacuum of modernism in high art fuels the cynical fantasy of popular media culture. For, if our high art depicts psychic trauma and a schizoid view of reality, our popular culture wants to run away from that as fast it can. It thus provides further fuel to the disintegration of the collective psyche in a fantasy of identity confusion, exhibitionism and false intimacy. The worst 'pop' art deals in ephemera and denies its audience's potential for development by preaching nihilistic morality and destructive hedonism. The decadence of popular culture is perhaps the inevitable outcome of a high art that is not interested in the masses, and by implication despises them. So, modernist high culture and consumerist 'pop' culture, are both anti-cultures, denying the potential

of all individuals to grow and attacking any sense of collective
identity.

A way forward

If our contemporary art is atrophied and meaningless, because of a
collapse of collective identity, can anything be salvaged from the
wreck of European culture, or have we to accept its demise? Yet to
accept this state of affairs without question is a failure of intellectual leadership. What hope the rest of humanity, if its most brilliant
minds retreat to an enclave of indulgent nihilism and use their creative gifts to tell the world and themselves that there is no point in
trying? What hope is there, if those who try to posit something
more constructive are condemned to the margins as cranks pursu-
ing a chimera? We are obliged to try. We must strive to make sense
of our predicament and to create the climate in which art can flourish. We should, however, never see art as the cause of the problem.
It is only symptomatic of a wider malaise, and any answer will
require the psycho-spiritual transformation of society: a reawaken-
ing of higher purpose in the collective awareness. Artists are
well-placed to guide that process and bring it into consciousness.

So what may or even must the music of the future be like? It
must be corrective, transformative and renewing for the collective.
Music must therefore grow out of archetypal impulses, be rooted
in the creative desire for growth beyond one's current boundaries,
but not disruptive and uprooting. It should not be iconoclastic in an
age of revolution and fast change. On the contrary, it should affirm
identity and encourage growth by steps. People need an anchor to
stabilise themselves in difficult times. Music must not perpetuate a
false reality, but it must point towards a higher reality beyond ourselves. It must not reinforce false and destructive notions of self or
society, but heighten our empathy for 'the other'. Music must
touch people, and lots of people. Anyone who wants to grow
should find something in music that at once is part of him and yet
carries him beyond himself. Music must elevate people, and belief
in the possibility of elevation, of a transcendent hierarchy of value,
is the only moral basis for art. A new music must be an art that

unites and does not divide; an art that seeks to put us in touch with the fundamental truths of our existence and experience; an art that stirs and transforms. To do this, the composer must find that point of convergence in himself, where his own individual struggles are archetypal and thus collective. Then his individual development will become a paradigm for the collective, to which either individuals or groups can respond. While the mass populace may not instantly recognise the quality of such music, this art must not set out to exclude them from appreciation. Great music, because it springs from the archetypes that define our collective identity, should have the capacity to communicate meaningfully with a large number of people over a long period of time.

The modernist paradigm, which explores the material of music as a thing in itself, has run its course. It is modelled on the methodology of science, which requires the alienation of the observer from the object. This undermines the true nature of music as a magical metaphor of the unconscious realm, requiring the dissolution of boundaries between subject and object. Modernism demands the impossible, for even in the most objectified work, the human reaction is to try and hear beyond the material into its transcendence. Human beings want and need to believe in 'the beyond'; a mysterious reality beneath the surface of things, beyond the material world and beyond individual consciousness. There are dangers associated with music that draws upon mystery and the well of the collective unconscious. It is an entry into a rich, but sometimes dark world. Primitive fears and insecurities are lurking there, and such an art could easily attract the projection of many unhealthy collective aspirations for simplistic and irrational solutions to complex problems. Consciousness must remain in control, checking these fantasies as unreal and potentially evil. That, after all, is the function of classicism in art; setting limits to feeling, balancing the power of the irrational with the common sense of practical reality. The archetypes emerging from the unconscious must be transformed by consciousness into something clear and meaningful. Art must both acknowledge and set limits to dark forces in the human mind, thus preventing them from doing their terrible work.

The continuing development of human consciousness is an act of Nature and irresistible. It would therefore be unrealistic to suggest that a return to a golden age of unknowing could provide a solution to the modernist impasse. The breaking down of a cultural consensus in Europe is a fact of life. One must then distinguish between the advantages this individuation brings for our personal freedom and self-knowledge, and the spurious claim that it provides evidence that man has achieved an autonomy which releases him from his past. The latter idea is a modernist fallacy, which justifies an unrealistic and dangerous cult of progressiveness. The modernist is thus fanatical and inflexible in a situation that demands the opposite. Jung writes:

> Nothing is easier than to effect a consciousness of the present. A great horde...of people give themselves the air of being modern by overleaping the various stages of development and the tasks of life they represent. They appear suddenly by the side of the truly modern man as uprooted human beings, bloodsucking ghosts, whose emptiness is taken for the unenviable loneliness of the modern man and casts discredit upon him...Many people call themselves modern, especially the pseudo-moderns. Therefore the really modern man is often to be found among those who call themselves old-fashioned...he emphasises the past in order to hold onto the scales against his break with tradition.
>
> *The Spiritual Problem of Man* (1933)

Jung recognised that any progress in psychological development is hard won. There is a price for progress and we should err on the side of caution, letting things proceed at their natural pace. Our past is more important than ever, as we take the tentative steps to a new level of development. If consciousness contrives growth out of a fashion for modernity, then considerable psychic damage can be done, as patterns of thought and behaviour are forced upon an unwilling unconscious. As a result the individual personality and society begin to fragment and descend into crude fantasy. The consequences of embarking upon such a path can be witnessed in the damage done by the spread of a depersonalised and invasive global culture. As a legitimate counterweight to these disruptive and disorienting patterns of change, our common past, its lessons of experience and inherited knowledge of the human condition, is all we have to provide a much needed source for group identity and social coherence.

In times of collective aberration, the composer must choose the lonely path of reality, which means acquiring scepticism before the illusions of modernity and a rare humility before the miracle of creation. Any delusion of omnipotence must be shed, for we are weak, mortal beings, dependent upon Nature; the source of all that we have. If we surrender to that, our anxiety may be the less for confronting such difficult truths collectively, without dissembling and denial. Music must be rooted in subjective identity and reject the impersonal, mechanistic view of the human organism. This means acknowledging and trusting the unfathomable creative forces at work in man, which constantly express anew the fundamental truths of existence and give them beauty of form. The Muse is our guide to this end, and she cannot die, unless we choose to destroy her. The reviving of the Muse will be the outcome of a transformed inner attitude. Composers have to rediscover the mysterious relatedness of man and creation, of which tradition, our assimilable past, speaks with profound eloquence. It remains as a rich well for the future: the Muse's obvious dwelling-place. As modern Europeans, we have to try to become more fully human, to celebrate our vulnerability and immense creative potential, for they form the core of our common humanity. Through our interaction with each other and by touching the deepest core of our being, we must struggle to find out who we really are, and to forge from that knowledge an identity, which expresses harmoniously both our separateness and our mutuality.

BIBLIOGRAPHY:

Fischer, Ernst *The Necessity of Art; A Marxist Approach* trans. of *Von der Notwendigkeit der Kunst,* Verlag der Kunst, Dresden, 1959 (English trans. by Anna Bostock, Penguin Books, London, 1963)

Jung, Carl G. *Picasso* from *Wirklichkeit der Seele*, Rascher, Zurich, 1934 (English trans. by R. F. C. Hull *The Spirit in Man, Art and Literature*, ARK Edition, London, 1984)

Jung, Carl G. *Psychology and Literature* from *Gestalungen des Unbewusten*, Rascher, Zürich, 1950 (English trans. by R. F. C. Hull *The Spirit in Man, Art and Literature*, ARK Edition, London 1984)

Jung, Carl G. *The Spritual Problem of Modern Man* from *Seelenprobleme der Gegenwart*, Rascher, Zürich, 1933 (English trans. by W .S. Dell and Cary F. Baynes, *Modern Man in Search of a Soul*, ARK edition, London, 1984)

Laing, R. D. *The Divided Self, An Existential Study in Sanity and Madness* Tavistock, London, 1960, rev. Penguin, London, 1990

Lévinas, Emmanuel *Time and the Other*, Paris 1947. (English trans. by Richard A. Cohen, Duquesne University Press, Pittsburgh, 1987)

Pruslin, Stephen Scenario and Libretto to *Punch and Judy*, an opera by Harrison Birtwistle, Boosey and Hawkes, London, 1967

Weil, Simone *The Need for Roots L'Enracinement*, France, 1949 (English trans. by A. F. Wills, ARK edition, London, 1987)

8

Recreating the Classical Tradition

John Borstlap

Old and new

When Giorgio Vasari wrote his *Lives of the Great Artists* around 1550, he had to explain time and again what he meant by 'modern'. The rediscovery of the culture of antiquity as a source of inspiration and as a standard of quality was felt, in Renaissance times, as something totally new and dynamic. The influence of antiquity can be traced back to the twelfth century, when conditions favoured a more refined and sophisticated civilisation. This was not the first wave of Renaissance thinking, for Charlemagne had already stimulated interest in antiquity in the early ninth century, in a spirit of constructive reform, after the worst of the barbarism of the seventh and eighth centuries had subsided. Later on, in the medieval world, Italy was dominated by northern and eastern influences and for many people, at that time, 'modern' meant the latest developments of medieval culture imported from the prosperous north, especially Flanders. The concept of a 'modernity', based upon ideas that were more than a thousand years old, was still controversial, but for the intelligentsia the works of poetry, science and the visual arts of the Greco-Roman world were all superior to anything produced by contemporary culture. The presence of Roman monuments, mostly ruined, reminded the Italians of a glorious past and inspired them to dream of a possibly comparable future.

The Renaissance interest in antiquity as a civilising influence is something totally different from modern thinking. In the twentieth century, progress was understood as a confident leap into the future; a projected Utopia, only made possible by a drastic break with the past. The past stood for reaction, and the future for progress. By comparison, the Italian Renaissance gives us a totally opposite picture. Although the immediate past was felt to be stagnated, the future held the possibility of recreating a distant past from a mythological era, which had already profoundly influenced the European intelligentsia. Was the Italian and, in general, the European Renaissance a reactionary period? Certainly not. It meant the restoration of a spirit of invention and an aesthetic sensibility, which lasted until the nineteenth century, when this broad wave of civilisation found a premature death through its codification in academic institutions. The rebellion against this petrified academic culture was the cradle of modernism: the creative forces left the territory of 'official' culture, which suffocated innovation, and moved to the margins of society, where neglected artists struggled to find new and freer ways of expression.

The same landscape may reveal very different aspects, depending upon the position from which it is perceived. The past can also take on different meanings, changing with the perspective we choose. Marguerite Yourcenar, author of the celebrated historical novel, *Memoirs of Hadrian*, was well aware of the ambiguities of historical perception. She commented in a late interview:

> If we look at history closely...leaving behind the academic and ideological clichés of our time, we conclude that every period had its own way of interpreting life... Although the human emotions are always more or less the same...they are open to thousands of variations, thousands of possibilities. So, if you like, the immensity of musical expression can be

related back to the seven notes of the scale. You see these possibilities not only taking shape from century to century, but from year to year. After all, we don't think the same as in 1950 any more, and it is fascinating to find at a precise date in the past, the way in which problems have presented themselves, our problems, or problems parallel to ours... In this way, history is a school of liberation. It liberates us from a number of our prejudices and teaches us to see our own problems and our own routines in a different perspective... The past does not offer us an asylum, but a series of junctions, of different exits along the same way. If there is a 'escape', one could sometimes even talk about an escape into prominence... The study of texts from antiquity was an 'escape' for Renaissance man, saturated as he was with medieval scholastic thought. The study of the Middle Ages was — up to a certain point — an 'escape' for the romantic generation, bringing it back to the sources of popular poetry, to the original, European phenomenon, after the clarity, but also dryness, of the 18C.

Entretiens radiophoniques avec Marguerite Yourcenar

In the new millennium

The 'modernist period', which has dominated most of the twentieth century, seems to have run its course. How has this happened? It is often the fate of revolutionary movements to become dogmatic and suppressive, because advocates are forced to adopt polarised positions and to dismiss even the most reasonable points of view of their opponents. Once a new world view has been established, the representatives of the old one have to be persecuted to keep the new faith pure and to help it take root. Dogmatism and propaganda are effective instruments to achieve this goal, and the academic attitude is soon restored, disguised by a new flag and new slogans. In spite of its rhetoric of progress and continual renewal, modernism became academic as soon as it was 'received'. In the twentieth century, Modernism gained official approval and state subsidy in the universities and academies, much as bourgeois art had done at the end of the nineteenth. Indeed, even promotional organisations were set up to create a 'survival kit' for an art, which was too difficult for audiences to understand. The remnants of a once living art, once again, became petrified into empty gestures and unimaginative repetitions. In other words, art became conventional.

Officially approved art generates conformity, because career drives begin to determine artistic choices. The difference with the nineteenth century situation is, that the official art of today is not supported by a wide audience and thus is not economically viable. This lack of viability combined with the avant-garde's ideological justification of modernism as a quest for Utopia, has convinced the political authorities of their responsibility to gamble on supporting great artists, who are claimed to be ahead of their times. The irony is that elected political authorities have to reflect their own times, so by definition they can never recognise a *real* avant-garde artist, who would inevitably wish to distance himself from the establishment to preserve his inner freedom. The ideals of the subversive avant-garde, once accepted as norms, created the breeding ground for conformism: the very same creative stagnation against which the early stages of modernism were themselves a strong and legitimate protest.

For the supporters of modernism, the acceptance and funding of modernist art may have seemed a grand victory over the philistines. But there are two fundamental flaws at the core of this victory, which form the seeds of its own disintegration. The first can be found in the modernist philosophies, which presume endless revolution and a fundamental break with the past motivated by utopianism. In such a climate, it is impossible to build a tradition of convincing norms because a tradition can only develop out of some sense of continuity and permanence. Progress and innovation cannot provide enduring standards of quality. Indeed, progressive ideologies create a feeling of continuous expectation, which can only lead to disappointment, when it fails to fulfill its ambition to transform cultural life.

The second flaw is the relative absence of an audience. There is no civilisation which had or has an art that did not over a period of time become relevant to an informed or educated public. It has always been implicit in modernist art, that it was, in terms of practice, replacing the traditional art forms. Therefore, the continued presence of traditional works of art from the past, the so-called museum culture, was perceived as a reason for anger and frustration, which inspired iconoclasm. Modernism was supposed to be the successor of traditional art, and the art of former times was a distraction from the new art, which was the only appropriate expression of the modern world and the existential condition of the modern human being. The modernist establishment wished to abolish any remnants of past practice, and condemn their exponents to the margins. Hence Boulez' proposal to burn down the opera houses in the nineteen-fifties, and the wish of others to demolish the museums, which guarded the great traditional collections. But traditionally orientated art was — and still is — being produced all the time alongside 'official modernism', in spite of its supposed irrelevance to the modern world. Artists have continued to paint figuratively, to mould figurative sculptures and to compose tonally. From the point of view of modernism, these trends were — and still are — considered reactionary and dangerous to the modernist project, as long as the public has not fully embraced it. The possible acceptance by the public of a new art still rooted in tradition is considered by the modernist establishment to be a nightmare; a degeneration from elevated ideals to primitivity, a betrayal comparable to the dance around the golden calf. Yet, in spite of the silencing of traditional artists and the support for modernism by the authorities, i.e. in the *most* advantageous circumstances, modernism has still failed to realise its ideals. It has *not* obtained the place within society, which it claims to deserve.

As long as the rhetoric of the ideologies intimidated the uninitiated, modernism was not really challenged. However, when it gradually became clear that much of its eloquent propaganda was not credible, its various forms were required to justify themselves before a critical public without the defence of revolutionary ideology. The ideologies no longer worked. The only modernist artists with any chance of survival were those who concentrated upon artistic quality and thus, in spite of the language of their art, in one way or another by necessity developed towards a more traditional position.

The cultural situation in which we find ourselves at present in the western world is probably the oddest in history. The great collections of traditional art, including the first waves of modernism, such as impressionism, are enshrined in museums which have almost obtained the status of religious institutions. Traditional musical life offers us old, tonal music as a ritual providing emotional and spiritual nourishment, or else as a luxurious and high-brow entertainment. Modernist music has never found a status beyond the more or less obligatory interruption of these rituals and pleasures, often enforced by the conditions of subsidy. This reluctance by the mainstream of concert life to embrace modernist music has forced contemporary music to develop a separate circuit, where modernism could not conflict with traditional norms. Only the museums of modern art, which house the 'classics' of early modernism, can count upon some popularity. The museums organising exhibitions of more recent developments are, with a few notable exceptions (usually connected with sensationalism), only visited by a clique of initiates and are otherwise overlooked. By comparison with visitors to the old collections, the audience interested in real contemporary art is a small minority. More than half a century of strongly promoted and subsidised modernist art has not led to general acceptance. So we have the ironic situation that modern art has failed to compete for the attention of the audience, and probably served to increase the general public's interest in the art of the past.

This state of affairs can only be seen as unnatural and unhealthy, reflecting the existence of some profound problem in our present civilisation. The enduring appreciation, across many generations, of traditional art cannot merely be because of its conventionality or the 'philistinism' of the bourgeois public. It must also be the art form's intrinsic qualities, which perpetuate its existence. Traditional art has obtained the status of a guarded collection of icons, even physically attacked now and then, as if they were living beings. Da Vinci's cartoon in London's National Gallery was 'shot', for example, and there has also been the 'stabbing' of Rembrandt's *Nightwatch* in Amsterdam's Rijksmuseum. The important question is, whether it is still relevant or important for us to experience traditional art, which emerged from a society so different from ours and from circumstances and a world view, which seem alien to the present.

It can be argued that traditional art emanates a meaning which is difficult to define, but which is capable of transcending limitations of time and place. This meaning is directly experienced through the works of art themselves, and although we may need explanations for a deeper understanding, we hardly fail to experience its impact, its presence. Despite stemming from different times and places, traditional cultural life may be, at present, the only possible place where meaningful art can be experienced. To interpret its continued popularity as a sign of decadent and reactionary attitudes is to miss the point entirely. Is it reactionary to find cathedrals important enough to restore them, or to keep libraries intact, or to read books at all, or to maintain the motorway network, or the telephone system, or even to keep an eye on one's health? The human psyche needs the reassurance of a sense of continuity, which is why we preserve that which seems precious and necessary. It is also true, on the other hand, that the human mind has a capacity for flexibility and agility of reaction in order to adapt to change. Curiosity for the new and delight in the unexpected are natural characteristics of human beings. However, the moment we are confronted by the cruelties of life and all the existential questions they generate, then, flexibility, agility and curiosity for the new are too superficial. We turn at such moments to enduring values. Here, the prior experience of others is of crucial importance, and traditional art and culture contain that body of shared experience and enduring value, which are of unequivocal significance to our deepest well-being. The apparent lack of any 'great' contemporary art has always been explained by the claim that our faculties of understanding are inadequate. But is this the only possible explanation? Could it not be that many contemporary artists simply lack the depth of character or personality which allows art to have universal meaning in relation to life's existential questions?

The increasing status of the traditional art of the past seems to indicate that it provides something that modernist art cannot. It is experienced as something very precious for our cultural identity. Without the art of the past, it is as if we might cease to be what we really are. As Europeans with a long and complex history, is it not perhaps just inevitable that the past will be part of our culture? We cling to works from the past, because it is all we have of this tradition, because as a living, contemporary cultural phenomenon, the European tradition seems no longer to exist.

Does the art of the past lose its meaning because it is old, and does our historical awareness distort our perception of its true aesthetic content? We visit museums to see the masterpieces of painting. We go to concerts and listen to the works of dead composers. But do we *really* understand what we see, what we hear? To what extent is our vision and hearing corrupted by more recent layers of artistic experience and our interpretation of history? Has our aesthetic appreciation been informed and enriched by these? Are we, in fact, like medieval Italians, walking around the equivalent of a ruined Roman temple without really understanding what it is, yet still impressed by its grandeur and beauty? We must find a path to the reality of the work of art, be it old or new, without the distraction of a polemic at the conceptual or historical level. Art has an historical and conceptual dimension, but is much more than these. Its aesthetic content is able to transcend these notions.

The re-creation of a lost tradition is not possible without a context, a framework rooted in society. Over the last years, evidence of such a framework has begun to emerge. Firstly, the European Union is aspiring to its own distinctive cultural identity, albeit still only vaguely defined. Secondly, the awareness that civilisation is unthinkable without concern for the Nature (which is itself fundamentally cyclical and 'traditional' and cannot be subjected to utopian manipulation without the serious danger of upsetting the delicate balance of eco-systems). These ideas reflect the need for a redefinition of priorities in our culture. A renewed interest in spirituality is another point of orientation. Spirituality is a natural aspect of human experience and indeed the basis of all civilisation, often now expressed through involvement in either traditional religion or in the many new, more free forms of religious dedication. So, here are three good reasons why artists could make a case for a new interpretation of the idea of a European tradition. The keyword here is roots. People can only be creative and constructive, if they have roots, if there is a minimum of psychological and emotional continuity and stability. A modern world which has no roots in the past is prone to sink into destruction, because of the lack of a framework for making value-judgements. We need to use the accumulation of human experience as the basis of our understanding of reality.

In the course of time, modernist art always loses its more ephemeral aspects like 'historical significance' and 'revolutionary qualities', and is judged increasingly by more universal standards: its power to move, to create meaning, to enrich our lives. It is perfectly legitimate to admire Picasso's *Demoiselles d'Avignon* for its revolutionary nature in the context of its own time, while also acknowledging that it is an aesthetically inferior painting. His *Guernica* on the other hand has much more to offer in terms of expression and aesthetic quality. The *Demoiselles* is only intelligible in the context of the suffocating bourgeois taste against which it was a subversive scream; a scream from the suppressed jungle of instincts, like the novels of D.H. Lawrence and Henry Miller. They and figures like Freud, Picasso, Schoenberg, the early Stravinsky are all a product of and reaction against the repressive European cultural climate of the nineteenth century.

If modernism no longer offers an artistic stimulus, what follows? If tradition is reactionary and modernism exhausted, where can new inspiration be found? With what has the artist to break to find a new freedom, and yet to create an art, which touches the heart of the public, while also individual and free from dogma and commercial restrictions? Here, the lesson of the Italian

Renaissance comes to our aid. If we can remove the polemics surrounding concepts of the traditional and the modern from aesthetic
judgements, and recognise these categories for what they really
are, i.e. psychological attitudes, then we can see our own times and
the past much more clearly. It would then be possible to see the
twentieth century as a kind of dark age, when barbarism threatened
to destroy a delicate and sublime culture. Only by recognising the
disruptive nature of this period, may it become possible to recreate
or restore traditional European culture, much as the Italians did in
the Renaissance with their reanimation of antiquity. Re-creation,
however, is something very different from repetition, since all
meaningful art contains both elements from the old and the new.
The polemical debate, the dialectical struggle between traditional
and the modern can never be resolved within a purely aesthetic
context, so we are rightly forced to focus upon the psychological
origins and purposes of creative endeavour.

Music is, of all the arts, the one that can find access to our emotional life in the most direct way. We can shut our eyes to avoid
seeing an ugly canvas, we can turn a page with uninteresting information, but it is much more difficult to avoid being touched,
pleasantly or unpleasantly, by music. It is so close to our emotions
that they are directly stirred, often without rational interference.
The problems of modernism are thus experienced more acutely in
music than in the visual arts. Also, notions of 'meaning' and 'spirituality' lie closer to musical experience, and thus it is music which
will be the focus of the rest of this essay.

Modernism and beyond

The notion of being 'modern' has been a continuous strand in
musical development since late Renaissance times, when new
ways of composing, which eventually led to the figured bass practice, were called the *secunda prattica* or *stile moderno*. The new
style was distinguished from the *prima prattica* or *stile antico*,
which designated the older, polyphonic methods of composing.
Musical ideals and styles in the past were soon outmoded, and —
by contrast with painting and architecture — masterpieces of the

past were soon forgotten. In periods of transition, the differences between old and new modes of thought could be quite drastic, as for instance during the transition from baroque to classical styles in the eighteenth century. These transitions meant a re-thinking of the handling of existing material and the development of some new means of expression. These new developments were not always motivated by a need for more adequate expression of emotional intensity, as the often childlike simplicity of eighteenth-century musical classicism shows. The 'modern' was, in this sense, about defining one (more recent) style in relation to another pre-existing style; it was a question of a change of interest, of fashion, not about idealising and condemning. In fact, much of the 'old' lived on in new forms. The 'modern' was not intended to describe an ideological revolution, with the aim of supplanting the old.

In the twentieth century, a very different kind of being 'modern' developed. By stepping outside the gravitational force of tonality, Schoenberg initiated a fundamental break with the tradition of musical composition, as it had existed since early medieval times. In the wake of Schoenberg's twelve-tone method, which became general practice among composers in the nineteen-fifties, thousands of composers, worldwide, contributed to a repertory, which on the whole found a place in libraries and the archives of organisations, which had been created to support the case of such music. The problems surrounding the successful promotion of new music in the course of the twentieth century are well-known and hardly need to be elaborated again. The basic principles of this self-conscious style of 'modernism' are strongly interrelated and can be summarised as follows:

- Breaking with the past, especially nineteenth-century romantic aesthetics and any manifestation of tonality.
- Revolution instead of evolution; new music as the province of an avant-garde, isolated from 'outdated practices' in traditional concert life, because it is ahead of the times, pointing towards a Utopian future, of which new music was an expression or

symbol. Attacks upon any continuing attachment to tonality and traditionally informed aesthetics.

• Historical determinism: technical innovations are evaluated on the basis of perceived historical significance, justified by the implicit direction of past events towards a future climax of modernity.

• Identification with science and its processes of experiment, analysis and objectification; musical composition as acoustical research; the composer as an explorer and researcher engaged for the benefit of cultural life and society as a whole, thus justifying government subsidies.

• Music defined as the abstract exploration of musical material; creation of new materials, technical innovation such as the development of new tone systems and new sound generators (electronic music, computerised processes).

• Abandonment of the intuitive and sensual aspects of music; concepts of expression, melody and narrative are rejected because of the link to nineteenth century aesthetics.

• Political engagement; music as a stimulus for and reflection of revolutionary developments in society; politicisation of musical material, i.e. triads and scales as symbols of right-wing reactionary attitudes, atonal chromaticism representing liberation from a conservative past.

Modern music, in its twentieth-century form, was gradually exhausted and the historical determinism, which was its motivating force, evaporated with the growing awareness of how implausible and unsuccessful the outcome of this so-called 'logical development' actually was. Hegelian notions of history were replaced by the postmodern imperatives: the end of 'the grand narrative' and even 'the end of history' itself, as described by Fukuyama. Thus twentieth-century modernism began to be felt as an historical period with a beginning and an end, like the baroque or romantic period, and valued in some cases for its aesthetic qualities, rather than its ideological claims. From the nineteen-eighties onwards, tonality, even triadic tonality, discretely began to return to new music, as did spirituality, in often a rather naive form. This rediscovery of tonality had hardly anything to do with traditional tonality. Its sources were from exotic cultures and 'pop'music, and its most obvious manifestation was in repetitive or 'minimalist' music. Gradually, however, various elements from the past were absorbed into minimalism to create more extended and complex forms, including European classical music (John Adams) and polyrhythmical textures from African cultures (Steve Reich). Music was rather cautious in these developments, while in the visual arts and architecture, the eighties brought an immense variety of styles and collages of styles, in which elements from modernism were placed alongside material from the past, the present, other cultures, or from sources outside of art altogether. Some architects even dared to use a straightforward classical idiom, something almost totally absent in music. Under the increasing influence of the media culture, with its consumerist drives, style became the focus of attention: not what something *was*, but how it *looked*. In all the arts, trends moved towards a situation, where there were no norms whatsoever and where a work of art consisted of the ideas behind it (conceptual art) or its references to other works or fields of experience (postmodernism). It could be called a mannerist phase.

In music, many young composers turned towards absorbing some elements from pre-modernist music and 'pop' in an attempt to inject some emotional energy into their work and to make it more accessible to audiences; or else they tried to find new audiences altogether, who often turned out to have no interest in traditional European classical music. In the nineties, contemporary classical music became something like a diluted version of the previously mainstream modernism. Non-modernist gestures sweetened the pill of modernism, but were not fully integrated with it. Gestures were borrowed from pre-modernist music, but not developed from a real understanding of the principles behind their former functions. By comparison with the public reverence for and familiarity with the repertoire of traditional concert-giving, it became obvious that it was extremely difficult, if not impossible, to compose new tonal music capable of emotionally communicating with the mainstream audience for classical music. In addition, modernism remained the general outlook among the education institutions and funding organisations. In effect, the basic principles of modernism seemed to be the only possible norms available to a composer looking for a professional career.

The gradual development into a more pluralistic culture in the seventies and eighties, which could also be called the post-modern situation, exposed the myth of progress in music, i.e. the necessity for continuous innovation. In art there is change, but not progress, as there is in science. The claims of the self-proclaimed modernist avant-garde to be the single focus of musical development were evaporating, because the utopian future of music stubbornly refused to realise itself.

Qualitative judgements in art are subjective by nature, but it is still possible to arrive at some objective judgement through subjective means, i.e. a judgement which seems to fit reality and can be shared by a wider audience. However, modernist utopianism, without roots in the past, postpones the question of judgement for ever, and if new music has now to be judged upon its qualities or 'relevance' (whatever that might be), there is no framework with which to do so, apart from the verbal claims of the composer. These cannot be used as a basis for aesthetic judgement, as they are an attempt to create an artificial critical consensus, which does not rely upon the reaction of the wider audience. It must be possible for quality eventually to be shared and acknowledged by others, if it is to be accepted as somehow objectively valid.

Does this mean that stimulating new developments in contemporary music has become impossible? Not necessarily, but the collapse of modernist ideals has left a vacuum which is, at present, filled by a flood of images from the media, originating in consumerism or naive New Age fantasies, which have grown up in opposition to it. Contemporary composition needs a space, a serious philosophical background, where the imagination can freely flourish again.

We can only see the immense range of sources available to

living composers and their value as legitimate stimuli for creation, if we leave historicist thinking behind. Music does not evolve in a single line of development, and so it is not true that Schoenberg and Webern inaugurated the only possible way forward for twentieth-century music. New music, since 1900, was a delta in which post-romantic music spread into a wide network of different developments, each with its own characteristics, but connected to the great river from which it came. With the development of twelve-tone music, Schoenberg left the delta altogether and tried to irrigate a barren territory, claiming that *this* was the only way the river could flow. His bold claims, which were welcomed among those radical intellectuals appalled by the cataclysms of the last century, have fundamentally distorted developments in music ever since.

Modernist music did not appear from nowhere. Its cradle was a tired musical culture. After the towering and thus discouraging pinnacle of Wagner, a degenerate Romanticism and an academic view of classicism seemed to suffocate all authentic innovation. The first steps out of that impasse were motivated by psychological rather than purely musical insights (like the increasing distaste for excessive emotionalism and pomposity) and they opened-up a host of new musical possibilities. The highly sophisticated freedom of Debussy, which was iconoclastic at the time, but which did not challenge the foundations of European music, provided the springboard for the tempestuous innovations of the early twentieth century. This led to an enormous broadening of the available means, including the older tonal tradition, as the works of Ravel, Bartók and Stravinsky show. Within this context, the Schoenbergian development, which generated, together with Webern, the first wave of musical modernism in its 'pure' form, was only one of the many different trends. Its fundamental break with tonality made it attractive to the generations after World War II, who wanted to sever links with the past altogether. The association of tonality with a decadent culture, which led to two devastating world wars, made the idea of creating a totally new and thus untainted musical universe ideologically attractive.

However, the survivors of this catastrophic disintegration of
European civilisation in the twentieth century carried with them
the fruits of their former history, which still had the capacity to
define a contemporary cultural identity, in a way which modernism, resulting from revolution and breaking with the past, could
not. Despite the claims of modernism to the contrary, the evidence
suggests that the old European art can and must live in the present,
and for good reason.

The present availability of all kinds of music, traditional or
modern, European, Asian or African, has created a unique situation. The availability of so much excellent music in traditional
concert life, as well as access to almost every other conceivable
type of music in the form of recordings, has created something like
a musical supermarket. Nowadays, music consumers simply take
from the racks what they like or what makes the best impression
upon them or that which allows them to identify with a desirable
lifestyle. Distinctions in terms of time and place have become
irrelevant. Similarly for composers, everything is potentially
usable as musical material: music of the past including sounds
drawn from modernism, romanticism, classicism, the baroque,
renaissance and medieval periods, and all existing music, including 'world music', folk, pop, jazz, (although romantic and classical
idioms are still found embarrassing, because of the modernist
taboo).

Within this context, traditional European music (including the
'suspect' masterpieces of classicism and romanticism) is still the
most popular and venerated type of music in serious concert life.
Yet — is it still the flagship of Western civilisation? Obviously not
in a direct way, since this repertory was written long ago. Thus,
while the mechanics of traditional, tonal music are known and can
be learned, until now no new music with a comparable impact and
expressive sophistication has emerged. It is a tradition, which has
seemingly died, and the cultural context from which it emerged, all
but disappeared. It is still very much present as a symbol and a
model for what we mean by the term 'classical music': that genre
of aspirational, high-quality musical art, reputedly one of the

greatest achievements of the human spirit. A vital, rather painful question emerges: does 'classical music' as a serious genre, still have a future in a pluralistic and relativist culture, which has lost the consensus of values from which this remarkable art form developed?

The spiritual dimension of music

It is a fact that the developments in twentieth-century music have generated a wealth of means and many composers have done interesting things with them. Observed from some distance, this richness consists mainly of a wide differentiation in terms of 'sound material'. Its complexities and subtleties mainly operate at this surface level. However, there is another type of subtlety and complexity, which is not so obvious: for instance, a Haydn quartet or a prelude by Chopin or Debussy offers a richness in psychological and musical meaning, which is not directly perceived in the often quite straightforward textures. It takes a close acquaintance and a 'growing' into the work's sound world to become conscious of what is often initially only understood as a multi-faceted world of psychological nuances, references and ambiguities. This world is created by listening to the works themselves, it seems to emerge as an autonomous entity from the listening process. It is a most miraculous phenomenon and cannot be dismissed as an entirely subjective projection from the side of the listener. It is certainly a subjective process, but a process through which it is nonetheless possible to reach a level of objectivity, since the experience can be shared and compared. Although some general information may help remove prejudices, verbal explanations provided by the composer or references to biographical or historical circumstances will not make this world accessible, if the piece itself does not reveal its presence and meaning in the listening process. This dimension of a musical work, which is psychological in nature, but musical in substance, can be called — with metaphysical overtones — the spiritual dimension of music.

The process through which the listener enters this dimension is psychological, and takes place in the region of the mind where the sensual and cerebral aspects of music are fused into one. It is also spiritual, because this very process is a metaphor of transcendence: an intimation of a realm where thought and feeling are integrated into a superior mode of being, where the distinctions between subject and object dissolve and the underlying unity of existence is directly experienced. Such an experience touches the core of our personality and gives us a profound sense of meaning and identity. The highly subjective nature of this dimension makes it very difficult, if not impossible, rationally to define it; the soul of a musical work articulates the twilight of our own souls; it holds up a mirror in which we see a reflection of our deeper selves, that part of the self which existed before we had words, before we developed a consciousness. If we had no rationality, it would still be fully understood (this is the reason why music is so powerful in music therapy). It shows us what is immortal and spiritual in ourselves. It also shows us what we could potentially be and the direction in which our psyche wants to develop. This explains why the moments in traditional music, which express spiritual aspiration or a longing for a higher existence, are so moving. The deeper self is irrational; it is the 'dark', instinctive being, the mysterious element which came into the world through the infinitely complex vehicle of physical presence. It is not itself physical. What the body is in relation to the human psyche, is the physical sound in relation to a musical work: a vehicle for an irrational, non-physical presence. As prosaic language is inadequate in the irrational territory, until it becomes poetry, so sounds have to be stylised and structured in such a way that they can create a spiritual context. They thus become music.

Does modernist, genuinely atonal, music have a spiritual or, at least, psychological dimension? Its advocates claim that it does. The suspicion is, however, that this is an example of an 'intentional fallacy'. When psychological and/or emotional states are expressed by atonal means, more information is always needed to support the meaning of the performance, to make the work understood. Meaning which cannot be transferred by the music itself needs verbal explanation. At best, atonal music does not go beyond decorative sound patterns, which of course can be a sophisticated form of art and which can evoke emotional reactions (as abstract painting can). There is nothing wrong with this, but its emotional impact is of a very different nature, and very far from the world of psychological nuances and references, which were a *conditio sine qua non* of pre-modernist music.

There is one type of emotional experience, which is strongly related to modernist music. For people, well-accustomed to tonal music, the most conspicuous expression in mainstream modernist, atonal music is a generalised state of stasis, inner fragmentation, an inability to feel or communicate: in essence, a mood of emotional isolation, emptiness and despair. In combination with a text, this can be highly effective, as works by Birtwistle demonstrate. His cycle, *Nine Settings of Celan* for soprano & ensemble, which uses Paul Celan's desolate, beautiful post-war poetry, or Morton Feldman's totally static opera, *Neither*, both express a state of total meaninglessness. It is an emotional world devoid of all psychological and spiritual energy: the world of the depressed and traumatised psyche. Yet its effect is rather poor, since there is no background against which this state can stand out, as there is, for instance, in Berg's *Wozzeck*, with its multi-layered emotional and musical complexities. To present such extreme emotional territory as a normal state of affairs for longer than ten minutes greatly reduces the expressive impact and eventually results in boredom and greyness. On the larger scale, nihilism as the basis of a cultural movement can never constitute the norm of a tradition without losing its effect. The negation of spirituality, the denial of any value *per se*, can never become a norm. A nihilistic and/or critical ideology can, temporarily, have its function, but once exhausted it must be replaced by another, affirmative principle to be suited to support psychological development. Life is essentially creative and nihilism is something like an invitation to death.

It is precisely the spiritual dimension of music which keeps the works of the past alive. They still have something very important to say to us, something different from most twentieth-century music. It is very easy to explain resistance by the public to 'modern' music as due to a lack of understanding and/or lack of acquaintance, or else straightforward philistinism. Certainly, twentieth century music is not played often enough for us to be sure that it is indeed flawed in its general aesthetic; but the reason why traditional repertoire again and again blocks new listening experiences is that older music gives audiences something that new music cannot. It is the audience's need for emotional and spiritual nourishment which makes the traditional repertoire relevant. The popularity of Monteverdi's *Vespers*, a work as different in sound from Tchaikovsky's symphonies as these differ from Stockhausen's *Gruppen*, is due to the spiritual dimension that this work is able to communicate across 350 years, despite fundamental changes in human life and society. A work like *Gruppen* seems, more than 40 years after its composition in 1957, to exist in a totally different world, one fundamentally different to those of both Monteverdi and Tchaikovsky. It is music from another planet, as we can guess its composer intended, but probably not in the literal sense in which it is actually experienced.

Great art communicates its quality in a direct way. It may take some time to understand it, but eventually its emanation will be decisive. A brilliant technique or great originality are not enough; these fade away, unless the composer has something meaningful to say, something which can transcend the barrier of time. Gifted musicians quickly recognise the inner truth of genuine music by responding naturally to give form to the spiritual dimension. This is mostly a purely instinctive process. A performer with a brilliant technique, strong stage presence and even some sensitivity to shades of expression, will fail to give a convincing performance of traditional music, if he or she doesn't understand the inner life of a piece: its character, expressive architecture, its mood and drama. In short, a performer must understand the work's meaning in psychological and spiritual terms. This understanding involves not only the rational faculties, but also, and more so, the emotional and intuitive faculties. Through this 'irrational' involvement, the piece is brought to life by the performer's subjectivity, which gives the performance authenticity and the power to move the audience.

One of the secrets of musical life, often discussed by performers, is the lack of understanding of pre-modernist music by many performers and composers from the 'modern circuit', who may be excellent craftsmen in their own right. Very often, for these musicians, the psychological dimension of music is just the romantic projection of an outdated bourgeois culture, the worst of nineteenth-century culture when — as they believe — audiences wanted to have their emotions massaged, but not be confronted by real experiences.

Atonal music, i.e. music in which the pull of a fundamental key or tone is absent, lacks an important means of creating structural unity, of defining different levels of structure, and especially fails to offer a means of experiencing a musical structure in more than one dimension as it unfolds in time. In an atonal sound world, unity has to be created through different means, like similarities of texture or intervallic references, or inaudible constructivist devices, which cannot prevent the acoustical result from sounding disordered to an extreme degree (as the serial works of the fifties and sixties mostly demonstrate). The early so-called atonal music of Schoenberg, such as the masterly *Five Orchestral Pieces*, derives its power from its symphonic rhetoric and its strong references to tonality. Its expression is only possible because, in the background, tonal symphonic music is present as a referential framework of norms and expectations. This framework is still present in his later orchestral *Variations*, a dodecaphonic work, but there the tonal framework intrudes all the time into the atonal foreground. The result is a painful example of Brahms with 'wrong notes', where two mutually exclusive sound worlds try to blend.

In the atonal music of the fifties however, all tonal referential frameworks were removed and since then, atonal music was no longer capable of creating a psychological context which created a space of its own: a space in which the musical processes can take place autonomously, i.e. unrelated to sounds from the environment and forming a coherent, self-contained musical and psychological experience. In atonal music, all musical processes operate on the level of pure sound. This can be demonstrated by the effect of noises from the environment. The sound of a claxon from the street will not easily be mistaken for a note within the texture of a Bach *Brandenburg Concerto*, while it can seem a natural part of the texture of a piece by Xenakis. The sounds of Xenakis' piece and the claxon are perceived as operating on the same level, both are perceived as pure sound, with no psychological or spiritual dimension and thus comparable in nature. This demonstrates that tonal, traditional music creates a psychological space, which is independent from the level of mere sound. This space is always structured through tonal relationships, however close or remote. It is this use of tonality which defines the crucial difference between Bach and Xenakis and in which the spiritual dimension of music is found. In atonal music by the likes of Boulez, Xenakis, Nono, the earlier Stockhausen and Berio, it is not possible to sense a musical space, nor is there any structural depth created by tonal relationships, where the fore- and background layers of the music can be *felt* and *heard*. In an idiom where the tones are not tonally interrelated, structural levels cannot be acoustically perceived. However complex and sophisticated the structure, in atonal music all elements are defined by physical parameters such as pitch, volume, colour, duration, dynamics and articulation, and any intentional multi-layered structure remains an abstract wish in the score. It can never achieve musical reality in terms of sound. [The difference between tone and sound, i.e. the distinction between musical and acoustical phenomena, has been explored in a thorough and revealing way in Roger Scruton's *Aesthetics of Music* (1997). It is the most authoritative work on the subject since Adorno and Boulez, and breaks new ground in addressing the problems which beset the musical world, while also offering new and profound insights upon our culture as a whole.]

Pluralism
The current availability of information, in all fields, has created a unique situation for the artist. He can choose from a range of possibilities, wider than has ever existed before. On one hand, this is truly democratic: he can make a selection of techniques or

principles which suit him best. On the other hand, the danger is that cultural forms are perceived as commodities, as objects which can be 'possessed'and perceived as something easily manipulated, as if they were separated from their history, and from their psychological, emotional, and spiritual meanings (which are not always immediately accessible). Hence the myth of the 'global village' is potentially destructive, since it restricts reality to a superficial present, instantly available for 'consumption'. It disguises the gestation process and complex context required to create a meaningful work of art, both of which demand a long time for growth and development. Those growing-up in such a environment often have no idea of what it takes to achieve something in the cultural sphere. The accessibility of the cultural object in the pluralistic culture's shopping mall suggests that 'buying' is the same as 'assimilating'. What is only to be bought, rather than assimilated, needs no meaning, which is why the spiritual seems totally absent in so much contemporary art. Meaning and inner content are often intended, but simply not present in such works of art, because the capacity to express a sense of interiority and value has not been developed. When the idea of expressing that which is experienced or lived-through by the artist is disposed of altogether, and the ideas behind the work of art become more important than the work's content, the intentional fallacy is exposed, because an ironic gap exists between intention and reality. Failure can be effectively disguised and critique prevented by the accusation that audiences have not grasped the meaning of the work, because they are 'behind the times'. In this way, serious discussion and especially, serious critical confrontation can be avoided. It goes without saying that in situations where financial interests are at stake (in music the subsidy network which supports modernism is its only significant patron), this strategy is a common instrument for maintaining the status quo.

Cultures are no longer restricted to a certain locality or a closed tradition. In the current pluralistic situation, many different cultural communities may live in one single town. Because European culture intruded into the east and the south, many people from formerly colonised areas have sought a future in the Western world. Sometimes one sees these different cultures living side by side, sometimes they seem to blend, sometimes there is opposition and conflict. In all cases, the boundaries between these cultures have become transparent, the 'other culture'has become 'visible'. This does not mean that the identity of each of these cultures has diminished, for cultural identity is autonomous, in the same way that a person has a distinctive and undeniable character. Although relations between cultures can erode each group's sense of identity, this is not an inevitable process — and neither is it something positive or negative a priori. The character of a traditional culture may have vague boundaries, but it has a definite nature. Just as a person with a specific character may evolve dramatically through life experiences and still keep his identity (or obtain a stronger identity), so cultures may develop in various ways without losing touch with their roots. This is an important consideration, because the continuity of these roots creates a core of stability and a body of values and norms, which make cultural development possible at all. The industrial age has done great damage by uprooting the identity of so many cultures and putting nothing back in its place.

The erosion of cultural identity and the human scale of life destroys the perspective accumulated from past generations. Their experiences lose their meaning in the new circumstances. If the cultural or social context is insecure, there is no place where new, durable insights can be developed, insights which can be interpreted for every individual situation, but which are based upon comparable experiences in the past. A strong cultural identity could offer, among other things, a point of reference, a centre of stability and permanence through which life can become meaningful and worthwhile; providing a background of values for understanding, development and action. In its absence, these no longer seem possible. It is here, that the role of the artist within society could take on a new form. Instead of an isolated individual, living and working exclusively according to his own, private norms and values, the artist can create the symbols through which a wider group of people can find their identity. It is the artist's capacity to define his identity within the referential framework of some kind of common culture which makes art socially relevant and important, because such an artist can share his experiences in a profound way with individuals, who can measure themselves against those expressions and thus literally find out who and what they really are. So, in the multicultural context of today, in which the artist can no longer simply embrace his inherited culture unquestioningly, his function as a creator of symbols of coherence, meaning and identity becomes more necessary to the spiritual life of the community and its individual members.

There are many cultures of the present and the past available to us, which often seem mutually exclusive. This contrasts with pre-industrial times, when the consensus of values was more or less intact. Now one has to choose from a whole repertory of cultural possibilities, many of which are distorted by commercialism and modernist taboos. The modernist project, the flagship of the twentieth century, began as very much outward-looking, thinking on a huge scale, and giving priority to changing the circumstances which would, in due course, improve the life of the individual. However, there are very different approaches possible to the problem of how to improve the quality of life. As Lao-Tzu wrote in the *Tao Te Ching*:

> Wanting to reform the world without discovering one's true self is like trying to cover the world with leather to avoid the pain of walking on stones and thorns. It is much simpler to wear shoes.

The modernist project in general has begun to disintegrate towards the end of the twentieth century under the weight of its own inner contradictions. Knowledge of the wider world has resulted in an awareness of the limits and relativity of Western thought and the dangers of utopian thinking. The passion for enquiry and riches led European culture to impose itself in places where it did not really belong. Disaster after disaster has revealed its weaknesses and forced us to concede the validity of other points of view. This confrontation with the variegation of the world has rightly generated doubts as to whether European culture has any claims to universality, since we have come to understand that each culture has its own intrinsic value and should be respected as such. The implication for modernist claims of historical determinism is obvious. There is *not* one history, which, by its own momentum, defines progress and the Western world is *not* its most powerful instrument.

For the artist, who lives in today's pluralistic culture, time and place have lost their original meaning. If he wishes, he can choose anything whatsoever as the basis of his art. No single cultural phenomenon can claim superiority over any other. The overwhelming presence of the cultural past thereby causes much frustration, since its popularity seems to thrive at the expense of the contemporary artist. By comparison, the living artist mostly seems to cut a rather poor figure. It would seem unreasonable to expect from him the kind of achievement, which was, in days gone by, the product of a very different society and a very different framework of values and beliefs, when the artist was still integrated within society and a respected contributor to its values. The revolt against tradition was in part born from the threatening presence of the masterworks of the past, which seemed to overshadow the achievements of the present. Yet by denying the past the artist loses the very soil in which he needs to grow.

In a more or less balanced culture, the past is the resource which informs the process of selecting models, providing stimuli for the imagination and technical examples. If all directions were equally possible, paralysis would be the likely result, because the very idea of choice becomes meaningless. It is thus necessary to make choices, which implies the need for value judgements. In former times, value judgements were not necessary at this fundamental level, since there was not much choice: one was simply a part of a cultural whole. But now, before embarking upon a creative endeavour, the artist has carefully to define for himself what his territory will be, based upon his abilities to identify emotionally with it. The context of a pluralistic culture is not necessarily in contradiction with this selection: the artist's field of work is his subjective right and even a necessity; an imperative for himself, but not for other artists. He has to create the fertile, personal world in which he can develop.

It will be obvious that the awareness of a surrounding pluralistic culture, in combination with the need to escape the presence of an impressive cultural past, may easily lead to alienation from the natural creative powers. If there is not a soil in which to grow, the artist cannot identify with his materials at an instinctive level. Without a soil, there is no context in which his subjectivity can obtain objective meaning, i.e. no means through which the work of art can be experienced by others on the same subjective level. The past is both a threat and stimulus and requires an indirect and even ambiguous approach. On the one hand, history may provide a basis for personal development; on the other, it should not determine the direction an artist takes in the sense of a pre-conceived, Hegelian obligation (as was often the case in nineteenth-century academic circles). History needs to be loved, as if it were a nurturing parent and begetter of the new, to be embraced as a referential framework, not as an authoritarian tyrant projecting its rigid expectations upon its descendants.

In pre-industrial times, the superiority of the European tradition was simply assumed, as there was no awareness of any valuable alternative tradition. In the nineteenth century, when large parts of the non-European world were colonised, Europe was confronted with other, often highly sophisticated, cultures. Western civilisation, the conqueror, had to believe itself vastly superior. As foreign cultures became more accessible, their stimulus to European art generated new possibilities for many generations. However, elements from foreign cultures were not imitated, but absorbed, as for instance in the work of Gauguin and Van Gogh and the music of Debussy. Later in the twentieth century, the attitude towards non-Western cultures showed a more enlightened understanding, as more objective research brought insights into the achievements and values of foreign cultures. Asserting the superiority of Europe now is rightly laughable; yet identifying with its way of life with love and loyalty, as it has evolved over more than two thousand years, implies no disrespect for other ways of life. It is not necessary to throw out the child of European civilisation with the proverbial bath water of its darker side. Our reluctance to love our historical roots is one of the results of the Nazi débacle and the second wave of modernist revolution which followed in its wake.

Cultural pluralism as a normal and even desirable state of affairs only applies in the field of practical politics. If applied literally to creativity, it uproots the artist and robs him of one of the most important instruments of creativity: his roots in history. For the artist, 'value-free' pluralism makes meaningful creation impossible. He will become stuck at the surface level of art and not be able to create something meaningful and durable. Fully to exploit his gifts, he will have to make choices based upon subjective value judgements, which will give him a sense of belonging, of continuity, with which he can instinctively identify. Within a pluralistic culture, he will have to choose his own tradition, the one with which he can best identify and which will provide the context for growth and development.

Serious, ambitious 'classical' music (classical in the sense of aiming at the highest artistic achievement in the perspective of traditional norms) is a genre. This implies that, within the genre, there are norms and limitations which must be observed to make successful creation possible. This is not a suppression of the natural impulses, but a *conditio sine qua non*. Where there is form, there is choice, selection, and judgement. As long as these judgements are restricted to the genre, there is no reason why they could not operate as such within a pluralistic culture. Also the delicate balance between following patterns and deviating from them, between more general modes of expression and the individual finger-print, are not possible without the framework of norms as an organic part of a tradition. In effect, an artist can only be original, if he is traditional. Following the norms blindly results in conventionality, while rejecting them totally, leads to incomprehensibility and sterility. Value and meaning can only be achieved through the struggle with the chosen norms and thus making one's own blend of universal and individual elements. This means that all of the composer's creativity has to operate in a unique context, where the limits are defined by his personal choice of a traditional framework.

The more the referential background is broken down, the more restricted the music. Because modernism has not been able to create a real tradition in the sense discussed above, its referential background is necessarily restricted. Mostly it goes no further than the personal taste of the composer or group of composers, and, at best, of a limited audience. However, this is not enough to generate the climate in which really great achievements are possible. Why has modernism failed to establish a normative tradition? Because the very notions of 'tradition', 'norm' and 'continuity' imply the idea of *normality,* as a point of departure: the concept of a more or less stable background of common practice, against which personal exploration can take place. Normality in modernist philosophies has always been perpetual revolution and continuous renewal: concepts which are by definition unstable and thus unsuited to provide a normative background.

On top of this, individualism or originality has been considered by modernism to be the ultimate indicator of artistic quality, which is a rather confused and superficial idea. Originality is a psychological category and not an artistic one. An artist can be mad and produce very original work, stimulated by his very private delusions, which nevertheless may be devoid of any artistic quality. On the other hand, a great artist has a natural originality as a person, which is reflected in his work. It appears as a by-product of his creativity, as a signature, *not* as an expression of artistic meaning. This twentieth-century confusion about originality has led us into an impasse, which has been one of the factors that prevented a modernist 'tradition' from developing. By comparison with modernism, the European pre-modernist tradition (still very much alive in terms of performance) offers an incredibly rich referential framework with numerous shades of styles, idioms, possibilities, and qualitative norms. It is the broadest and most highly developed musical tradition in Europe, providing a wide range of materials and expressive means. If this tradition were available to contemporary composers, which is a question of consciousness and psychological attitude, it might be possible to unlock rich possibilities for new development.

We can conclude that the cultural world of today is pluriform, i.e. consists of many different cultures, which all have their intrinsic value; none of them can be considered superior in relation to another. Within this context, traditional European culture is as valid as any other. How are we then, from this point of view, to consider the modern culture of the twentieth century? Is it indeed an outgrowth of European culture, one which cut itself off from its own historical roots?

Modernism in a broader sense is an agglomeration of beliefs predicated upon ideals of social justice, personal freedom and technological advancement: a utopian vision which dismissed ancient superstition in favour of faith in innovation, rationality and materialism. These beliefs stemmed from science, and achievements in this field have given the scientific methodology tremendous prestige in other areas of thought, such as philosophy, the arts, economics and the social sciences. The most visible change in the social realm was effected by modern architecture, where modernist ideas found their most drastic and often intrusive realisation. On a more day-to-day level, new technologies entered life everywhere. At the beginning of the twentieth century, technological progress made an immense leap forward and began drastically to change daily life. The trauma, moral collapse and sense of irrevocable break brought by two world wars did the rest, to create the impression that the past was in all respects a closed chapter. Interest in the past, in the concept of tradition and any sense of continuity, became synonymous with reaction, a lack of imagination and vision, fear of both the present and future. Utopias were to be built upon the idea that the past was forever buried and that a new human being was about to emerge from the struggle with conservative forces.

The new developments of post-war Western culture tried to disconnect with the very continuity that could have supported them and could have set limits to their unrealistic ambitions. Modernism became an all-pervasive movement: an ideology which was easily applied in different situations, because it had no roots. It can be argued that modernism is a way of thinking, a lifestyle and, in the eyes of many, an absence of culture, rather than a culture in itself. It is a manifestation of the new, rational human being, liberated from his spiritual needs and emotional vulnerabilities and all the props of metaphysics and religion. Unfortunately, there seems to be a link between this liberation and the current erosion of social cohesion, the triumph of mediocrity and banality and the demoralisation among the thinking élite.

Modernism has not only uprooted non-western cultures, it has also uprooted Europe itself. Real European culture belongs to the civilisation which existed before the rise of twentieth-century modernism, that is the old Europe before 1914, which had generated a last impressive flowering of art during the *fin-de-siècle* period. In this sense, European culture suffered — and still suffers — the same fate as traditional Indian, Islamitic and African cultures. The demoralisation of the European intelligentsia reflects the sense of being dispossessed, which inevitably appears in the wake of any modernisation. The modernist spirit holds, overtly or covertly, an aggressive stance *against* the past, *against* tradition, and hence *against* the roots of identity. It should be therefore no suprise that the impact of modernism leaves people in an inert state of mind, uncertain of identity or any sense of enduring value. Of course the modern world, with many improvements at many levels, has contributed considerably to human well-being, yet this should not close our eyes to the devastating effects of the modernist project on the human psyche. In the realm of high, serious culture, its effects have been visibly devastating.

Rescuing the concept of tradition
The taboos surrounding tradition are the result of a serious misconception: the association of 'traditional' with 'reactionary'. One can be very reactionary, no matter how progressive one's aesthetic

outlook. The transformation of modernism from a progressive position to one of convention has already been discussed. In the same way, a traditional attitude may acquire a progressive, i.e. innovative, meaning, according to the context. If a particular cultural movement has exhausted itself, any new direction can be described as 'progressive'. Questioning the status quo, which may at a given moment be understood as either modern or traditional, cannot in itself be considered reactionary. It is adopting a position where no innovative developments are possible, which is reactionary. Were the artists of the Italian Renaissance reactionary in their looking back to antiquity, or Beethoven when, in his late works, he absorbed baroque elements like fugue and canon? Was Wagner reactionary with *Meistersinger* or Ravel with the classicism of his string quartet, or Stravinsky in his *Apollo*?

As we have seen, the idea of a self-conscious modernity has a long history which reaches back to the early Renaissance. However, before the twentieth century, this urge for modernity was held in check by religious, spiritual and aesthetic instincts. Since traditional values were usually supported by the ruling classes, who often had an interest in suppressing the individual's freedom, including his freedom of invention, tradition became — in the polarising climate of the nineteenth century's revolutions — increasingly associated with conservatism and was thus compromised. By 1900, the notion of tradition had become devoid of meaning; it had become part of the façade culture of a morally bankrupt élite. Invention was only found, where the limitations of European culture were being explored and extended, i.e. among progressives, who wanted to renew tradition rather than destroy it. Only when the modern movement began to break with the basic assumptions about the role and meaning of art was modernism in its twentieth-century form born. Van Gogh still belongs to the European tradition in spite of the utterly original and progressive nature of his work. Mondriaan, however, crossed the threshold and belongs to a new and very different period. In music, Debussy, Scriabin and Bartók can be compared to Van Gogh in this respect; Mondriaan with the dodecaphonic Schoenberg and Webern. (This observation does not refer to artistic quality in itself, but to the ideological background from which artistic developments emerged.)

Although modernism grew out of European culture, it cannot be identified with it in a straightforward way, because a basic tenet of modernism was the rejection of Europe's identity, which had matured over many centuries. Exactly because modernism was based upon the denial of the past, it could so easily be transported to America and other parts of the world. Crucial to modernism was the rejection of tradition; the very notion of 'tradition' is a central anathema to the advocates of perpetual progress and innovation. Modernism by definition had to separate itself from the broader flow of tradition and create a different psychological territory with its own norms and values. The result divided the intelligentsia into two opposite camps: the 'progressive'and the 'reactionary'. In this climate of opposition, concepts of continuity and tradition obtained their pejorative meaning; a serious distortion which still obscures any objective evaluation of twentieth-century art.

The destructiveness, which characterises twentieth-century history, has also compromised the idea of tradition, because these catastrophes were supposed to be the result of the irrationality and decadence of a degenerate culture. Yet it is equally irrational and primitive to blame pre-modern European civilisation as a whole for causing two world wars and all the uprooting that social and technological changes have subsequently generated. If we want to restore the best aspects of European culture, it will be necessary to re-interpret tradition as a drastic, but liberating step forward from the atrophy of modernism; a fundamental renewal of our attitudes, comparable with the revived interest in antiquity during early Renaissance times. The paradox here is, that to break with the stagnation caused by modernist concepts of 'modernity' and 'renewal', one has to understand a return to tradition as a 'step forward', i.e. a form of progress in order to return to a more realistic and stimulating relationship with the past, and not as an end or quality in itself.

Of course, a straightforward return to a musical universe as restricted in scope and expressive range as, for example, Mendelssohn's, would seem unfruitful. It is not possible literally to turn the clock back without losing integrity, and without integrity one cannot create meaningful works. There is a great difference between naive escapism and selecting older material to develop it in a personal and authentic way. Composers can approach older traditions from quite unusual angles, as the works of Ravel, Stravinsky, Prokofiev and Bartók show. The later works of Bartók, for instance, with their synthesis of classical tradition and folk material, led to a universal and highly personal reinterpretation of tradition. So personal was Bartók's synthesis in fact, that it cannot be successfully imitated. His inner identification with both folk material and the classical tradition was so profound that both elements, which are, by nature more or less mutually exclusive, could blend perfectly well to create a new unity. The level on which this blending took place was not the material level, but a profound psychological one. His understanding of folklore and classical principles led him to develop very sophisticated structures and formal procedures, which were the outcome of an inner process, not themselves the aim. Bartók's later works are a perfect example of breathing life into existing material to create a living tradition.

It goes without saying that the pre-modern European civilisation had its dark and morbid sides, like the suppression of individuals or whole classes, the abuse of power by church and state, and the opposition between body and soul with the attendant suspicion of sexuality. In his disturbing book, *In Bluebeard's Castle*, George Steiner has pointed out that there exists a link between hierarchical thinking, which is a condition for any cultural achievement, and the suppression of the misfit, of which the holocaust is the most extreme example. A meaningful re-interpretation of tradition does not mean a blind return to a position which has proven to be dangerous as a social paradigm. In the process of selection, the modern experience will have to play an important role in making distinctions between what from the art of the past can be judged to be good examples, and what were the aberrations that inevitably led to the very stagnation which provoked the anti-traditional movement in the early part of the twentieth century. In this process, some ideas, which may seem at first typically 'modern', may appear to belong to an old tradition. A good example is belief in the freedom of the individual to choose for himself how he wants to live, which goes back at least to humanist writings of the sixteenth century, and is not an invention of modern times.

The various emancipation movements of the twentieth century have opened our eyes to the blind crimes of the past; but this awareness does not necessarily lead to the rejection of the greatest flowerings of past culture. In a socio-political sense, a Haydn symphony is a product of the *ancien régime,* i.e. a fruit of an unjust society. However, there is no reason to believe that an individual like Haydn could not have written his music in a better environment. And then, what is better? Twentieth-century New York City, where the nobility are now the barons of the media and real-estate? Steiner's point is that a work of art inevitably has a moral dimension, which can taint, say, Haydn's symphonies, because they were written, to some extent, reflecting a system based upon injustice and suppression. Of course, this is only true if a musical work is seen as a social phenomenon, when in fact a work of art is so much more. Great art transcends its material circumstances. As a social phenomenon, one cannot divorce a work of art from its environment, as it is inevitably rooted in real life. In this sense, innocent masterworks do not exist, for they are always tangled in a web of moral implications. The example of Wagner is often cited as a warning to artists, for although Wagner did not himself commit crimes against humanity, he greatly contributed to a climate in which certain paranoid ideas (like anti-semitism) became increasingly acceptable to the intelligentsia. Yet we should not judge such personal confusion and weakness too harshly, if it does not impinge directly on the aesthetic content of a work of art, since no artist is perfect and no historical period without its errors.

Of course, modernism is itself not immune to moral critique. The elevated ideals of modernism, just after the the second world war, were often used to justify creative repression, so that non-

modernist artists were attacked as the enemy for opposing the
gospel of new music. While modernism in the arts was supposed
to be the ultimate rejection of fascist crimes, it committed comparable errors of judgement, justified by a similar claim of moral
superiority. (Just look at what modernist architecture, for example,
has done to our cities, and to the lives of ordinary people shovelled
up into great housing projects of the kind recommended by
Gropius and Le Corbusier.) This intolerance was not a delusion of
grandeur, as one might expect, but the result of a total blindness to
the reality of cultural life outside the restricted, subsidised
modernist milieu. When the history of modernism, as both a
cultural and social phenomenon, is written, it will show itself also
to have had a dark side comparable to the totalitarian political systems of the twentieth century, which were also characterised by a
disregard for the moral implications of their ideologies. However,
it is Europe's humanist tradition, concerned as it is with justice and
human dignity, rather than progress and innovation, which makes
the pattern of intolerance visible. Respect and compassion lead us
to protect the vulnerable. Imperatives of justice and dignity keep
alive a continuing sense of moral caution. This awareness of moral
implications should inform any exploration of the past and the re-
interpretation of its values. Both tradition and modernism are
blemished, and so with the lessons of modernism behind us, we
should approach tradition carefully and knowingly.

Because there is still much confusion about the meaning of
concepts relating to tradition, it may be helpful to define these as
precisely as possible:

- *Tradition*: a practice, in which the role of example sustains continuity and quality. It is neither dogma, nor prescription. It is not
  laid down in a corpus of rules. It offers the instruments for personal development and achievement. The New Oxford
  Dictionary says: 'Tradition. Transmission of statements,
  beliefs, customs, etc., especially by word of mouth or by practice without writing; what is thus handed down from generation
  to generation; long-established and generally accepted custom,

practice, etc.; an immemorial usage.' Conspicuous here is the absence of a dogmatic text or body of rules: it means that the forms of tradition are flexible and open to individual interpretation. It follows naturally that the academic codification of culture in the nineteenth century, which was reflected in the regular norms in the conservatories, academies and official exhibition spaces was a quite arbitrary formalisation, motivated by the idea that art could be best understood and taught through a rationalistic approach to its material appearance. This idea was greatly stimulated by the impressive developments of science and technology at the time. The reaction against nineteenth century academic culture was thus fully justified. The true heritage was left *without* a testament; a living tradition does not lend itself to an archeological approach.

- *Conventionality*: A convention, in itself, is just an agreed way of behaving, which is understood and recognised by a social group. It takes the form of communicative gestures, and they are the basis of tradition. If such gestures lose their deeper meaning, a degeneration follows. Only the surface level of the work of art is present, often referring to other works of art for credibility rather than as a true model. The interest in a conventional work of art wears off, as soon as we have under-stood its nature. The forms of the surface are often contradictory and arbitrary without reason. 'Mannerism'can be considered another term for conventionality.

- *Historical awareness*: Knowledge and understanding of history, of the past. It is the perspective which makes a fruitful relation to the past, and an understanding of the relationships between the present and the past, possible. It acknowledges the necessity of continuity for the maintenance of quality and excellence. One is aware of the past as a reservoir of possibilities, *not* as a goal for which to strive.

- *Historicism*: An attitude related to 'conventionality'; a superficial application of historical information without under standing of the subtle interrelatedness of tradition, which provides continuity and meaning. Good examples can be found in nineteenth-century architecture and also in modernism since the Second World War (both being tainted with mannerism). The Utopian projection into the future is based upon the misconception that history can be 'made'as a self-conscious act in the present, as if history consisted of a single lineage, moving from A to Z, and were open to manipulation. Historicism presupposes an autonomous, yet predictable motor of progress, which is largely driven by mankind, which defines the direction history is taking. In reality history is the result of the unfolding of life, hence full of randomness and contradictions.

Tradition and historical awareness are informed by an understanding of the more profound levels of the human psyche; conventionality and historicism are characterised by a more superficial and materialist approach.

The true traditionalist attitude in art is one in which individual achievement and idiosyncrasy are welcomed within a language that can be understood by a wider audience — not necessarily the majority of people, of course, but a considerable proportion of the thinking and civilised élite. The artist functions as an individual within a greater group, for the good of that group. In such a context, the outdated conflict between the independent artist and the community is transcended. The ideas and impulses in the artist's subconscious, articulated in his works, need to be recognised (or even shared) by the community, if the work of art is to be meaningful. Within a cultural tradition, the universal problems and emotional struggles of the members of a community are represented and worked out in the metaphor of the work of art. Since human beings are formed by the past, biologically and psychologically, they carry it within them, whether they like it or not. It is this fact which makes the observance of continuity with the past a necessity. An individual artist may, by nature, deviate in terms of personality from the expectations of the group, but he will at least share the community's past. In that sense, he is not outside the group. In his art, the shared experience of the past becomes a powerful instrument of expression, possibly even a bridge from alienation to integration. If an artist is determined to express his individuality effectively, only an understanding of the workings of tradition can help him find ways in which he can touch the inner-most being of the members of his audience. In a society supposedly made up of free individuals, such a paradigm is a much needed potential source for social integration and the affirmation of individual identity in relation to the group. Obviously, within a tradition at any given moment, the extent of historical awareness, the level of individuation, the relative freedom of the individual within the group, the opportunity for communication, are all strongly interrelated. Any change in one of these elements affects the climate in which an artist must try to realise his artistic ambitions, i.e. it would alter the nature of the task.

Historical awareness should never become a straight-jacket of ideas and least of all, a tyrannical projection into the future. A tradition does not unfold according to historical laws, but is the natural result of the unfolding of life itself. If artists would fully dedicate themselves to the quality and authenticity of their works, the result would be an unfolding elaboration of historical precedent, that would be intuitive, more of an improvisation, than the rigid imposition of a preconceived order. It is not at all neces-sary to project developments into the future. They are not the artists' concern, but at most, speculations that may or may not be of interest to future historians. To live 'historically', seeing reality through the glasses of a hypothetical future historian, inevitably falsifies our perception of that very reality; subjective projections and wishful thinking detach us from the flow of life and the creative forces in the subconscious dry up.

It will be clear by now that an artist, working within a tradition, will be supported by numerous examples and stimuli, but only if he can see them as subject to his free choice. What about the indi-vidual freedom of the artist, as it was cultivated from the nineteenth century onwards? Indeed, an artist needs a space in which he can develop his personal taste and interpretations. This space should be in natural proportion to his talents and personality. Paradoxically, the total freedom advocated in the twentieth century merely undermines the artist's sense of identity. Only in the struggle with a body of examples and the need for touchstones of excellence, does the artist find his identity and discover the nature of his relationship with the community. An equilibrium has to be found between the use of a general 'language'and individual expression, but individualism should never detach the artist from a meaningful interaction with the group. Exactly because tradition does not provide rules, the artist has to explore the limits of subjectivity, which will be an evolutionary process, sometimes requiring correction and self-criticism. This continuous revision makes tradition a living process. Where individual freedom and social constraint collide and generate creative, challenging tensions, the unfolding of ever changing variations becomes possible. As Suzi Gablik describes in *Has Modernism Failed?* (1984):

> The fluctuating relationship between individual freedom and social constraint constitutes, for each society, a field in which it organises itself — that is why different societies have different moral densities.

One of the motivating forces behind modernism was the idea, that traditional means were exhausted. They had all been used up, worn out. All that was left were clichés. This may have been the impression at the beginning of the twentieth century or even just after the Second World War, but now, after such a long period of prevailing modernism, the culture of old Europe looks quite different. To begin with, our experiences are very different from those of pre-twentieth century people. Even if he tried to imitate a traditional example, a contemporary artist would inevitably infuse something of his personal experience, possibly including his experience of the intervening modernism, into his imitation and thus feel the need to deviate from the traditional model. Secondly, the idea of the exhaustion of artistic means is a psychological fallacy. The human imagination is inexhaustible in finding variations and new combinations of available material, because the human being is never quite the same and inevitably develops over time. The continuous change of perspective — even upon the very same elements — produce different experiences of what is materially unchanged. The creative fantasy sees new possibilities in any material all the time, because its position towards the material changes. Life is the passing of time, and accumulating experience gradually changes the interpretation of inner and outer reality. One of the phenomena which gives human life its tragic taste is its transitoriness. But we feel that there is an eternal core in our being, and thus we seek for things which endure and reflect this inner reality.

One can never assess the moment when the mind is really incapable of seeing a new perspective upon familiar things. The human imagination has no definable limitations. This can be shown by a familiar example. Before the revival of Vivaldi, one could not imagine that there was more to baroque music than was then known about it; a notion contradicted by the discovery of Vivaldi himself. So, in a hypothetical mental framework, first there is a limited number of possibilites which seem exhausted, then a new possibility enters from outside the framework and proves otherwise, thereby slightly changing the entire framework's nature. That is exactly what creativity is: to imagine the seemingly unimaginable; and history proves that it is possible. When artists feel that certain types of material are exhausted, it merely means that the psychological context can no longer fruitfully work for them and that their instincts stimulate them into other directions. In most cases, the proximity of great achievement compels subsequent generations to try to escape from its overwhelming shadow. Such was the reaction after Michelangelo and Da Vinci, after Handel and Bach (his own sons especially), or after Beethoven and then after Wagner. It is, however, an artist's psychological reaction, *not* the reality of an actual situation. One may feel at a certain moment that nothing can be done, but that does not mean it remains eternally the case, as an objective truth. It is merely the subjective experience of the artist at that moment.

How can a tradition maintain its character, when there is no body of rules? There is a very striking case, which clearly shows how a tradition functions, namely classical architecture. A rather small repertoire of basic ideas and formal elements was sufficient to create infinite possibilities of variation, transformation, refinement and expression. Greek, Hellenistic, Roman, Renaissance, Baroque, and Classicist architecture present different worlds of experience, in which can be found an almost endless number of variations and interpretations. Yet there is continuity and an underlying unity of meaning. From daring idiosyncrasy to the impersonally formal, from the dynamic to the static, from the intimate to the public, from dramatic conflict to peaceful harmony, it seems that all kinds of balances between innovation and norm are possible. If one looks through a book with pictures of classical architecture, one cannot fail to be struck by the enormous diversity, the exuberant innovation which exists within the accepted fundamentals of the 'classical' style. It is a language with a network of references that extends over immense distances of time and place. It may be instructive to quote from the fascinating study by Alexander Tzonis and Liane Lefaivre, *Classical Architecture, the Poetics of Order* (1986):

> Classical architecture...is based on formal conventions that can operate perfectly without being explicitly stated. Being able to design or see classical architecture is like being able to speak or understand a language; one joins a cultural tradition, a social universe. It implies the incorporation of formal conventions into a larger receiving structure in the mind. In real life, people are not shown the classical canon and all its levels and schemata. They simply come into contact with buildings, with events related to buildings, with representations of buildings and discussions about buildings. Only slowly is the canon and its schemata crystallised ...Bringing this implicit canon to the surface is not an easy matter...the definition of the classical canon, when it comes to many details, is subject to many versions and revisions. The idea of it as something frozen and monolithic is an abstraction toward which many have aimed, but which has

always remained elusive...The formal system of classical architecture has been a domain with blurred boundaries; the classical canon has been constantly modified, like any social convention. The classical building is an expression of this evolving canon that it confirms. At the same time, it is the product and the creator of the canon.

In the context of a pluralistic culture, a revival of the concept of tradition seems fully legitimate. Reabsorbing the European tradition, by re-interpreting pre-modernist values and ideas, could reconnect new music with a past which is living all around us. It could provide new stimuli to the existing traditional performance culture and its audiences, by bringing new life into an art form which has — as a contemporary expression — seemingly died. Above all, it could provide a framework of reference to composers and audiences alike, thus restoring the lost credibility and meaning of new music in the public's mind: the basis for the more or less natural interaction between composer and audience, which existed before the modernist schism. Modernism should be left a niche to make clear that it created a separate territory of musical experience, but did not replace the European musical tradition. Such a revival of a living tradition would provide certain standards of quality, which would avert the dangers of both commercialism and cerebralism. Only by restoring the classical tradition can a climate prevail, where the highest ambitions of musical creation can, once again, find new realisations. It is the only way in which those, able and inclined to use traditional methods of composing, can be mobilised.

European integration: artist and community
The slow and often painful integration of Europe into some kind of interrelated agglomeration of nations and cultures has underlined the strong need for cultural identity. If the new Europe turns out to be an immense, bureaucratic machine, in which the individual is an uprooted particle, manipulated by forces beyond its control, the project will certainly fail. There is only one way in

which the notion of an integrated Europe is acceptable, and that is in the context of respect for traditions, which can function as a powerful and inexhaustible psychological reservoir, compensating and counteracting the dehumanising side-effects of this integration process. We see already, while the borders of the nations are getting less and less important, that certain regions, which overlap more than one nation, have an identity of their own. Here, local customs, ways of life which have long roots into the past, function as references for cultural identity. While certain types of government develop towards supranationalism, others take on an increasingly local character. It is rare that a political system or the boundaries of a nation-state can fully match the complex ethnic and cultural pattern of even a small region. This problem grows, as the scale of government stretches across a vast territory like Europe. Here art offers a potential solution, because sophisticated culture can contribute to a sense of self-affirmation, relatedness, empowerment, independence, responsibility and freedom, thus providing meaningful expression for subtle aspects of identity that political systems cannot address. The collections of pre-modernist art and traditional concert life would not be adequate alone to fulfil this function, although they are perhaps the most important emblems of a common European identity that we have. It is through contemporary creation that audiences can find something of their own realities in symbolic form and their struggles resolved. There are, by definition, no rules for the way in which contemporary art might play this role. It is a territory to be explored; one of the important tasks ahead. Nevertheless, there are examples of many different kinds of traditional integration to be found in the past. Seen from this point of view, the cultural past becomes, as Marguerite Yourcenar believed, a treasure trove of possibilities, instead of a closed museum. With a European future in mind, artists could explore these riches and find their own, innovative solutions to the many problems, which undoubtedly will come their way.

A successful integration of Europe should go together with a successful re-integration of the artist within the community. Only the living artist can, through his own personal integration with tradition, find the right articulation point, the right symbols, the right expressions of cultural and thus personal identity. This territory has become very problematic, not only because of the problems of modernism, but also because the role of the artist has been, since the revolutionary times of the late eighteenth century, increasingly ambiguous and insecure. We should acknowledge the freedom that an artist needs to develop his vision, but acknowledge that real isolation from society can only result in sterility, because it makes an integrated role for art within the community increasingly difficult. Suzi Gablik again writes:

> In the Renaissance, the artist's mission was twofold: a direct one imposed by the requirements of city, church, or patron, and an indirect one arising from the need to express individuality and to find originality within an established order. A work of art was an individual achievement *and* a social fact, the affirmation of obedience to an established order, and the transcendence, through originality, of that obedience.

In other words, the apparent dialectic of traditionalism and originality, fulfilling a community's expectations and answering one's individual inner needs, could and should be resolved and integrated within the boundaries of a work of art.

Re-creating the classical tradition
Compared with the riches of tradition, postmodernism is too poor as a source of ideas, because of the lack of normative features. A philosophy that promotes the principal equality of all musical material (ignoring tradition and context) creates a cultural supermarket. A selection of materials, on the basis of a relativist freedom of choice, makes the infusion of and identification with the artist's subjectivity more or less impossible. Equally, blind imitation of pre-modernist musical forms cannot be more than an exercise. As we have seen, the notion of tradition as a living process makes it impossible to set precise limits to the idea, so its

essence can only be approached indirectly through the works of art themselves, together with a clear awareness of the ambiguities involved. The European tradition is implicit in its individual works, which confirm and extend their own context and referential framework.

Also, it is possible to detect traces of tradition within modernism, and it would be revealing to discover how much of modernism is, in fact, unwittingly informed by tradition. In any case, the precise distinctions between modernism and traditionalism cannot be drawn so clearly at the level of the actual works. It is, for instance, possible to handle a thoroughly atonal idiom and use a rhetoric which stems from tonal structures, with its phases of beginning, transition, interruption, development, repetition and closing, as can be found in some works by Jonathan Harvey (his cello concerto of 1990, for example). It is also possible to compose with thoroughly traditional techniques and still arrive at a very dissonant and uncompromising result, as in the case of the Englishman, Robert Simpson or the Dutchman, Hans Kox.

Being modern can be translated as being in touch with the collective unconscious of the times, intuitively understanding the *Zeitgeist*, the needs of the present and giving form to that which is still invisible beneath the surface of reality. In relation to artistic quality, this is irrelevant; but it may be a psychological motor, which motivates the artist to choose the unusual rather than the conventional path, and which may thus lead to very personal results. The form which this path takes is not bound to certain specific idioms. As we have seen, a revival of past practice can be very modern in a context where modernist utopianism itself has become conventional. This whole territory of reinterpretation should be explored by composers and theorists alike and poses a great challenge to fill the vacuum left by the evaporation of modernist ideals.

What is generally considered to be the European 'classical' tradition'? The main line of the pedigree: Bach, Haydn, Mozart, Beethoven, Schubert and so on, is an invention of the nineteenth century. The codification of a canon of 'classical' works with normative weight however, has done much damage to the very works which it sought to elevate to immortal status. The veneer of being 'classical' made it quite difficult to enjoy the works for what they really were: superior outbursts of creativity, full of life, a manifestation of the best in the human spirit. In nineteenth-century musical life, they often seem to have been presented as precious objects, venerated rather than enjoyed; a misunderstanding which unfortunately has not totally disappeared in our own times. Thus the wild flowers of creativity turned, for many people, into dried bouquets, which decorated the stuffy salons of the bourgeoisie. The nineteenth-century bourgeois and academic cultures, which had a strong tendency to suppress the natural and the human in favour of a rather dry rationalism, saw their values reflected in a view of the 'classical' masters, which turned their freshness and originality into icons of respectabililty. This in turn provoked the romantic artists to subversive fantasy. The entire romantic movement of the nineteenth century took place in artistic and intellectual, but not academic, circles. Society in general kept Romanticism's excesses at bay. So, if the European tradition is considered as a way forward, the nineteenth-century idea of that tradition, which is academic and restrictive, should be avoided. In fact, respectability has nothing to do with works of art. This is confirmed by the fact that many works, now considered 'classical', were quite subversive at the time of their entrance into the world.

The European tradition embraces the entire development of music from Gregorian chant up to and including the best of twentieth-century tonally orientated works (such as Ravel, Bartók, Stravinsky, Britten, Prokofiev, Shostakovich). It encompasses some exotic branches like Gesualdo, Monteverdi, D. Scarlatti, C.P.E. Bach, Berlioz, Chopin, Wagner, Debussy, Scriabin and Berg. A wide range of the interpretation of basic principles (as far as they were available at the time) was possible, in which conformist and deviant elements could blend in individual ways, as in the music of Schumann, for instance, but also in Tchaikovsky, Mahler and Ravel. Even material which was originally unrelated to the European tradition of art music could be digested and absorbed, as the music of Stravinsky, Janáček and Bartók illustrates. If one could dispose of the old-fashioned nineteenth-century idea of tradition, certain contradictions which apparently existed in former periods between tradition and individualism would disappear. For example, if one listens to the chamber music of Haydn and Beethoven with ears trained by the late sonatas of Debussy, one appreciates the textural and colouristic qualities of the older composers in a new way. It is even possible to hear both types of music as belonging to the same musical continuum, in which they each form a separate, smaller world. Instead of forming a historic line reaching ever further back into history, older works can be heard as temporary manifestations of the same plasma, which can take on different forms in the hands of any different composer. The relationships and references which naturally exist between the works within a tradition, create a presence in which the historical order, in the form of measured 'real time', has no place. One is reminded of the German composer Bernd Alois Zimmermann's idea of a *Kugelform der Zeit*, a hypothetical concept of musical reality where there is no longer a distinction between past, present and future. On a spiritual level, all composers thus become contemporaries.

Although it is not possible, and not desirable, to lay down a canon of European classical works, it may be possible to sketch-out the boundaries by which the European musical tradition could, even with the greatest reserve, be defined. While these boundaries should never be precise or prescriptive, music which goes beyond them in a fundamental way should be easily recognisable. It could be argued that a new form of traditional music should encompass the following characteristics:

- The principle of tonality, i.e. the musical structure is related — directly or indirectly — to tonal centres which makes it possible to experience the entire structure as a whole of interrelated tones. This can be achieved through different organisational tone systems like modality, major-minor tonality, chromaticism, or mixtures of them. Even atonal elements can be integrated into the tonally informed whole.

- The work has more than one structural dimension, i.e. there is a structural background which informs larger units, in which foreground material fills-out shorter periods. This creates the possibility of structural articulation, narrative and the construction of larger forms.

- The work has a beginning and an end and defines itself as an entity separate from its environment. This makes the presence of the work possible in different environments without its identity being affected.

- The presence of a psychological, and/or spiritual, dimension (as discussed before), which unfolds within the space created by tonal interrelatedness.

- The essence of the work, its identity, consists of the structure which is formed by the notes, which can be enhanced by additional instrumental or acoustical colour, but cannot be replaced by it.

- The notation is focused upon practicality and has no aesthetic *musical* status of its own, apart from decorative value, unrelated to the acoustical presence of the work. The score represents the work, but is not its presence; in the first place, it is a body of instructions for performance.

For musicians, working in traditional concert life, all this is just common sense. But if one reviews the changes which have been proposed since the *Darmstadt* explorations, the practical value of defining these boundaries is again underlined.

It will be clear by now that the change in attitude, which is needed to see tradition in a new light, is psychological in nature. The two main problems are, how to get under the skin of tonal composition without falling into the trap of repeating what has already been done, and how (and which) lessons of modernism might be integrated into the European tradition. An archeological approach to pre-modernist music would lead to sterility, because it would leave no space for the composer's subjective interpretation and the fruitful 'misreading' of models. Incorporating any fundamental modernist principles, which are incompatible with those of tradition, will lead to paralysing conflicts. Here, the need for research, experimentation, exchange of ideas, and discussion makes itself felt. We need a new *Darmstadt*, based upon very different ideas and with a very different undogmatic philosophy, to explore this wide territory. The potential advantages are obvious: restoration of new music's credibility with audiences, a new stimulus to performers, an injection of new ideas and repertoire into concert hall programming and the recording industry. Above all, it might make possible the renaissance of a miraculous art form, celebrating the dynamism and creativity of the European spirit, so badly needed in a world of crumbling values. This vision does not break again with the past, but embraces it; the need for synthesis may be the fundamental lesson of twentieth-century modernism.

BIBLIOGRAPHY

Eliot, T.S. 'Tradition and the Individual Talent' from *The Sacred Wood; essays on poetry and criticism*, Methuen, London, 1920

Gablik, Suzi *Has modernism failed?* Thames and Hudson, New York and London, 1985

Lao-Tzu *Tao te ching* (English trans. by D.C. Lau, Penguin, London, 1963)

Steiner, George *In Bluebeard's Castle,* Faber&Faber, London 1971

Tzonis, Alexander and Lefaivre, Liane *Classical Architecture, The Poetics of Order*, Massachusetts Institute of Technology, Boston, 1986

Yourcenar, Maguerite *Entretiens radiophoniques avec Maguerite Yourcenar*, edited by Patrique de Rosbo, Mercure de France, 1972 (English trans. for this essay by John Borstlap)

9

Renewing the Past: some personal thoughts

David Matthews

An individual composer cannot predict the course of musical history, nor can he or she tell others how they are to compose. But since composers are no longer the natural inheritors of a tradition and of a musical language which they can unthinkingly adopt, they must choose their own particular language themselves and also work out their relation with the past. In doing so, they will inevitably acquire an overall view of what music, from their perspective, should be. My own view is founded on a few central principles, which were unfashionable at the time I began to write music in the mid-1960s, but which now, at the start of the twenty-first century, have come to seem quite legitimate, except to those diminishing few who attempt to hold on to the rigid prescriptions and proscriptions of modernism. My principles are: that tonality is not outmoded, but a living force; that the vernacular is an essential part of musical language; and that the great forms of the past, such as the symphony, are still valid. The remainder of this essay will attempt to elaborate and justify these three propositions.

It hardly needs to be said now that the proclaimed dogma of the post-Second World War avant-garde that tonality was dead was mistaken. Tonality flourishes again everywhere, and by no means only in the simplistic form adopted by the minimalists. My own attitude to tonality is straightforward: I hear music tonally, so it would seem perverse to resist what I hear. Although many passages in my music move away into regions where a sense of tonality is lost, I am always compelled eventually to bring the music back to a tonal centre. I am conscious of a balance to be preserved between stability and instability. When I listen to non-tonal music, it is very difficult for me to hear it except in relation to tonality: non-tonal music seems fundamentally unstable. This seems quite reasonable, if one hears music as an expressive language, as I do. The alternative is to hear it as pure sound, which my ears will not allow.

The temporary eclipse of tonality began with Schoenberg, who obsessively pursued the advanced chromaticism of *Tristan* and *Parsifal* to its logical conclusion, where extreme emotional states could be expressed by means of a totally chromatic musical language, free from any sense of tonal stability. His Mosaic, lawgiver's personality led him to codify this Expressionist language, which had been an ideal vehicle for the nightmare worlds of *Erwartung* and *Pierrot Lunaire*, and to propose his new method of composition based on the equality of all twelve notes of the scale as a wholesale replacement for the tonal system. Schoenberg's authority was such that he and his successors have had an enormous influence on the music of the second half of the twentieth century. This is a curious phenomenon: as Deryck Cooke remarked, it was 'as though the whole main modern movement in literature had taken Joyce's *Finnegans Wake* as its starting point.'[1] Schoenberg's belief in the comprehensiveness of his system ('every expression and characterization can be produced with the style of free dissonance'[2]) was, however, mistaken: the musical modernism that stemmed from him is almost invariably limited to a narrow range of expression, which stays at a pitch of high tension, and cannot naturally evoke states of joy, gaiety or exuberance.

This might be called the common sense view of Schoenberg, but it is nevertheless true. It is, of course, a simplification, ignoring, for instance, the deep attachment Schoenberg retained for tonality, which means that none of his serial works — the late ones especially — are entirely free from tonal references. He did not go as far as Berg, the modernist composer whom everyone loves. Berg reconciled serial technique with tonality by deliberately choosing twelve-note rows with tonal implications and using these rows with great freedom, and was thus able to combine Expressionism with late-Romantic eroticism and tenderness. The purist Webern, on the other hand, abolished all sense of tonality, and his serial works really do breathe the air from other planets. Other, later classics of serial modernism such as Boulez's *Le marteau sans maître*, Stockhausen's *Gruppen* and Stravinsky's *Aldous Huxley Variations* inhabit a world of intellect and refined sensation, but one remote from human feeling. It was a path that, pursued further, could only lead to sterility; and it is interesting that Boulez (for instance in *Rituel)* and Stockhausen (in *Inori*), have both made some accommodation with tonality, and Stravinsky in his final work, *Requiem Canticles*, partly reverted to the harmonic world of his earlier music.

Modernism in all the arts has often mirrored the isolated, anguished state in which the twentieth-century artist has found himself. While a sense of isolation is almost inevitable, given the breakdown of a common culture, does it follow that all serious artists must also be afflicted with existential angst? There is a genuine art to be made out of existential despair (such as the early works of Peter Maxwell Davies), but composers should beware of the self-indulgent use of an extreme language, which should not be an easy option. On the other hand, it seems particularly difficult nowadays to take an opposite standpoint. In writing tonal music and trying through it to express the sheer joy and exuberance I often feel at the fact of being alive, was I simply being naive, out of touch with the modern world? I was encouraged in what I was attempting to do by hearing the music of Michael Tippett and reading his writings on music. Tippett in the 1930s opted to be a tonal composer of a strongly conservative kind, using melodies derived from folksong and aiming at a classicism modelled ultimately on

Beethoven. In an article of 1938, he had written:

> An artist can certainly be in opposition to the external 'spirit
> of the age' and in tune with some inner need, as, for
> instance, Blake was. A composer's intuitions of what his age
> is really searching for may be, and probably will be, not in
> the least such obvious things as the portrayal of stress and
> uncertainty by grim and acid harmonies. The important
> thing ... is that he should be in some living contact with the
> age.[3]

Tippett associated tonal stability with psychological wholeness,
which he himself achieved through a rigorous course of Jungian
self-analysis. The split psyche associated with modern man found
its most appropriate means of expression in atonality. What Tippett
said, and the music he wrote that demonstrated his beliefs, such as
The Midsummer Marriage, made perfect sense to me, though ironically, in the late 1960s, he seemed to betray his ideals in a quest
for novelty. It is significant that he later regretted some of his more
extreme experiments, and in old age reverted to a more stable kind
of music, culminating in his last piece, the serenely beautiful *Rose
Lake*.

Although as a young composer I had no wish to follow Boulez
or Stockhausen, I was as a romantic adolescent immersed in the
early work of Schoenberg, Berg and Webern, in Scriabin and
Szymanowski, in Strauss' *Salome* and *Elektra*, and above all in the
symphonies of Mahler, who was the most important influence on
the music I began to compose. My music became highly chromatic
and had a strong flavour of prewar Vienna. I sensed the need to
purify this language with a strong dose of classicism, but I was not
clear how it was to be done. In the early 1970s, I reached a compositional crisis, and for several years was unable to finish a work
that satisfied me. Around that time I met the Australian composer,
Peter Sculthorpe, and became his composing assistant for several
years. In 1974, he invited me to come and stay in his house in
Sydney. Living there for several months, as far away from Europe

as it was possible to get, had a profound effect on me. I was able to look at Europe with a detachment never before possible. From Australia, with its relaxed way of life, its burgeoning new culture and its strong belief in itself, the contemporary culture of Europe seemed exaggeratedly neurotic. Hearing European modernist music in Australia, it sounded bizarre: why all this tension and agitation? I was not so laid-back as to imagine that music could do without tension altogether, but a certain redressing of the balance seemed necessary. Peter's own music, which combined European and Asian influences, achieved an equilibrium of romantic expressiveness and classical poise. Peter reminded me that contemporary European music was an exception to the rest of the world, where a stable, tonal basis to music had never been called into question. While the particular manner of his music has always seemed an ocean's distance from my own, Peter has been one of the strongest influences on my subsequent development, and I hold his own compositions in the highest regard.

D. H. Lawrence's perception of Australia as an untouched land where life 'had never entered in' but was 'just sprinkled over'[4] remains largely true, and the real subject of all Australian art is that continent's extraordinary landscape. But the European artist cannot free himself entirely either from history — of which our man-made and man-ravaged landscapes speak eloquently — or from musical history. Minimalism, a born-again tonal language that disregards the past, is not really suited to Europe. Though a product of New York, it seems most at home in California, where the sun shines and the burden of history weighs lightly. Minimalism is a secular, hedonistic music. The so-called 'holy minimalism' we have in Europe, in the music of Pärt, Górecki and Tavener, is different in essence; but these composers have also tried to escape the past, or at least the past since the Renaissance, reverting to medieval Christian ideals much as the pre-Raphaelites tried to do in the nineteenth century. Like pre-Raphaelitism, theirs is a somewhat artificial stance, though the strength of all three composers' religious convictions gives a depth to their music, which might otherwise sound dangerously thin. I recognize the value of traditional religious faith to provide a foundation for art. Those who have such faith are enviably secure, and their art will reflect this (in music, Messiaen is the best recent example). Speaking for myself, however, I cannot ignore either the Renaissance or Romanticism, both of which represented huge and irreversible strides away from Christianity and its central doctrine of man's reliance on God and the Church for salvation, and towards a conception of man on his own, self-reliant, though able to discover the divine element that is within us. This was already inherent in the humanism of the Renaissance, and became the philosophy of Romanticism. Because of its over-optimistic idealisation of human potential, Romanticism failed to bring about the wholesale transformation of mankind that many of its proponents hoped for, but that does not mean that there is any other real substitute for its essential beliefs.

Beethoven still seems to me the ideal of the modern composer, for Beethoven won through his personal anguish towards a profound spirituality in the *Missa Solemnis*, in the late sonatas and string quartets, that is the equal of the unselfconscious spirituality of medieval music, but which Beethoven achieved by himself. Beethoven's dramatic use of tonality within sonata form, whose parameters he expanded enormously in his late works, made his spiritual quest in music possible. Wagner attempted a similar path, expanding Beethoven's forms still further into music drama. Wagner's great achievement was the comprehensiveness of his musical language. He developed chromaticism to an unprecedented level of expressive power, so that for the first time the overwhelming force of sexuality finds its full musical equivalent. Alongside this precarious chromaticism is a stable, elemental diatonicism. In *Parsifal,* the struggle between eroticism and spirituality is finally resolved in the latter's favour, in a sublimated A flat major. Whether Wagner achieved true spirituality in *Parsifal* is still a controversial topic, which it is impossible to pursue further here, but the immense yearning for transcendence in the work cannot be denied. The same conflict between body and spirit, between disruptive chromaticism and stabilizing diatonicism, is found in Mahler, Wagner's truest successor. Mahler was less in thrall to sensuality than Wagner, and there is a more natural spiritual quality to his music. Mahler's attitude to tonality, as a drama mirroring the drama of life, is, like Wagner's, indebted to Beethoven: the drama is eventually resolved triumphantly in the majority of the symphonies; tragically in the Sixth; and transcendentally in the last works, *Das Lied von der Erde* and the Ninth. This dramatic approach still seems to me to be valid, even if one chooses not to work on such a large scale as Mahler - which is wise advice for most composers.

What I should like to suggest (once again to compress a huge topic into a few sentences) is that, if tonality is to regain its full power, it must be used dynamically again. Most contemporary tonal music is static; but stasis, it seems to me, is ideally a condition to be achieved, as for instance in Beethoven's last piano sonata where the static, contemplative slow movement is heard as a consequence of the dynamic drama of the first movement. The dynamic use of tonality will involve both modulation and the rediscovery of dissonance as a disruptive force. Although one can no longer easily define the difference between consonance and dissonance, it is still possible to conceive of harmony as either stable or unstable. Unless there are real harmonic contrasts in a piece, it cannot have dynamic movement. Perhaps, because our most frequent experience of movement nowadays is as a passenger in a car, train or plane, observing the landscape speeding by while we ourselves remain still, most fast movement in contemporary music, whether tonal or atonal, is merely rapid motion without any involvement of physical energy. Fast music in the past was related to the movement of the body, walking, running or dancing. The fundamental importance to music of dance is something I shall return to later.

Schoenberg also brought about the other revolutionary change in twentieth-century Western music, when he renounced the use of the musical vernacular. Throughout its history, European art music maintained a close contact with folk music, on which its modal and diatonic melodies were based, and there was no unbridgeable gap between serious and popular music, right up to the beginning of the twentieth century. Schoenberg himself had used diatonic melody naturally and skillfully in his early works, notably in *Gurrelieder.* In the scherzo of his Second String Quartet, the work in which he brought tonality to its breaking point, Schoenberg quotes the well-known Viennese popular song, 'O, du lieber Augustin', and makes a point of repeating its refrain, 'Alles ist hin' — 'it's all over'. For Schoenberg now, the use of the diatonic vernacular was indeed over. He banished it from his subsequent, non-tonal music, except once or twice as a ghostly, poignant memory (as in *Pierrot Lunaire*). Schoenberg still based his music on melody, but on the chromatic, synthetic melodies he derived from his note rows (it is impossible to believe they are not in some way synthetic). Webern, once again, went further than Schoenberg in virtually excluding recognizable melody from his serial music, and the postwar Darmstadt composers, under the influence of Adorno, turned Webern's composing principles into a creed. Adorno's neo-Marxist argument was that 'mass culture', which includes popular culture, based on tonal clichés, is another bourgeois-imposed opiate; a device for keeping the masses in subjection. Serious composers, therefore, should have nothing to do with this corrupt musical language and so must embrace its opposite; serialism, an esoteric high art music for the elite.[5]

This was a drastic oversimplification: tonal clichés and bad popular music are one thing; to reject all post-Mahlerian tonal music, including Sibelius and the neoclassical Stravinsky, as Adorno did, is quite another. Just as with the arguments against tonality, we can now see that these ideas, which for a time sustained modernism at least as a valid musical style, are, as general principles, simply erroneous. Jazz and popular music are an integral part of twentieth-century art and Gershwin and Ellington, for instance, are two of the century's most significant composers. Tippett, who was the last major British composer to use folksong as a foundation for his music, was also one of the first in this country to realise that blues and jazz — and later, rock — could be a viable alternative vernacular to folksong. This idea had already been adopted by the *Neue Sachlichkeit* composers of Weimar in

Germany. By the time Tippett began to compose, folksong had died out as a living force, except in the remotest parts of Britain, but it did not simply disappear into the museum culture of the Cecil Sharp Society and morris dancing. In the 1950s and 1960s young, mostly urban people began to revive folk music at the same time as they began to listen to and to play rock, the new popular music derived from black American blues and white Country and Western music. Blues, rock and folksong from Britain and North America united into a common new vernacular language. It is a true vernacular, for its new music has largely been written by the musicians who sing and play it, unlike the popular music of the first half of the century, which was for the most part the product of non-executant composers.

Tippett's use of the blues as a vernacular, for instance in *A Child of Our Time* and the Third Symphony, is successful because he grew up with the blues as a natural language. He was less happy with rock, because he did not grow up with it, and I find his introduction of the electric guitar into his opera *The Knot Garden* faintly embarrassing, even if I warm to his intentions. My own generation, those born during and immediately after the Second World War, encountered the beginnings of rock as we were emerging from childhood into adolescence, and for many of us it was a crucial event. Some of my earliest genuine musical experiences were of hearing mid-1950s rock — Elvis Presley and Little Richard. The effect on me of this wildly orgiastic music, so different from anything I had encountered in my cosy suburban childhood, was overwhelming. The Beatles were hearing and absorbing this music at the same time, as well as older types of popular music, and they seem to have inherited the folksong tradition instinctively (although Paul McCartney has told me that he did not remember hearing any folksongs while he was growing up). One of the earliest recorded Beatles' songs, 'I saw her standing there' is, as Wilfrid Mellers has remarked, pure folk monody: an utterly simple four-note melody with prominent flattened sevenths.[6] It was through hearing songs like this that my generation were reintroduced to the folk tradition.

By listening to rock music, I rediscovered the elemental power of tonality. Rock musicians, ignorant of musical history, used the triad as Monteverdi had used it at the start of *Orfeo*, as if it were a freshly-minted sound. Taking their cue from rock music, the minimalists too used the triad in this way. Both showed that even the most over-exploited musical cliché can be renewed from a state of innocence. The majority of composers, myself included, are not innocent in this way, yet any language handled with real confidence can have validity: conviction can overcome self-consciousness. I agree with Alfred Schnittke when he wrote: 'Contemporary reality will make it necessary to experience all the musics one has heard since childhood, including rock and jazz and classical and all other forms, combining them into a synthesis ... The synthesis must arise as a natural longing, or through necessity.'[7] Schnittke's own work went a long way in putting these ideas into practice. Many others are thinking along similar lines. The vernacular has indeed been rehabilitated, and if all is again open to us, then the renewal of melody, which is contemporary music's most serious need, may be possible. The loss of accessible, singable melody in the music of Schoenberg and his successors was a devastating blow to music's comprehensibility. The masterpieces of European music in the past all had an immediately accessible surface layer, which was primarily the melodic line. The fact that the majority of the musical public are as likely to miss the deeper, structural level in Beethoven as they are in Boulez is not an argument against the desirability of an accessible surface, for Beethoven's melodies give access to the deeper levels of his music.

The contemporary Western vernacular may not be much help here, for contemporary rock music demonstrates an increasing impoverishment of melody (as Roger Scruton has convincingly argued in *The Aesthetics of Music*[8]) and indeed of rhythm and harmony, so that it now offers meagre rewards to anyone who wants to make use of it. My own generation was more fortunate. It may be that the necessary renewal of melody will come from outside Western culture, from parts of the world where a living folk tradition still flourishes, one that has not yet been exploited and corrupted by commercialism. Whatever way, it must happen, for unless our musical culture is once again founded on melody, it is moribund.

Postmodernism, then, permits a return to music of all the elements that modernism proclaimed were done with for ever. But if we are all post-modernists now, we should not be superficial in our attitude to the past, parading styles like dressing up in old clothes. Much post-modernist art ransacks the past indiscriminately with little sense of history. A more responsible attitude is to attempt to integrate the present with the past by reestablishing a continuity with those forms from the past which contain the greatest accumulation of historical meaning. I have been much concerned throughout my composing life with two of these forms, the symphony and the string quartet. The first is a public form, the second private, but they share the same Classical archetype, which is so well-known that almost everyone who listens to music will have some notion of what a symphony or string quartet should be. According to Hans Keller's useful theory, the richest kind of musical experience is provided by 'the meaningful contradiction of expectation'[9].This assumes that the listener will have some idea of what to expect, so that he will be pleasurably surprised by the contradictions that an inventive composer will provide. If on the other hand you attempt to be wholly new, then no real surprises are possible. To write a movement in sonata form is somewhat daunting, as you are competing with, and almost inevitably failing to equal, the many supreme examples of such movements from the past. But it gives you access to a world where meaningful contradiction has been practised for two-and-a-half centuries, and although many of the devices of confounding expectation have been overexploited and have themselves become clichés, it is possible to renew them by inner conviction, and there are still new games to play!

One game nineteenth-century composers played was with the repeat of the exposition. Up to Beethoven's time, this was a formality. Beethoven was the first to dispense with it, for instance in the first '*Rasoumovsky*' Quartet, op.59 no.1, where he pretends to repeat the opening of the exposition, then, just when we have accepted this, the music sheers off into the development. Throughout the nineteenth century composers either continued to use the repeat convention, which, because it was no longer taken for granted, could itself become a surprise, as in Mahler's First Symphony; or else they devised cunning ways of disguising their intention not to repeat — an outstanding example is in the first movement of Dvořák's Eighth Symphony. In the finale of my own Fourth Symphony, a modified sonata movement, I have taken the game a stage further. The exposition begins to repeat, but after three bars it goes off into what sounds like the development. After less than three bars of this, however, there is a pause, and the exposition material begins again, though not quite exactly as before, so there is still a little confusion ... but after six bars of this we are finally launched into a proper repeat, after this triple bluff. Except that it is a quadruple bluff, for this repeat is not quite an exact one, though the changes are so subtle I should not be surprised if they are not noticed.

My Fourth Symphony contains two scherzos in its five-movement scheme, both of which have connections with the contemporary vernacular. The first, in a hard-driving tempo, is based on fragments of melody which could be from rock music, while the second is a tango, which I thought of as a contemporary substitute for the Classical minuet. The tango form has been used by composers (including Stravinsky and Martinů) since the 1920s, and it seems to me to be an ideal archetype, with its infectious rhythms and erotic overtones, once possessed by the waltz and the minuet, but which have been dulled by time. What is crucial is that dance rhythms must find their way back into contemporary music. Dance was another of postwar modernism's puritanical exclusions, because of its supposed tainted association with populism. I am tempted to abandon rational argument here, throw up my hands and cry, 'what nonsense!'. Music began with song and dance, and however sophisticated it becomes, it must never lose touch with these essential human activities. The Classical symphony achieved an equilibrium between mind and body by following an initial sonata allegro, where the intellect was dominant, with a song and a dance movement. The finale was then often a movement of play: the body's energy enhanced by intellectual games.

Because the Classical style produced nothing of great value in this country and our own symphonic tradition only truly began with Elgar, it may be easier to write symphonies and string quartets today in Britain than in Germany or Austria. The symphonies of Vaughan Williams and Tippett, and the string quartets of Tippett and Britten, represent outstanding innovative attitudes towards these forms. It is not fully appreciated just how rich a quartet culture there is currently in Britain, with many young ensembles of the highest quality keen to include new works within their repertoire. The typical concert in which a contemporary string quartet is played alongside works by Haydn, Mozart, Beethoven or Schubert is, to my mind, a most rewarding experience. The new work often gains in juxtaposition with the old, through the stimulating contrasts in style and technique within an identical medium. The string quartet, perhaps even more than the symphony, seems infinitely capable of renewal, and I should be content to write nothing but string quartets for the rest of my life, since the possibilities for variation within this most satisfyingly balanced of ensembles are so rich. In my recent Eighth Quartet, I cast off long-held inhibitions and introduced not only a folksong, as part of a modern Pastoral — alive to the precariousness of modern landscape as well as to its beauty — but also a fugue, as the middle section of a slow finale. The fugue is the most apparently exhausted of all forms, as many perfunctory fugues in twentieth-century music appear to prove. Yet Tippett was able to renovate the form in his Third Quartet, which contains three fugal movements, as was, more recently, Robert Simpson in his magnificent Ninth Quartet. It depends, once again on conviction and, of course, on technique. In my Ninth and latest Quartet, a tango is succeeded by a *moto perpetuo* which ends with a reference to the style of the Irish Reel: a folk form that is still exuberantly alive.

Composers can never know how their audiences will hear their music; they can be certain that it will not be as they hear it. Although I do not think of the audience when I am composing, but only of the notes I am writing, and sometimes of the players I am writing them for, I do seek a creative dialogue with my audience, and hope for some kind of appreciative understanding of what I am trying to do. The deliberate refusal of some composers to engage with an audience, and the consequent unintelligibility of their music is a sad feature of contemporary musical life. It has never been the attitude of more than a small minority, but it has done great damage in making the very notion of 'contemporary music' a frightening prospect for many listeners. Repairing the damage has always been one of my chief concerns, and I dream of a time, when, as in the past, contemporary music will once again be the focus of interest for the majority of concert audiences. It is probably a fanciful dream, but its only chance of fulfillment is in the hands of composers.

NOTES

[1] Cooke, Deryck *Vindications,* Faber, 1986, p.195

[2] Schoenberg, Arnold *Style and Idea*, Faber, 1975, p.245

[3] Tippett, Michael 'Music and Life'from *Music of the Angels,* Eulenburg Books, 1980 p.33

[4] Lawrence, D. H. 'letter to Else Jaffe, 13 June 1922'from *The Collected Letters of D.H. Lawrence*, ed. Harry T. Moore, Heinemann, 1962, vol.2 p.707

[5] see Scruton, Roger *The Aesthetics of Music*, Oxford, 1997, pp. 469-472

[6] Mellers, Wilfrid *Twilight of the Gods*, Faber, 1973, pp.34-5

[7] Schnittke, Alfred 'Tempo 151', December 1984, p. 11

[8] Scruton, Roger *op.cit.*, pp. 500-506

[9] a full explaination of the theory can be found in Keller, Hans *1975 (1984 minus 9)*, Denis Dobson, 1977, pp.136-9

10

Old Practices, New Ideals: the symphony orchestra in the modern world

John Boyden

After many years, working in the classical music business, I found myself increasingly frustrated. Something fundamental was being forgotten in orchestral life, so I decided to take steps to recover it, by founding my own orchestra; one that could preserve and draw attention to many rapidly disappearing performance practices. The idea behind the New Queen's Hall Orchestra, radically different from the standard symphony orchestras of the late twentieth century, did not appear in a flash, but emerged after a number of years of recording classical music. Indeed, the seeds for its appearance were sown as long as fifty years ago, during my early teens. The Long Playing record made its cautious appearance in 1950 and remained a rarity for several years. There was no stereo, no FM, no cassettes and virtually no tape. Anyone wanting to hear great music at the highest level had no choice but to buy a ticket for a concert, which I did by making my way down London's Victoria Street, in those days still a Victorian street, to the Ernest Read Concerts in the Central Hall of a Saturday morning.

When it came to owning records, life was not so simple. In common with most Londoners I was genuinely poor, which meant that I could not afford many new 78s at 7/6d each, some £3.50 in modern money and quite a price for eight or nine minutes of music. So I usually ended up searching for bargains among the second hand records displayed in the street outside Foyle's bookshop in the Charing Cross Road, which came mostly from the pre-electric period of the 1920s. I recall my joy at assembling most of Beethoven's Fifth from a mixture of discs by the Royal Albert Hall Orchestra under Sir Landon Ronald and an outfit claiming to be the Royal Philharmonic. My doubts about this band's legitimacy stemmed from the fact that my father had been a member of Beecham's RPO since its formation in 1946, and I fancied I knew enough of the origins of London's premier orchestras to question the authenticity of this apparent usurper.

The performances on those old records were quite unlike those being broadcast by the BBC. Indeed, they were even different from the ones I had at home by Beecham and the immediately pre-war LPO, only a dozen years or so earlier. Yet, despite their heavy string portamenti and the apparent lack of energy of their wind and brass, these old discs managed to convey the spirit of the music to ears more than willing to be delighted.

The London orchestras of the 1950s seemed better than the old ones, only in the sense that they were more positive in their professionalism and in the way they aped Hollywood soundtracks. In common with so many commercial 'products', orchestras were moving closer to the anonymity which follows internationalism. Performers had always learned from one another, but now, instead of comparing notes, face-to-face, they were being steered down a path to conformity by radio and records. Contact was no longer to be personal and local, but detached and multinational. As a result, some players were already suffering from the uncertainty of wondering whether their own contribution to a performance would any longer fit the greater whole, either because they did not have the latest and most fashionable instrument, or because their style of playing failed to match their colleagues' changing approach to performance.

Thirty years earlier, when, for instance, Sir Landon Ronald had made a recording in London, his players would have played like Londoners, with all the certainty, which stems from a unity of approach based on shared experience. I very much doubt if any of them would have given a hoot for the stylistic fashions to be heard in Vienna or New York. No one would expect a modern London orchestra to sound any different from those in Manchester. Yet, in the 1920s, the LSO sounded quite unlike the Hallé, not least because the LSO had French bassoons and the Hallé had favoured German instruments, ever since Richter's time as their chief conductor. Until 1930, when the newly formed BBC Symphony Orchestra hoovered-up many of the best players from the provinces, Manchester's orchestra outshone London's, and the citizens of England's second city took as fierce a pride in the reflections of its glory as they now do in those of its football teams. The Hallé's individuality rested as much on its choice of instruments as it did on its approach to string playing. Orchestras were different from one another, and expected to be so. On the other hand, in the autumn of 1930, when half the LSO moved to the BBC, the band being advertised as the London Symphony Orchestra was made up of half the Hallé Orchestra!

Neither, when Sir Landon directed a recording, did he have a record producer to prod him towards the consensus, which record companies would later believe produced a more saleable product and which consumers would accept as an ideal. Had such a creature been around, his advice would almost certainly have been rejected for being nothing but an interference with the conductor's choices and with the personality of his performance. I rather doubt that he would have asked, as a conductor once asked me, 'How would you like me to do the ending? Like Toscanini, Walter or Klemperer?'

Until recording came along, there was little chance of anyone asking such a question, if only because interpretation, as it is now understood, could not have existed without everyone being equipped with total recall. Stripped of such a blessing, audiences were more likely to be swept along by a more generalised set of sensations than modern concertgoers can be expected to allow themselves. Any suggestion that they might sit in a concert hall and make detailed comparisons was inconceivable.

These days, committed enthusiasts often do not bother to go to concerts for fear of the disappointment, which they believe must follow a performance, and which challenges the ingrained expectations of their favourite CD. Recording has endowed the average enthusiast with the power of a god and given him the means to join the pundits on Radio 3 on Saturday morning in the ritual dismemberment of recorded performances. Without irony, experts with the instincts of quality control managers, analyse every beat of a record in pursuit of deviations from the set of conventions holding good at the time. Devoid of humility, they parade the superiority of their grasp of the composer's intentions over that of countless performing artists.

But, while the ability to replay half a bar of a CD in pursuit of an 'error' may be very recent, the insight into recording's potential for standardisation was grasped soon after serious music was first recorded. By the 1920s magazines, such as *Gramophone*, had established record reviewing as a quasi-science; one in which comparison assumed a greater significance than merely reacting to the music's emotional message. From now on, recorded performances were to be weighed and measured, as though they were industrial products, with individual qualities being held against a definitive model, so that x's disc might be rated against y's. Under such pressure the enthusiast's taste soon became conditioned by a handful of opinion-formers, which led to recordings being bought under instruction. Such a switch in the evaluation of musical performance was so profound that the long-term effects of the recorded music industry, once known as the 'industry of human happiness', needs to be questioned.

Records and broadcasting were not the only novelties to threaten the sound and concept of musical performance. Standing on the runway was the modern airliner. First, conductors and soloists, and then great orchestras began to travel the globe, taking their sounds and prejudices with them, offering the players and audiences of less important towns a pattern against which to draw comparisons. The trouble was that fast travel and rapid communications may have brought exotic orchestras to otherwise parochial concert halls, but such contacts also helped to thin out the regional styles of playing which had been one of music's subtlest glories. A glance at Charles Burney's writings shows how eighteenth-century Europe had flaunted as many styles of musical performance as it did languages and dialects. Cross a river and the language or dialect changed; cross another and the flute or oboe, or the way in which they were played, also changed.

Since the 1950s matters have degenerated in a typically twentieth-century way. For example, pan-European orchestras are a reality. Forty or fifty years ago, when the Viennese gloried in their quirky oboes and horns, and Parisian woodwind still produced the most individual of colours, the possibility of combining players from such different traditions would have been dismissed as an impractical joke. Today, the Vienna Philharmonic may stay loyal to its oboe, but the young Viennese oboist knows that, if he wants to travel the globe, he must also master the Conservatoire system. In France, the position of the old-fashioned bassoon, with its great character, has been usurped by the bland German bassoon, while the narrow bore French Horn with pistons has been eclipsed by the wide bore German horn with rotary valves. Such changes followed the introduction of records, radio and the jet-setting conductor, who, together with the record company executive, hankered after the standardisation which had been theirs, since being exposed to a handful of landmark recordings in childhood.

I remember an American conductor who inserted a cymbal crash in the first movement of Rimsky-Korsakov's *Scheherazade*.

'It's my tribute to Stokey,' he explained. I was beginning to suggest that the piece was fine without it, when a percussionist entered the playback room.

'The last time I played that were for Stokey in 1963,' he said. The conductor's face lit up.

'You played cymbals on the 1963 record?' he asked.

'I did,' he said, 'I thought it were daft then, and I think it's daft now.'

The conductor looked crushed, and it was with obvious regret that he agreed to leave the cymbals out. This little story shows how this conductor had grown up with Stokowski's famous recording and identified with it so much that it carried more significance for him than the composer's score or with anything he might have brought to it.

To return to my own story: by the late 1960s, I was making a living from recording. Because I had only two microphones, my efforts were of a purist nature, which was no handicap because I wanted my recordings to have a point of view, with the performance being heard, as it were, through an open window. Such an approach led me to spurn the convenient artificiality, which comes from using lots of microphones; a technique which often leads to an orchestra sounding as though its instruments have been spread in a straight line between the speakers, deprived of any sense of depth.

I even managed to convince myself that consumers would share my approach. Unfortunately, the bulk of LP buyers were as unfamiliar with live music as CD buyers are today, showing that classical music has developed two distinct audiences: one, which enjoys the communal realities of the concert hall, and another which prefers the isolation of electronically recalled performances, with an occasional trip to a concert.

In 1970, I managed to create the chance to record professional orchestras, which was when I discovered the limitations of a purist recording technique. It is one thing to sling a pair of microphones in front of a choir, or a string quartet, but quite another to get really fine results from a modern orchestra. To begin with, a first class acoustic is necessary, which was in short supply in London (and still is). Secondly the orchestra must have an ideal internal balance. That is to say, one whose instruments relate so well to each other, that their volumes and tonal qualities allow each to be heard according to the composer's indications. No such orchestra existing, I bought a mixing desk and a few extra microphones instead, and learned to distort what was happening in the studio into a convincing whole for the finished disc.

I had discovered that the imbalance of modern orchestras worked against the record producer, but also, which was far worse, it also worked against the composer. The relative loudness of musical instruments had changed so much over the forty years since their composers' deaths, that making a recording of the orchestral works of Holst and Ravel, so that the brass and percussion did not obliterate the woodwind and strings, called for the active intervention of a balance engineer.

One of the most likely reasons for these detrimental changes was the acceptance of fashion, which musicians are as willing to follow as anyone else. Even though Wagner and Bruckner had probably never heard such things, metal flutes had now replaced wooden ones. Indeed, Wagner's attitude to the changing nature of flute playing was made clear in 1869, when he wrote that flautists 'had turned their once so gentle instruments into veritable tubes of violence – a delicate sustained piano is hardly to be attained any more'. Which does make one wonder what Wagner would have made of the industrialised machines which slam out his music today.

In a similar pursuit of fashion the German bassoon had chased the French from the stage even though it was the latter's character which had inspired Stravinsky and Ravel. Metal strings had replaced gut, and all the brass had developed an obesity which brought bigger, but ever less focused sounds to the platform. All these changes had arrived with such stealth, that they had gone largely unnoticed. Players no longer seemed to remember a time when violas and second bassoon parts were heard as a matter of course, even when threatened by a squad of brass. Nor could anyone, apparently, understand why Elgar had marked the dynamics of his trombones so heavily that counter-melodies, which he must have been convinced would match the rest of the orchestra, now swamped it. Indeed, in continuing to develop the power of brass instruments long beyond the point of common-sense, science has not known when to stop, forcing many orchestral players to save their hearing by wearing earplugs or sheltering behind plastic screens. Even Swift would have been hard pressed to satirise the self-deafening orchestra.

The trombones, whose massive bells now lord it over their colleagues, were not intended for symphony orchestras, but had been designed to add even more firepower to the rip-roaring dance bands of post war America. If it were not for their shape and design, these fat instruments would bear little resemblance to their skinny predecessors. The bore has widened so much that, apart from being far too loud in *fortissimo*, the new trombones produce a sound in *piano* which is usually inappropriate to the context. The same situation applies to trumpets and horns, whose loudness can be increased by widening the bore without affecting their pitch.

Faced with such evidence, my mind went back to the heavy, shellac 78s of my childhood, and to the gentle, expressive performances which Wagner would have recognised. Before long, I became preoccupied with the idea of forming an orchestra to bypass the problems of modern instruments and which would restore the balance and colour anticipated by Romantic composers. On its own, such an idea would produce immediate benefits, but it would not be enough.

The actual instruments of the early 1900s would solve problems of balance, but, for complete success, the players would have to undergo a sea change in their mental approach to playing. I think it was Oscar Wilde who said something about a man revealing his true nature only when wearing a mask, which was the effect I hoped these unusual instruments would have on musicians suddenly freed from the need to conform. For example, modern instruments deliver an aggressive power which many listeners find stimulating, and even orchestral musicians fail to question a situation in which half of them might as well be playing behind a plate-glass window, for all the chance they have of being heard. None of this is to be heard in early recordings.

Another reason for the high tension of modern playing is the widespread use of vibrato. By removing vibrato completely from the woodwind, and by rationing it among the strings, a significant step would be taken towards restoring the sense of peace and tranquillity which lies at the heart of much great music. Little joy is to be found in a cello section, whose members strain after little but intensity, their left hands thrashing in a frenzy of promised commitment, as though striving to rid their fingers of sticky paper. Jelly d'Arányi remarked: 'Variety of tone....was what Joachim and all of us stood for, and which is ignored by many prominent violinists, who just establish a vibrato and stick to it'.

Players in the new orchestra would also need to come to terms with the radical proposition that discipline is not, of itself, an artistic concept; an especially hard proposition to accept, when the paramount goal of training for the modern orchestra is excellence of ensemble. For fourteen people to play the violin as one, tells the listener nothing about the music. For the members of an orchestra to be drilled into holding a single and highly rehearsed view of a work, under a dictatorial figure verges on fascism. Yet I would suggest that all orchestras, whether large and traditional, or small and 'period', embrace such a spontaneous approach. The adoration of discipline and precision for their own sakes seem to me to be the antithesis of artistic expression and to lead to the unpleasant subjugation of the individual.

This is why I believe the market should be able to sustain at least one orchestra of people, encouraged to bring their individualities to bear on the music at hand. To witness eighty or ninety players delighting in expressing their personalities, within the framework of a common cause, is life-enhancing. As the *Birmingham Post* wrote of the New Queen's Hall Orchestra: 'the general sense of freedom which comes out of these performances is as joyous as that of pit-ponies liberated out into the sunlight'.

Finally, I had to confront the question of the modern conductor, who has suffered just as much under the 'system'as his orchestras. In the days before air travel and electronics, many conductors worked with the same players day in and day out, and developed their particular style, so that the Concertgebouw was seen to be Mengelberg's and the Berlin Philharmonic was synonymous with Furtwängler. It would be hard to think of a present day orchestra whose sound and personality were so individual that it could be identified within seconds as the product of one man's genius.

Conductors spend too much time travelling the world for them to
have a lasting impact in any one place. Equally, orchestras have
developed lives of their own as units of employment, and are less
and less willing to risk dependence on a single figure.

Indeed, many bands have developed such a powerful idea of the
way a particular work should go, that no conductor can shift them
from it. A few years back, one well-known (and maverick) maestro
walked out of a rehearsal of an equally well-known (but less
maverick) German orchestra, because the players refused to accept
the possibility of an alternative view to the one they had grown into
during fifty years of repetition. One of our more eminent musical
knights once told me that he had recently recorded a standard
symphony with one of the London orchestras. 'They all knew it
perfectly well and, as there wasn't much I could say, I let them get
on with it, and we all went home.' Courtesy prevented my asking
whether he pocketed the fee.

Because we are now taught from an early age that when something cannot be measured it cannot exist, the very existence of
something as personal and as transitory as musical performance, is
bound to be called into question. Which is why so few modern
performers see the composer's manuscript as a staging post on the
journey between the composer's imagination and the audience's
ears. They seem happier with the notion that it is an end in itself;
as something akin to an engineering blueprint, with quavers standing in for rivets and the metronome replacing the tape measure.
Such an approach is embraced by many conductors; especially
those unwilling to risk exposing their lack of a personal viewpoint.
They would rather put their faith in such earthbound goals as
precise ensemble, mechanical dynamics, 'tick-tock' tempi and the
comfort of repeating precedent.

How has such a condition been reached? How is that, within a
span of not much over fifty years, the once vaunted idiosyncrasies
of Leo Blech have become anathema and been replaced with the
inevitabilities of the bog-standard, international hamburger performance? Why do the world's flautists, almost to a man or
woman, mimic the vibrato of Marcel Moyse? Why do so many

violinists imitate, as nearly as their talents will allow, the mannerisms of Heifetz?

To begin to understand the reasons for this predicament we need to go back to the twenties and thirties; to a time of widespread competition; to a time when someone was always breaking a world record, so that even musical performance might be turned into a branch of sport. Why not set one orchestra against another, as though they were machines with measurable performances? Suddenly, with improved travel and the availability of recording, the LPO was being compared with the Berlin Philharmonic and the Philadelphia with the Boston Symphony Orchestra, and so on, until orchestras invoked any number of inappropriate comparisons. Such habits die hard. In the 1970s I remember one well-known London journalist telling me rather proudly, that he thought the LPO was a Rover and the LSO was a Ferrari!

It is true that such changes appeared at different times in different places. For example British and German orchestras of the late 1920s sound sloppy and uncompetitive to our ears, even under such big names as Elgar, Strauss and Pfitzner. But I doubt that anyone will suggest that such geniuses had lower standards than the present readership of CD magazines. Perhaps the truth is that these great men were not interested in technical matters as ends in themselves? Perhaps they were more excited by the idea of performance as a human canvas of spontaneity; one upon which the precise colour and shape of the images was only determined at the point of delivery?

Yet, when one listens to American orchestras of the 1920s something utterly different is to be heard. In their attention to detail, and in their efficiency, they sound almost modern. Precision of ensemble and brilliance of execution are things with which we immediately feel at ease. In an age which adores precision, the American approach was sure to triumph. The sheer professionalism of a string section, trained to play as one man, was a sight even unmusical people appreciated. But virtuosity alone seldom satisfies the deeper elements of a music-lover's life. Where can one go, once a finale has been played so fast that it can never be played faster? Or when an orchestra makes more noise than Concorde?

The noisy brilliance of a modern symphony orchestra does not necessarily tell us anything profound about the music. Yet, by accepting the quality of its sound and the nature of its dynamics as being inevitable, we agree to be blinded to the potential of the score's message. Ten cellists, moving with the precision of a machine tool, come no closer to conveying the composer's message to us than a single player with nine mirrors. But, once we realise how persuasive the sloppy, free-bowing orchestras of the early years of the twentieth century were, both in the possibility of spontaneity and in the risk of danger, we may begin to identify the stultifying consequences of discipline on the modern orchestra.

'It's not together!' players will exclaim, on listening to a play-back at a recording session, 'we can get it better than that. Let's have another go.' Off they troop to ensure that a particular beat is 'together' and, in doing so, ensure its growing similarity to all the other recordings of the same piece. What worse crime can there be than for a performance to suffer a looser ensemble than that indicated by the stiffness of printed notation?

'It's not in tune!' players will murmur under their breath. Could there be anything worse than an out of tune chord? Of such basics is the virtuoso orchestra constructed: a mixture of whiplash ensemble and superhuman tuning. Because of the need to patch a recording with inserts of identical weight, colour and tempo, the modern orchestra is an impersonator and not the original. Playing has become so technical, and so taken up with detail that no one should be surprised when orchestra members resort to drugs in an attempt to cope with the pressure of a life spent in 'getting it right'. When such hard-won virtuosity is used to display music which we instinctively feel to be too deep to be treated as a vehicle for showing-off, or too vulnerable to be exploited by a stone-faced professionalism, it tends to deter where it sought to attract.

Such a situation is not helped by the demands made by so much modern music on the virtuosity of orchestral players. Instead of offering them extensions to the repertoire which they studied at college, and which prompted their original passion for music, so much of the avant-garde has accelerated their descent into being cogs in a machine, and stripping them of the chance for self-expression. Such a position would be easier to tolerate, if the demand for perpetual dissonance had been sustained by public demand. It has not! The truth is that very few people have any enthusiasm for challenging new music or for the judgement of the handful of overseers who stand with a whip in one hand and the state's purse in the other, while they second-guess which composer will be seen as Beethoven's heir fifty years after their deaths. Buying forward in the market is often risky. In the middle 1970s I had a meeting with the BBC's head of music, who claimed that 90% of the BBC Symphony Orchestra loved playing the avant-garde music for which it had recently become so famous throughout the European Broadcast Union. When I passed this information on to my old friend, Jack Gorowski, a violinist in the BBCSO, he laughed and began counting the number of his colleagues who enjoyed it. He stopped counting before reaching the thumb of one hand.

One of the ideas behind the New Queen's Hall Orchestra is to guarantee the expressive content of its concerts and the individuality of its performances, so that a new deal may be entered into with its audiences. Such a deal is meant to restore trust in the Orchestra's taste and judgement, so that new composers and new works may be introduced in the atmosphere which once existed between orchestras and their audiences, and which has been so damaged by decades of subsidy. The fact that no piece of the avant-garde appears in Classic FM's top hundred favourite works may please those of us who despise popularity, but it also delights those of us who believe that the arts should occasionally be concerned with communication.

Which brings us to spontaneity. Most musicians will agree that musical performance should be spontaneous, but only once every step has been taken to see to it that ensemble and tuning are as precise as an edited recording, and that everything has been locked into a metronomic tempo, with each bar given its full weight of beats. As Wilhelm Furtwängler, wrote, in 1924: 'Nothing can be said against precision, except that it practically eliminates the most important thing about playing, the intuition of the moment'.

In any case, why be so literal to the score? Few composers believed their notation to be so perfect that they were in a position to hand over complete instructions to the performer. Any text remains open to variation, even when the variables are no more exciting than the temperature and humidity of the hall, the time of day, tiredness, one's heart beat and the feelings of the audience. What seems to be a good *allegro* in the morning may be out of sorts by the evening. Yet I have known famous conductors note down the 'perfect' tempo, so that, thirty years on, they reproduce the 'perfect'performance at will, as though there were a mould into which the composer's ideas might be poured and remove responsibility from the shoulders of the so-called maestro. I have seen many a score, in which a conductor has written in a large hand the number 12, 20 or whatever, to show that he must beat twelve bars of four beats or twenty bars of something else, before needing to adjust his gesticulating to a new pattern. A cheap black box with a flashing light would do just as well.

Such approaches are misguided. More than that, they represent the betrayal of the individualism of performance. One of the chief attractions of great music lies in the impossibility of achieving a definitive performance. Yet radio stations and record companies continue to make unrealistic claims for their pasteurised products, and many music critics (as well as record critics) turn in reviews which do little more than list lapses from the 'perfection' of the printed score; hence the perceived need for a CD to be 'perfect'. Indeed, the chief function of digital editing techniques lies in its ability to sustain the image of the artist as infallible genius, sometimes to the point of blasphemy, even though most consumers must have some idea of the crafty trickery of the post-production technician and his boxes of flashing lights. No wonder there is a widespread conviction that filtering out 'mistakes'(often only tiny deviations from the printed text), automatically leaves behind perfection. All of which is profoundly unnatural. Furtwängler again, wrote: 'The thing that has outstripped the "natural" for us, is the "new". But one can't dismiss the fact that the new quickly becomes old, while the natural always stays natural.'

Modern listeners have been trained to believe that errors mean loss of perfection; that a horn split can no longer be endured. Yet it is these so-called errors, which endow a performance with its humanity and which ensure that it has more in common with a craftsman's hand thrown pot than with a melamine tea-set. Where is the humanity in a recorded performance whose integrity has been undermined by having been glued together from several performances? Worse still, where is the artistry in one whose smooth continuity depends on the skill of the engineers and not on the genius of the player? Sometimes a CD is cobbled together from a thousand snippets according to the record producer's preordained plan, which leaves the performer where? The realisation that the finished CD contains a performance, which was never given, seldom clouds the judgement of the critics, who happily endorse the result for being nothing less than a triumph; a case of the end justifying the means.

How do musicians deliver the consistency of tempo necessary for a process, which blends so many different takes into a seamless, manufactured whole? To start with, the bloodless beat of the recording producer's metronome ensures that the mosaic of performance may be stuck together, as though by numbers. Such inevitability leaves almost everyone happy. The artist delivers all the notes (but not necessarily in the right order), the producer offers a string of 'suggestions'which, he hopes, will bring his tape into contention with all the other CDs of the same work, while the tape editor is thrilled at not having to spend too much of his time in sustaining the artist's reputation for never ever doing anything individual. On its own, such a situation would be bad enough, but it becomes far worse when the consequence of all these tricks appears on the concert platform and is paraded as an artistic experience. Stiffness of tempo, and the skill to reproduce a machine-like intensity of sound, time and time again, may be great assets in the studio, but they certainly add nothing to a live concert. The capacity to deliver such high professionalism suspends the performance as though in aspic, and works against the elasticity which would allow us to sense the moods of the performers on their journey through a work; qualities which we know from a combination of anecdotal evidence and early recordings were the norm before recording triumphed over the real thing. I remember a concert at which a conductor and orchestra played a piece, which we had recorded earlier, only to be amazed when they delivered a fine imitation of an edit, which I had been forced to insert into the master. I doubt if anyone else noticed the minute disturbance in the even flow of tempo which this join had introduced, but the conductor had obviously become convinced that it formed a part of his interpretation and ensured its survival in the concert hall.

The New Queen's Hall Orchestra has been re-formed to correct such commonplaces. If the NQHO sounds like an ordinary orchestra, and repeats a performance because its players have decided, that 'this is the way it goes', then it has failed. Elgar, for example, was concerned that his music should not be imprisoned in little boxes. He wanted something fluid and rhythmically expressive: music with its own organic life. In common with other composers of the romantic era, he coated his scores with instructions, yet still complained that conductors missed the point. The briefest comparison of his recordings with those of his present interpreters will show how right he was.

So, what finally prompted me into re-forming the New Queen's Hall Orchestra? In 1991 I had a meeting with Andrew Cornall of Decca, during which I described my vision of an orchestra of old instruments and old freedoms: an orchestra with musical, historic and geographic points of view; based on a London orchestra of the first twenty years of the twentieth century, playing at Philharmonic pitch. Not a general purpose, all things to all people, period orchestra, which claimed to be authentic to whoever wanted to book it on any Wednesday afternoon. Rather to my surprise, he said that Decca would use it for a recording of Vaughan Williams. So I left Andrew's office and formed the NQHO. Apart from issuing gut strings to the players, the first string rehearsals were straight forward enough, but those for the wind and brass skirted comedy. Into a freezing room above the old Sadlers Wells Theatre appeared a motley crew of players, clutching brass and woodwind instruments which may have escaped from the set of *Steptoe and Son*. No one really knew quite what to expect, and initial efforts were splendidly anarchic.

By the time the new orchestra gave its first performance, a few days later in February 1992, everything had settled and the players of the whole orchestra were enjoying an experience, unknown even to their own fathers. For the first time in seventy years each player could hear his own contribution and those of his colleagues, even at fortissimo. For the first time in thirty years, no one had to wear earplugs to protect his hearing from the onslaught of his colleagues. For the first time in fifty years, pure expression came top. The concept worked.

The strings of the New Queen's Hall Orchestra play with gut top strings, and covered gut elsewhere. The players are encouraged to reduce the amount of their customary vibrato, and to use more portamento. One or two hardy souls even go so far as to use their own bowing and fingering, as would have been the case in London in the 1920s. Indeed, uniform bowing was such a new idea in England in the 1920s that a Manchester audience 'was so startled with the stark discipline of the strings of the Berlin Philharmonic when they visited the City under Furtwängler that they could not hear the music for watching the up-and-down-altogether of the bows'. Again, in a 1944 history of the Queen's Hall, the author noted 'The New York Symphony Orchestra, under Walter Damrosch, appeared in the summer of 1920. The fine playing of the woodwind and brass and the almost excessive discipline of the strings were a notable feature'.

These two quotes suggest that English audiences were accustomed to string playing which harked back to the previous century. Indeed, shortly before the first concert of the re-formed NQHO I had a meeting with Margaret Harrison, whose more famous sister, Beatrice went into the Surrey countryside and recorded her cello there with the sound of nightingales. Without hesitation she declared that the essential difference between string playing in the early 1900s and that of ninety years later was the complete lack of fantasy in the modern style! She condemned the most famous players for being nothing more than heartless, unimaginative technicians.

Because the arts are concerned with human expression, assumptions of progress are questionable. The idea that musical instruments are endlessly improvable requires an exceptional leap of faith, especially when some instruments are more open to development than others, and when every so-called improvement takes an instrument further and further from the sound anticipated by the bulk of composers. This is why it is sometimes necessary to call a halt to 'progress' and to question the wonders being served up to an innocent public.

With appropriate instruments and players the NQHO simplifies the conductor's job at a stroke. Without needing to resort to any tricks, the orchestra delivers a balance between its instruments of such perfection that rehearsals are taken up with matters of expression, instead of being bogged down by the need to find answers to difficulties never imagined a few decades ago. After all, in the orchestra of one's dreams, every instrument would be concerned with phrasing, with all lines forever growing or dying, and never simply lying there, inert.

Such delights are enhanced when delivered inside a hall with a wonderful acoustic, which has not been available in London since the bombing of the Queen's Hall, in 1941. London may claim to be the world's capital of music, but it is a claim which is hard to justify when it lacks a single large building to do justice to its many orchestras and choirs. This is why plans for a New Queen's Hall are so exciting, and why the provision of a great and beautiful acoustic is every bit as significant to the spiritual impact of profound music as the choice of instruments and the emotional engagement of the individual. The dry, unsympathetic sound of the Royal Festival Hall, which Beecham so roundly condemned at the time of its opening, has delivered fifty years of aural starvation and stifled the development of a home-grown orchestral sound of the highest quality. For a performance to envelope audience and performer in the same swirl of sound brings an unimaginable uplift to the listener.

With the arrival of the New Queen's Hall, London's audiences will be able to hear orchestras and choirs creating spiritual experiences, unmatched by any broadcast or recording, no matter how faithful. Society, of course, may decide that it no longer cares about differences between reality and unreality. I don't accept such pessimism, preferring instead to be cheered by the signs of growing enthusiasm for musical performance now appearing in those regional centres of excellence, such as Birmingham and Manchester, which have invested in concert halls with fine acoustics and where their integrity grabs the heart and speaks to the soul.

11

Looking Sideways for New Music

Edward Pearce

A steady moan can be heard about the concert hall. Audiences are often thin, there is a sense of ennui. Classical concerts seem, as the great British boxer, Henry Cooper, used to say about himself on a bad night, 'to have lost their snap.' Such statements can be put alongside outbursts from people like Gavin Bryars, who hopes that one day Brahms will never be performed again. Bryars's own opera *Dr. Ochs*, when staged by English National Opera, induced quite a few members of the audience to stop listening halfway through; a case of the serious public, one willing to give new and supposedly weighty things a whirl, doing their own 'Never again'! Bryars hates what he thinks of as war horses, but if new music is not created which pleases as much as Brahms's Second Symphony, we will continue to play that work rather often. One way to diversify concert programming would be to promote neither modernism, that corpse exhorted by cheer leaders, nor minimalism — tired before it starts (witness the unenjoyed and thus uneconomic music of Gavin Bryars), but to play more frequently the two delectable, but rarely played Serenades of 'Ah', Brahms.

It is no good approaching music with flippant political slogans about things being 'new, exciting and vibrant,' and saying, 'this is a young country'. In fairness, what for the empty, wittering politician is an empty, wittering slogan, is for many commissioners of music, a fervent doctrine, sustained with dervish-like intensity: unless music develops, amends, changes all the time, it will be, can be of no intrinsic value — we say so — be quiet! There was Bach, who was one thing, Mannheim and the *galant*, followed by Haydn, which was another thing, followed by the classical-romantic shift, which was yet another, then Wagner from whom all blessings flowed until, in the early twentieth century, until the early twentieth century when this succession became both apostolic and compulsory for posterity.

This is the central doctrine of Schoenberg and those who still follow him. Its consequence has been that whatever is clearly new, in however unappetising a fashion, however uninteresting, however rebarbative, however stayed-away from, however hermetic, however alien to the sort of people who, in their doomed, stupid, rank-and-file way, actually hope to enjoy music, is to be saluted. The praise must come, even if the teeth are clenched over the salutation. Such an outlook misses the chief function of notes on a stave, the pleasing of fallen man. If the working programmer sticks to a lot of war horses, it is because people still say 'Aaah' — and want to stroke their noses.

The fallacy of music as progress sees the composer as *Flying Dutchman*, doomed eternally to seek new and generally Antarctic waters. We might instead distinguish between what changes in ways lastingly recognised as beautiful, as steps that can be stood on, and what changes under command from the critical requirement that there should be change. Schubert modulated in ways that would have startled the Mozart of 1790; and across the songs and the late piano sonatas, the effect is perfectly and entirely wonderful. Not being a professional critic, I don't have a better word for what happens, but a note is struck which wasn't expected and which is certainly startling, but also beautiful and true in ways to set you quoting Keats. Listen to the latest hyped and bullied-for piece by Benjamin or Adès and, sorry, whatever their inherent musical talent, it will be none of those things.

Now minimalism, which has enjoyed some success, works on a different principle. It is a direct rejection of the modernist approach, and those modernists who are not also *politiques* tend to loathe it. It is not new, nor does it change — not from bar to bar, frequently not from page to page. The acreage of dinning repetition represents one obvious, standing up and hollering thing — a homage to Pop. Repetition works at the gig in the marquee for the hairy boys with hand-held microphones. From *She loves you yeah, yeah, yeah* on, it has been clear to a brilliantly successful commercial market that a little will go an incredibly long way. I am not surprised that Adams's *The Chairman dances* is genuinely popular, though Adams, Glass, Reich and all are as far from the Schoenbergian injunction or the doctrines of William Glock as very well can be. It is comfortable to the point of numbing.

But the relative success of minimalism shows that the public has needs utterly different from those of critics, Radio Three apparatchiks and the assorted popes of music. Modernism is impossibilist, minimalism a withdrawal of demands. We are caught between the poles of the market and producer-led art or, if you like, between free trade and protection. And I doubt if polar life is much fun. Music surely belongs in a temperate zone.

But the market has done strange things in art, proper in this time of the unmade beds of un-maids, and of butcher's installations that turn art into a picked mutton futures market. The market has taken over modernism and made money out of it. Shrewd men with distinctly plastic aesthetic impulses like Charles Saatchi have discovered that a brick or a dead farm animal, bought at a modest point in the market, will appreciate very agreeably. A solution of formaldehyde does wonders for the P/E ratio. Great numbers will turn up to see glazed-over excrement offered as art (and comment on art) because publicity, promotion, sensation replace the usual occasions for attending an art gallery. All it lacks is a Max Clifford to sell the story to the tabloids.

Happily, I think, no such public taste for sensation has been found in the serious music field. We have no such five-star charlatanry, except for the candy-striped futilities of operatic production. In assembling a concert programme, we stick with works of obvious public rapport, including very great music, virtuosic stuff, plus the tried and trusted (often terribly tired) and a tiny sprinkle of the money-losing modern. If that means a lot of Haydn, Mozart, Beethoven, Schubert, Brahms, Dvořák, Sibelius, Strauss and Elgar, it is for good market reasons. But there have also been changes over thirty to forty years, changes now so well established that the join can scarcely be detected. Bruno Walter laboured hard in mid-century to gain attention and performances for a composer he had known and greatly admired, but who had never quite found his place on the roundabout, Gustav Mahler. If one thing is a certainty in the concert hall and record industry, it is that since the mid-fifties Mahler has been arterial blood. It was very recherché of R.A. Butler, the British Chancellor of the Exchequer introducing his budget for 1953, to describe its sweets and penalties in terms of the German directions to a Mahler symphony. But from about that time onwards, Mahler has grown exponentially. He has never been a personal enthusiasm — too much self-indulgent schmaltz, when not too grandiose, but purely personal is all that opinion is. Mahler, born in 1860, has functioned as a new composer in ways that Harrison Birtwistle, born in the thirties, never will. Mahler has been music lately added to the repertory and embraced by a large, enthusiastic public. The only thing worth saying is 'Hurray!'

The same process is almost as true of Anton Bruckner. Bruckner had some status and was played to a degree, before the late and heroic Robert Simpson disinterestedly used his position at the BBC straightforwardly to promote him; interestingly, a Socialist championing a Catholic. Simpson understood Bruckner's greatness, and Bruckner, since the early seventies, has been full-scale mainstream. To put it plainly, there has been enough public response, enough name-recognition for a concert hall programmer to feel commercially safe in undertaking to have those great galleons enter the water. The third name, and in Britain almost entirely Simpson's doing, is of course Carl Nielsen, surely a very great composer indeed and incidentally someone whose changes and progress actually matter, actually enhance. We barely noticed his existence until the late seventies. Today major standing is no longer contested.

Incidentally, we keep doing this to Scandinavians, as if admitting Grieg and Sibelius was very good of us, but really they mustn't think we can indefinitely let in bogus asylum seekers. For Nielsen this is still true in the opera house. A single, silly director-marred Opera North production of *Maskarade*, which Michael Oliver rightly described as 'the best comic opera after *Rosenkavalier* of the century' — as for *Saul and David*...? But most opera houses, with their 'watch me mum'exhibitionist directors and turnspit repertories, are less responsive than concert houses. Nielsen was born in 1865, Bruckner in 1818. What we have with these three, Mahler, Bruckner and Nielsen, thanks to sedulous playing in front of uncertain audiences, is the *Alt-Neu*, what I would like to call *lateralism*, an intelligent going sideways to find music of then, which falls on the ears of now, and is found good.

Imperceptibly, the scope of the repertory has been widened by going back to the half-known, and in Nielsen's case, the precious little known. The recovery, even the very career of Nielsen, defies Arnold Schoenberg's historicist dogmas, and the continued domination of Mahler and Bruckner over their successors certainly stretches them. These latter two owed heavy debts to Wagner. Bruckner in his own lifetime was looked upon, with the Seventh Symphony interestingly excepted, as a muddling derivative of Wagner; and his own sweetly naive devotion to that master did nothing to see off the canard. This is not the place to argue what their degrees of derivation were, only to say that nothing they acquired has diminished (may even have strengthened) their appeal to the large audiences, desperately needed audiences for music that is both new and enjoyable.

Lateralism worked here. It has worked on a larger scale in the cult of the Baroque. The fictional, cultivated detective, Inspector Morse, an avowed Mozart and Wagner man, was to be heard in one of the television dramatisations speaking scornfully of Vivaldi.

You could scrap the lot of it, as far as he was concerned, he said, sounding like Inspector Bryars dismissing Brahms. But Vivaldi is as new as Mahler, and Vivaldi was born even before Bach and Handel, in 1678, and people love him!

Don't lets get too prissy about popularity. I can defer to the many who love Mahler, not least because he will be a bridge for them to so much more music. The *adagietto* of the Fifth Symphony is classical music which reaches people who didn't think they liked classical music. They heard it in *Death in Venice*, Visconti's cult film based on a yet better, because more or less perfect novella. And, if it speaks its melancholy in a way too close to *kitsch* for many of us, what the hell! It speaks and is heard. A parallel is with the poetry of A.E.Housman, whom a whole generation of dismissive academic pronouncers tried to bury, but who has stayed continuously in print for a hundred years, conveying his own encapsulated, epigrammatic *tendresse;* the musical equivalent of the falling thirds and sevenths of Edward Elgar — and scorned by the same sort of people.

It is reasonable enough to grumble about the excessive popularity of Vivaldi's *The Four Seasons*, but not because there is anything wrong with it as music. It simply marks the extreme trepidation within the limits of wholly accessible music shown by dull-minded fillers of space. It is what the telephone companies put on as 'holding music'(the great Mozart clarinet concerto stands in the same grim position). The gap between BT and Classic FM is not as wide as it should be, and Raymond Gubbay promotions further show us how narrow the repertoire might become. Given that people do like Baroque music, there is a great volume of it, a great volume of Vivaldi for that matter. Where a promoter has before him a name known to and trusted by his target audience, he could, if he dared, with reasonable commercial confidence push on to vastly more of that composer's unfamiliar work. But so often he dares not. Ian Rankin, in one of his detective stories, has a character called *Feardie Fergie*, the circumspect model of un-enterprise. The concert circuit knows him well. At one end, we suffer from modernist arrogance and, at the other, from the promoters of the timid and piffling so called 'popular classics', like the pathetically debased outdoor picnic concerts or those indoor non-extravaganzas, for which the *New World Symphony* or bits of it, take over, where *The Four Seasons* leaves off.

It is not so long since Vivaldi was an utterly forgotten figure with only a single piece in print as sheet music. The rediscovery of the red priest was the work in the nineteen twenties and thirties of the Turin scholar, Alberto Gentili, who identified manuscripts at a monastery as those of Vivaldi. Then with further help, he found a huge amount more in the archives of the Durazzo family of Genoa. With generous contributions from two industrialists, he was able to buy the manuscripts for the Turin Library, though this took years and Vivaldi didn't come to public attention until after the Second World War. A pity, after such tribulation was faced in order to unearth the compositions, that concert programmers should gag after comparatively few and they by no means the finest works. A handful of pieces have become over-sucked humbugs; a great repertory exists, wind and string concerti and much more church music. There are also operas, championed by no less than Cecilia Bartoli. Of course, much is now on disc, but the concert repertory remains dismayingly limited.

The point of *lateralism* is to strike a compromise between what will sell and what ought to be explored. One recognises that the public is given to clutching the handrail, when edging upstairs and, in that knowledge, we should hold out points of affinity and comfort. Glock did this with his famous sandwiches of Mozart, Birtwistle and Tchaikovsky. It let the unwanted ride pig-a-back on the familiar. But if this were regularly done, where the music thus sold was actually sellable, then we should be talking the potential for a really extended repertory that the public could take to their hearts.

Into any concert of familiar Baroque music, I should want to insert something by Johan Friedrich Fasch. I read a snooty review in one of the record magazines, dismissing Fasch as a minor follower of Telemann, an example of what the academic mind at its most futile gets most wrong. Fasch, born near Weimar in 1688, is vivid, individual, combative and fresh to the ear — listen to his music for the trumpet. Once in the public domain and pushed a little, you would have a natural favourite. After all, if the young gentleman in the record magazine discounted him, he at least has the consolation of having been admired by Bach.

Staying with the Baroque, when will we have decent promotion of one composer who perfected his style in this country? It may be a dubious claim to be the finest London-trained Swedish composer of Italian music, but Johan Helmich Roman (1694-1758) was a devoted follower of Handel. Listen, to get a sense of him, to Anthony Robson's recording for Musica Sveciae of two of the oboe concerti. This is pure lilting, skipping melody, active, no reservations about pleasure and quite progressive, leaning forward into a classical/ galant style. Listen as well to *The Drottningholm Music*, recorded recently by the Uppsala Chamber Orchestra for Naxos. Roman is derivative alright, derivative from Handel, with the same instinct for melody, the same driving style. *The Drottningholm Music* is in the full tradition of Handel's *Water Music* and *Firework Music*. Roman for me is a composer waiting to become a major popular favourite.

Seriously obscure, and crying out for attention and display, is Jean-Féry Rebel. As a general rule, French Baroque music can be heavy going — too much religion, too much formality, not enough of Henry Cooper's 'snap'. The passion for the gloomy bass viol makes Saint-Colombe and Marin Marais, blessed by a recent fine film, rather a dark undertaking, though very worthwhile. But the Baroque violinist, Andrew Manze gave us, only last year, a record (from Harmonia Mundi) of this same Rebel, previously unknown to me, who though he regularly touches the melancholy of his con-temporaries — he was born in 1666 and played privately for the morose Louis XIV — can soar up in the way of a well-lit, floating Baroque staircase: the sort of thing which suggests the French Regency and its painters, Watteau and Fragonard. These are sonatas supported by harpsichord and viola da gamba; try the *visté* (track four) or some of the gigues and sarabandes making up the disc. They are seriously worth anyone's trouble, though there are complex moments, when Rebel sounds more like Bach than anyone else.

The caution of the concert hall does not apply to the record company, especially not to the smaller and newer companies. So much has been done in the last fifteen years that concepts of the minor and major will have to be revised because Hyperion, Naxos, ASV and Harmonia Mundi have shifted so much music off the library shelf and on to steel disc. The odious priestly quality which tells us 'We say what shall be played' grows harder to sustain. There is a lot more music, neglected by historical accident or a fringe-location, than the purists would have us believe, and in places like Turku, Zagreb, Dublin, Bratislava and Košice, there are also musicians of good quality able to perform competitively, who now turn up regularly on the smaller labels. The lateral transformation is taking place, although public and broadcast performance limp behind what is pressed and retailed.

The pioneers of this sort of thing were two linked companies; Turnabout and Nonesuch. From one of them there was a recording, perhaps twenty five years ago, of a cello concerto, another of a bassoon concerto, delicious dancing stuff by a certain Danzi: Franz Danzi, German-speaking son of an Italian musician in the famous Mannheim orchestra, where the classical style, symphony and concerto were finally wrought. Danzi was a close and corresponding friend of Weber, whom he influenced and was a man widely liked for his general good humour. With him, thirty years younger than Haydn, we are in the classical midstream, no romantic dark enveloping him, rather a recurring levity. He is a bit of a musical card, but listen to the quartets for bassoon and strings. What again would speak, if exposed to a general public would be the melody; sharp, quirky full of zest. It isn't grand music. Never does Danzi, a working professional in the despotic service of the stroppy King of Württemberg, seem to have had portentous views of himself. But he was an inventive, unexpected, compelling composer. And unlike Vivaldi, he is crying out for more sources to be researched, published, performed and recorded.

Sometimes a composer was relatively obscure in his own time, sometimes exalted, then thrown down by posterity. Bach after all, was quickly dug over with earth after the salutations of Frederick the Great in his last years. Danzi, born 1763 for one, was part of the culture from which Mozart and Beethoven arose. To rescue and listen to people like him is not to deny distinction, only to say that beside great music lies commonly very good or very enjoyable music, which its own age knew and esteemed. Oblivion is a lottery. An uninventive composer, writing at third hand for the school of the day and bringing to it no flair or personality of his own is legitimately discarded. Though technical progress is not a warranty of appeal. Johann Wenzel Stamitz moved the symphony forward from a perfunctory three movement interlude and influenced people like J.C.Bach, Boccherini, and Cannabich. The English critic, Dr Burney thought the world of him, but there is no great joy in Johann Wenzel, whereas his son Karl, who did not add another sleeper to the theoretical track, wrote, especially by way of woodwind concerti, things which you want to whistle. Johann Wenzel is for scholars, Karl for listening.

A musician like Danzi or Friedrich Kuhlau in Copenhagen or the Englishman, Capel Bond, the crazy, but invigorating Florentine, Francesco Veracini — 'One God, One Veracini,'— like Leopold Hoffman or Franz Krommer — ought to be looked at in terms of the ability to please their own times and their potential for being brought back to please us. Below the producers of very great music, which is to say behind the sort of composers Mr. Bryars wants never to be played again, are the names listed here. But when heard, each one offers a voice of his own. It will be interesting to see how names, once perfectly obscure, may come into light. They have before them the example, not only of Vivaldi in the Baroque but, in the purely classical era, of Luigi Boccherini. It was typical of the patronising style which flourished at the BBC some fifteen or so years ago, when Boccherini was given the Composer of the Week slot (he has had it again since, done very much better). Each programme was introduced with a variant of the famous millstone 'minuet', including a steeple carillon set to it. On the whole, the BBC has been very good in handling composers before the

1940 watershed, but with columns in the catalogues and a row and a half in the shops Boccherini has had his revenge. The trajectory of his take-up is something for Danzi, Hoffman and the others to emulate. The image was the minuet taken from an early quartet long ago and given the *Auld Lang Syne* treatment, also the Grützmacher concerto adaptation, nothing more. The breakthrough came, well before the BBC extended its good will, with a recording by August Wenzinger of one of the nine guitar quintets.

Probably Boccherini, who made leg-pulling remarks about civilising the Spaniards, among whom he spent his life, did not greatly value the arrangements he had made of string quintets for the modest talents of the Marques De Benavente on the guitar. They were distinctly manageable, for a noble patron to play, but they were so captivating that versions of the eight other surviving quintets followed. Add to these, the *echt* unadapted cello concerti, quintets, quartets and also symphonies, lightly scored, but richer in feeling than quite expected, especially the lovely D Major one from 1765, which has been admirably performed by the Ensemble 415 under Chiara Banchini. Add also a solitary choral work, the very moving *Stabat Mater*, and we have a rich source of new repertoire.

Boccherini didn't develop in a very notable way, though he, with Haydn, shared the creation of what we call chamber music; especially string quartet and quintet — there are also sextets and some perfectly heavenly settings for oboe and three strings. But all the market points made above apply strongly to a composer whose exposure, however late, has come ahead of most of the names touched on here. Do people like it? Yes, they like it. There is no joy in acknowledging Margaret Thatcher, but as she said — you can't buck the market.

Incomprehension between generations is nothing new. Boccherini was spoken of pityingly — 'Can you call that music?' — by an uncomprehending Louis Spohr, for whom such tender sentiment and unassertive melancholy, best understood by French critics, was quite alien. Spohr was an odd judge. He was appalled by late Beethoven, yet early on, discerned greatness in Wagner. He became as great a victim of misapprehension himself. A Paladin in his own lifetime, by the end of the nineteenth century, Spohr had descended to old hat. Because he was accomplished, smooth, efficient and adored in his own time, reaction is understandable, but quite wrong. He is thought of as an establishment man, which musically he probably was, having a thoroughly apostolic view of Mozart. But, though respectable and upright as a citizen, Spohr was a lifelong radical. Regretting Beethoven's breaches of orthodox harmony, the 64 year-old went out in the streets of Kassel in 1848, Herr Kapellmeister that he was, and mounted the barricades built by students against the gendarmerie and troops of Elector Wilhelm II.

But to test the enjoyment principle, listen to the two discs from Hyperion of Spohr's four double quartets. They are indeed smooth and accomplished, but also wall-to-wall pleasure, ensemble music as capable of giving delight as anything in the field. The single quartets, which Spohr steadily wrote all his life and which Marco Polo are working through, have the same effect, especially some of those written towards the end of his long life. Then there are the four clarinet concerti written, as the clarinet pieces of Mozart and Brahms, for an individual player, in Spohr's case, Johann Simon Hermstedt. They are, says Andrew Marriner, who greatly admires them, hellish to play. To miss the music of Spohr and to let dismissive chat about blandness stand in the way of that endless melodic invention is plain silly.

Missing from general view, despite an excellent recording by the Bamberger Symphoniker and Rickenbacher, is the single symphony of Otto Nicolai. Everyone says, 'Ah, Nicolai — the *Merry Wives of Windsor* overture'. I find the opera itself, though worthwhile, slightly anti-climactic after all that zip and fizz, but the symphony in D is quite gorgeous. It is like the very best of Schumann's orchestral work, and if only it were played, then it would certainly be taken up and loved.

But the biggest omissions from the concert repertory probably come later. The paradox of Mahler's popularity is that it cries out to be matched by his bitterest enemy, Franz Schmidt. Here we are going beyond the pleasure principle, and music heard for the sheer delight of it, to very serious claims. Hans Keller and Harold Truscott (and somebody should be fixing performances of the fascinating music of that unselfish scholar!), both musicians with real and profound understanding, thought of Schmidt as quite simply a great composer. They would put him alongside Bruckner, his admiring teacher and Mahler, with whom he had a great and often furious rivalry.

The first symphony with its Straussian shimmer, and the last with its lamenting trumpet call, as he summoned the student practising in the Perchtoldsdorf woods, the loss of a wife through madness and an only daughter dead in childbirth, seem to this nonexpert as the sort of thing which, with a blind disregard of Schoenberg's orders, music was meant to go on doing. If music like this, following the broadly settled rules, was no longer supposed to be possible, how could Schmidt have written this stupendous stuff? Elgar's favorite marking, *nobilmente*, is not actually used in the Schmidt fourth symphony, but it belongs. The language, at the tragic summit, is very much the language of Elgar. In the open and sunnier country below, it recalls Richard Strauss. Schmidt has had some attention, not least from a patriotic Franz Welser-Möst, who is a great advocate of the oratorio written in 1938, *The Book with Seven Seals*. The BBC has been quite friendly, after a long freeze, but the revival has not yet been properly done.

If we are talking not just of enjoyment, but of inherently great music, which must be set down before music lovers, then to Schmidt must be added the name of an English composer. Anyone who does not know the symphonies of Edmund Rubbra should start with the fourth, a great dark cathedral, though not of very great length, and complete the great middle with numbers five and six. Vernon Handley has made a fine recording of the fourth coupled with the third, and Richard Hickox is performing a public service with a cycle of all eleven. They take up where Malcolm Sargent left off and the incredible malice of William Glock began — malice which was to make Rubbra an un-person for the last twenty-five years of his life. He never, unlike George Lloyd, found constructive friends in America or had small recording companies take an interest, as Lyrita and then Albany did in Lloyd.

From having every new symphony performed with some panache by Sargent, Rubbra was put to silence. 'That sort of music,' as Glock told the very different and equally discriminated against Berthold Goldschmidt, 'cannot be played.' For the last quarter of his life, Rubbra was a former composer. Given the quasi-monopolist promotional authority in classical music of the Radio Three in this country, Rubbra and those like him were not better treated than Shostakovich was in the Soviet Union. Shostakovich though bullied, was played. Edmund Rubbra has to be taken out of the silence imposed, and one act of repentance open to the present apparat keen to take credit for a mild thaw, would be for his symphonies to be played at the Proms. Is that too much to ask?

But the destructive insolence of Glock and his successors, though unavoidable, is not the theme of this account. That simply accelerated, to grotesque Zhdanov-like lengths, the process of loss and waste, which critical opinion has always effected. Bach ignored, Vivaldi lost, early music (whose revival is the great triumph of the last fifty years) forgotten, most of the Baroque simply put on one side. The irony is of course that before the mid-nineteenth century, most music was contemporary music. If anyone changed the outlook, it was probably Brahms, proper scholar as well as annoyer of Mr. Bryars. Brahms delved and looked back, influenced by Mendelssohn, who had rescued Bach (forgotten since Frederick the Great's 'Up gentlemen — old Bach is here'.) We are knowledgeable about the sixteenth century, and earlier, in ways which fifty years ago looked simply eccentric. The Dolmetsch family and then, David Munrow, changed all that. Dowland, even Dunstable are mainstream. The magnificent John Sheppard is an even newer composer than Mahler. We go back to the Eton Choir Book and hear music composed in the medieval reign of Henry VII, which still has full force with us. In *Lucky Jim*, Kingsley Amis portrayed the early music enthusiast as Neddy Welch, an academic grotesque toting a recorder, all of which was,

in the way of Kingsley Amis, brilliantly unfair. I could though for-
give him everything for the sublime line, as Jim Dixon creeps
away from the musical evening — 'But you'll miss the P. Racine
Fricker.'

   We have the choice laid out before us, but we lack generally
disseminated knowledge. The concert promoter could and should
be braver than it has been, doing musical sandwiches, letting the
good unknown ride on the shoulders of the well-beloved. What we
probably need most of all are regular programmes on a less prim
Radio Three or a less timorous and cowering Classic FM: programmes to play and gently push for the music of which these
composers are a mere sample. *Lateralism* is an outlook poised
between the market and private discernment, unwilling to dictate,
but keen to make available. Informed but unbound by seminary
dogmas, it advocates would give the public, not what it likes, but
what it need not fear and very well might like. If minimalism is a
response to Pop, the cry of *lateralism* should go up for a new kind
of DJ.

12

Building Blake's 'Jerusalem'

Sir Ernest Hall

As we enter the new Millennium, we are experiencing changes which I believe will prove to be as momentous as those which were the consequence of the Industrial Revolution. This revolution was the physical manifestation of the Newtonian Universe: a quantifiable and knowable universe, where order was good. This cerebral view of the universe developed from the seeds sown by scientists such as Sir Francis Bacon in the seventeenth century. Descartes' vision of the universe was dominated by mathematical laws in which there was little spontaneity and freedom and in which everything could be predicted. In ancient days, the soul and spirit had been regarded as more important than the body, but this soul-less vision of Mother Nature became the foundation of modern science and industry. The Industrial Revolution was in the view of the visionary poet and artist, William Blake, an expression of materialist ideology, in which matter triumphed over the mind and spirit, the machine over man, cruelty and exploitation over love and compassion. Worst of all, the Industrial Revolution resulted in the 'banishment of the soul'; the relentless pursuit of financial success, regardless of human cost, dominated the whole development.

Work was a form of slavery for men, women and children. The Industrial Revolution created a world in which an opportunistic few dominated the lives of the many and which established a concept of work as servility and drudgery. A sense of paternal authority predominated, and a dependency culture was the inevitable consequence.

This culture of paternalistic employment is coming to an end. Old style employment with jobs for life no longer exists. The expectation of certainty and security in employment is being replaced by a more realistic sense of uncertainty and apprehension. Many of the problems we are facing are symptoms of a society in transition from a culture of dependency and servility to increasing personal responsibility. These changes cannot be met by minor modifications; they demand nothing less than a radical rethink, because we are facing a new reality. The growing world population and the continuing reduction in conventional employment due to new technology have resulted in around 800 million people worldwide without employment.

The consequent growing divisions between the successful, motivated, confident and optimistic and the unsuccessful, disenfranchised, powerless and pessimistic are a major source of conflict. What are the forces which divide our society into such extremes, encouraging and empowering the one and discouraging and negating the other? These deeply conflicting and opposing attitudes have become so much a part of our life and experience that we have come to accept them without question. It is the way things are; some people do well and some do badly and to most people the differences which emerge are the inevitable consequence of human nature. There is a commitment to providing equal opportunities, but it seems there are many who are not prepared to respond positively. This failure is perplexing. Why do so many people, apparently given the choice, opt for indifference instead of interest, unhappiness instead of happiness, and failure instead of success? This division is serious, because it threatens the stability and prosperity of our society. If more people become purposeful, society becomes more successful, but if more sink into apathy and despair, society becomes self-destructive. It seems that the most important advantages and disadvantages are not a consequence of inheritance or circumstance, but of attitudes we develop during our lives and particularly our early years. This determines whether we become enthusiastic or indifferent, ambitious or without purpose, confident or diffident. The development of these positive and negative attitudes is central to our development and determines our view of ourselves, our future and our success or failure.

The ebb and flow of our confidence and certainty are forces which shape our future. Whatever gives us confidence to believe we can achieve our deepest heartfelt yearnings affirms our view of ourselves. Whatever threatens that view causes us to shrink and perhaps abandon our quest for success. Our instinct for self-preservation is at the heart of our constant search for love and admiration. Our survival instinct has developed over millions of years into expressing those qualities which evoke love and admiration in our parents, when we are physically vulnerable. The qualities of love and admiration have a dual role. They are inspired in people, when we succeed, and when we benefit from them, they give us that sense of confidence and self-worth upon which our ability to succeed depends. I believe that every child is desperate to succeed. Look at the faces of young children before these positive and negative attitudes have developed; they are full of eagerness to learn, they are trusting and vulnerable. They are desperate to win love and admiration and they want and need approval. They want to succeed more than anything and yet many of them will become low achievers and purposeless individuals. Why do they abandon their dream of success? What induces them to opt for failure?

It has to be a very powerful reason. No one who believed success was possible could or would opt for failure. If we believed we could achieve it, we would pursue it relentlessly. There is only one reason that we opt to fail, and that is that we have persuaded ourselves that our inherited nature and ability are too poor an endowment to sustain our quest for success. And for many people, it is the education process that delivers this message first. We desperately want to succeed, but the intensity of our longing for success induces an equally intense feeling of failure. We sense the vulnerability of needing something so badly, if the prospect of achieving it recedes. From the moment we enter school we begin to gain or lose confidence. We sense something predictable in a system dedicated to identifying superiors and inferiors, winners and losers. Our system of scholarships and prizes celebrates the success of the privileged few. In every subject we celebrate the achievement of the minority. Our obsession with ranking from best to the worst permeates every aspect of our system. We rank the pupils, we rank the schools, we rank countries and I believe, no doubt, that one day we will rank the planets. These divisions determine our future. From our earliest days in school, we hear words which suggest that we can only play a passive part in our careers. We are told that we either are or are not clever or talented or that either we have or do not have the ability. The idea of *becoming* clever or talented seems by definition to be an impossibility. In this way we are being persuaded continually that our achievements are the consequence of our natures and, regardless of our hunger for success, we are destined to do well or badly. The consequence for high achievers is the elevation of their aspirations into a kind of cosmic inevitability. They are motivated, not only by their own confidence, but also by the knowledge that they are regarded as special. It is hard to imagine a more powerful aid to success. On the other hand, for the unsuccessful, destiny becomes a respectable reason for failure. If we are powerless in the hands of destiny, we have no reason to reproach ourselves. In the first case, a belief in destiny is a powerful aid to success and, in the second, it is a powerful encouragement of failure. Of course, we are exhorted to do well, but our efforts are constantly compared with others to indicate that we are superior or inferior. If we are being persuaded that we are inferior, how can we be expected to feel excited about our prospects, to put every effort into our work; to be enthusiastic and motivated. This sense of inevitability in our lives and our powerlessness to transform failure into success are reinforced during the most vulnerable period of our lives. Once these divisions are created, it is almost impossible to change sides. If we are failing and persuaded that we will continue to fail, our only refuge is to embrace defeat and accept failure. There is some security in making no further effort.

Assume for a moment that every human being had the same amount of ability, the creation of the concepts of talent and cleverness conferred on selected individuals in an arbitrary way would lift these individuals at the expense of the remainder. One group elevated in confidence and self-esteem, the others diminished by the distinction. This is not to say that natural ability does not exist, it clearly does, but the way people with ability are elevated offers an advantage which inhibits the development of those who are slower to develop. The brightness of pupils we identify as talented creates a shadow in which many talented people wither as they lose confidence. Confidence is not an enhancement, it is what we need to express our true nature. To lose confidence is to lose the power to be ourselves. When we lose confidence, we are lowered in our own and other people's estimation and we become less than ourselves.

When we look at a primitive society and learn that the consequence of the Medicine Man pointing the stick may mean death for his victim, we feel pity and a sense of disbelief that a society can hold such absurd beliefs and superstitions. Why do we find it so difficult to recognise that the pointing of the same stick at a child by a thoughtless parent or teacher, in a way which conveys the life-threatening message — you are stupid — is as terrifyingly destructive in its consequence. In measuring achievement, we have failed to understand that the process may in itself influence the outcome. Boredom, poor teaching, indifference may contribute to a poor result, but that poor result may blight our lives. If being measured is painful, we will seek to make it irrelevant and avoid it as much as we can in the future. Up to now these divisions have been turned to advantage by society. Is it possible that they have been created by society precisely because they can be used for subjugation? A society, not yet technologically developed, has a need for human beings ready to perform the many subservient roles. An employment culture of dependency has been able to exploit generation after generation conditioned to believe that what they are offered is no more than they deserve. But a culture of dependency may create the conditions for dangerous social upheaval, when employment cannot be guaranteed. People who are prepared for work in true expectation that it will be provided have few resources, if they fail to get that work. If employment is no longer predictable and the paternalistic culture no longer appropriate, then we need a fundamental reappraisal of the role of education.

All governments seem to believe that education is the passport to the future. My concern is that, as Einstein once remarked, problems cannot be solved with the same kind of thinking that gave rise to the problems. Governments still talk about education as if its role is unchanged from the servitude of nineteenth-century industry. The clear connection being promoted between work and education is reducing the concept of education to being no more then a preparation for work. But, if we are in transition to a new society in which personal responsibility will be needed as never before, instead of education as a preparation for work, we need education as a preparation for life. The successful transition of society to a post industrial age demands the cultivation of different qualities from those prevalent in a society which has cultivated the dependency of paternalistic employment. The human robot, so essential to nineteenth-century industry, is being made progressively redundant by new technology. In the twenty-first century, eventually, the only role for people will be one where they can exercise the qualities of inspiration, creativity, imagination, commitment and ambition. This is the vocabulary of the entrepreneur and this is the only solution to the problems this new society is posing. Instead of schools and universities creating employees, they need to create entrepreneurs.

The simple truth is that conventional education will not provide employment for those 800 million people. Jung said that in his experience the greatest problems his patients faced were often fundamentally insoluble, and only when people developed higher and wider interests could they outgrow their problems. This is why in the world of the twenty-first century, divisions of ability will have no place. We must eliminate the label of failure from education and put in its place an understanding that ability is illuminated by the bright lights of inspiration, motivation and confidence. Without that illumination, measuring ability indicates nothing more than their absence. Then every human being can discover the limitless power which these qualities release. We must begin to recognise the dangers of our obsession with cleverness. To elevate the intellect above the spirit is to diminish the vital qualities of creativity, imagination and passion, which are the foundation for an enterprising new society.

This change demands a reduction in our confidence in the intellect and the development of the creative and spiritual side of our brain. It sometimes seems we have no difficulty in believing anything, if there is a persuasive intellectual case. The intellect inspires misplaced confidence in our judgement; it can even convince us that we are infallible. Nowhere is our confidence in the intellect more extraordinary than in its belief that it can devise an infallible method for measuring the power of the human brain. The ranking of children is itself an intellectual exercise, which excludes the possibility of miracles. This sense of order in ranking children may seem to be true, but to regard it as incapable of change is to deny our power to evolve. A belief in miracles is more important than reason. Our reason can destroy us; a belief in miracles can transform us. We need an unambiguous declaration of faith in every human being. Listen to the profound wisdom of that great musician, Pablo Casals, who wrote:

When will we teach our children in school what they are? We should say to each of them: Do you know what you are? You are a marvel. You are unique. In all of the world there is no other child exactly like you. In the millions of years that have passed, there has never been another child like you. You may become a Shakespeare, a Michelangelo, a Beethoven; you have the capacity for anything.

This transformation of education can only be achieved when we put the creative Arts at the centre of the curriculum. Usually any defence of the Arts in the curriculum is built on the growing recognition of the contribution they can make to education in other areas of work. It is increasingly obvious that an interest in the Arts aids young people's ability to do every subject in the curriculum. The *'learning of the imagination'* is a powerful aid to a successful and fulfilling life in any area of work. But the transformation of which I speak goes beyond serving the present system better.

I want to talk about the Arts and their power to spur on and elevate the human race, and about music in particular, because I am a musician. Perhaps I should make clear what kind of music it is which I believe has the power to transform education. It is not entertaining music. I sometimes like to be entertained, but the quality of this experience is very different from the experience I shall describe. We are entertained by popular music but we are rarely enriched. The popular arts tell us little we do not already know. They demand little because the language is one we already understand. The vocabulary is simple and accessible because these are the qualities on which its success depends. There is no new vocabulary to learn; no profound ideas which demand thought before we can understand the significance of the message. We are reading variations of the same story with the same limited vocabulary and with a limited range of feeling. Our real power will never be revealed to us. Our development will come to a stop.

The importance of great Art is that it enables us to experience and feel what we might otherwise never discover. It is Art which can elevate our sense of humanity and which at rare and wonderful moments can induce a feeling of ecstasy. It may seem that in giving this description and in applying it to music that I am looking backwards in preference to looking forwards. This is not because I am uninspired by contemporary music. I thrill to the sound of many composers writing today. In any case, the division between our cultural heritage and the work of living artists is in many ways artificial, because the past and present are always connected by each new generation of artists, who fight to keep the Arts of the past alive as well as to create new Art. To each generation the cultural heritage is as fresh and original as any work created in their own time. But perhaps we should also remember that the great achievements of the past are the only foundations on which we can depend. History clearly demonstrates the aberration of contemporary judgements. Only the passage of time makes clear the difference in quality between the work of two great composers such as Telemann and Bach. To many eighteenth-century musicians, Telemann was the greater composer. Many artists, admired and popular during their lifetimes, are now seen with hindsight as greatly inferior to contemporaries, who were perhaps derided. Even when composers are recognised by contemporaries, it is often only posterity which recognises their greatest work. The pinnacles of true genius tower above the landscape of human achievement, when we look backwards. They have withstood changing fashions and are built on foundations, which are relevant to every generation. These are the rocks which afford us a sure foothold and which we can climb with confidence. They are rocks on which we can forge our own careers, as well as being a lasting testimony to the greatest achievements of our civilisation. From the peaks, we can see the undiscovered territories of the future, and we are also nearer to hearing the music of the spheres. These mountains are evidence of humanity's yearning for immortality. It is from these peaks that we can perhaps converse, as Blake suggested we could, through poetry, painting and music, with paradise. It is this conversation which I believe is crucial to ensuring that the evolution of the human race is in the direction of the Gods and not a descent, which Blake suggested might result in the human race being no more than worms on the face of the earth. I believe that this collective aspiration towards the spheres is the only sure way to carry us in the direction of a sustainable, civilised society.

My own life was transformed by the creative Arts. I was born into a poor working class environment in the 1930's and might well have opted for failure. My parents took almost no interest in my education and my progress at school was mediocre. But on one occasion I was inspired and it was enough. I was nine years old, and one day a stranger came into the classroom with a gramophone and some records. I still remember the excitement that I felt as he described the music we were to hear: 'ghostly dancers mysteriously appearing and disappearing in the ballroom of a great fairy-tale castle,'and then he put on the record. I heard music that was beautiful and moving beyond anything I had ever experienced. Hildegard best describes the experience I had: 'Great flashing poured down from the open sky, setting on fire my entire head'. It was my introduction to the power of Art to reveal a new reality. Even though I was in a public place, I knew that I had made a unique and secret discovery that would change my life. The discovery of beauty is the discovery of a new world which continually reveals itself. From that moment I had an insatiable passion for more and more music. At about the same age, I discovered a piano on a visit to some relatives and my obsession and delight in playing it persuaded my parents to buy one. My passion to play was nourished by the inspiration I derived from listening to more and more wonderful music. No sound I made could match the quality of the music to which I listened, but the more beautiful it was and the more remote in miraculous facility from my own technique the harder I worked. It was Blake who resolved the gulf between listening and playing for me: 'Prayer is the study of Art, praise is the practice of Art'.

When I entered the Royal Manchester College of Music, it was like entering Valhalla. I lived on inspiration and dreamed of achieving beautiful things. My family, on the other hand, could not understand that work could be passion, purpose and pleasure. They constantly told me that when I came to make a living I would have to play dance music. This was because they knew I hated it, but for them that was the reality. If it was something you didn't hate, then how could it possibly be work?

My passion to play continued, but fear about the future began to increase. Was I good enough? The competition was intense, and I knew that supply was likely to exceed demand. My fate was settled when I heard that John Ogdon, a pupil of my own teacher,

Claude Biggs, was playing the three Bartók piano concertos at the Edinburgh Festival. These concertos are amongst the hardest in the repertoire, which put his achievement far beyond anything I had done. A sudden fear of compromising my ideals as a pianist and composer led me to look for a way to make a living outside music, and I found one in a textile mill in Yorkshire.

That lead to the discovery of enterprise, and from that moment, I sensed a new excitement. I had believed that commerce was ugly. My mother was one of thirteen children, all of whom worked in mills. Yet I quickly realised that designing and weaving fabrics and running a business was a similar creative process to composing music and satisfyingly productive. It was in this way that my interest in the connection between Art and Enterprise began. I believe that there is a profound connection between them. Both the artist and the entrepreneur see what might appear to be a sordid reality and transform it. Both the artist and the entrepreneur use the instinct more than the intellect. The successful transition of our society demands the cultivation of enterprise. Enterprise is not an intellectual skill. It is a powerful mix of confidence, creativity and courage. The intellect is useful, but the instinct is indispensable. It is this change which demands a transformation of education through the inspiration of Art.

But even in the Arts, we are not immune to attack from the intellect. The Arts in schools are more than the provision of a music teacher and musical instruments. I meet growing numbers of university-trained bureaucrats working in the Arts, whose views are essentially intellectual. I sense that their interest in the Arts has developed without the mystical experience of inspiration and that, because of this, they attach little importance to it. In the absence of this experience, it is not difficult to understand why there is a growing trend to promote participation in the Arts, isolated from the experience of creative listening, looking and reading. But I know from experience that purposeful participation can only be sustained by inspiration and that people can discover themselves more surely in creative reading than they can in creative writing. Reading, listening and looking are only passive, if we regard the mystical experience of inspiration as inanimate; if we believe that the playing of a musical instrument is more beautiful and fulfilling than the sound of the music itself. My concern is that this trend can reduce the Arts to an intellectual exercise, stepping from grade to grade, and never discovering the miraculous power of inspiration. In place of a system of education which measures achievement, we need a system which inspires achievement. Whilst our present system is dedicated to elevating and liberating, in practice it imprisons a great number of people, because we have under-estimated the vulnerability of the infinite complexity of mind and spirit. Our ability and genius do not have the qualities of a precious stone but of a tender plant, which needs to be given the right con-ditions, if it is to flourish. Only a system of education which respects our vulnerability and the organic nature of ability can serve the needs of this new society. My own experience has con-vinced me that it is through the inspiration of great Art that people can become a part of this new society. The experience of inspira-tion feeds and nourishes our deep seated need for beauty. It has nothing to do with liking and disliking. When we encourage people to believe in the importance of their own views, we encourage their egos to become insurmountable barriers to their progress. Only the awareness of the limitless depths we can strive to experience can lead us to discover that we will never achieve our 'potential'. I often hear in schools and universities the commonly expressed aim that they want to help people achieve their 'potential'. But the word in this context no longer conveys a sense of infinite possibil-ities, it has become instead a barrier which draws ever nearer. There are no surprises in achieving this 'potential', indeed once it becomes the achievement of what we believe is possible, the word itself destroys our real power. Our aspirations must have no ceiling; only the ambition to achieve the mediocre becomes self-defeating. It is the ambition to achieve the unattainable which can continue to excite and inspire us.

My own life and experience are testament to these ideas. I have described how I dreamt of a life of music, but decided to set that dream aside for a career in business. Yet the dream did not perish, and my successful business life served only to strengthen my determination to realise my dream. As I approached 65, the age at which most are considering retirement and the decline of old age, I asked myself a challenging question. If John Ogdon, playing Bartók concertos, had been enough to convince me that I would never be a pianist when I was 25, could I vindicate myself by playing and recording these same works at 65? It was a daunting challenge, but I did it nevertheless and made one of the most exciting discoveries of my life. I discovered that what was impossible at the age of 25 was achievable at 65. Spurred on by this, I have now embarked on another major recording project; the complete piano works of Chopin. In my 70th year, I am more confident and ambitious than at any time in my life so far.

The human race has never had the prospect of living longer, and yet it seems that the opportunity to change the pattern of human achievement is not being taken. The evolution of the human race depends on the discovery of new possibilities. We need innovators who will change our sense of what is possible. The first four-minute mile was not simply a breakthrough for an individual, but for the rest of the human race. That kind of breakthrough needs nothing less than the courage and ambition to attempt the impossible. My concern is that the language of educators has progressively and unintentionally limited and lowered the horizons of many people. We not only need to change the way in which people see themselves, but we also need to change the way in which we see them.

In a materialist society, we increasingly come to believe in the power of money and less and less in the power of ideals. I know how hard it is to hold on to ideals, if our experience is continually persuading us that they are unrealistic, but ideals should always dominate our thinking. We must not allow our thinking to become the victim of experience. The power of highest ideals, when we trust them, is that they can transform our lives. They can inspire, motivate and lead us to our greatest achievements. When I started to redevelop *Dean Clough Mills* in 1983, I created the concept of a 'Practical Utopia' to guide me. The concept may at first have seemed remote from reality, but increasingly it has illuminated the way forward. A pedestrian development of buildings has been transformed by a dream of the impossible. In commercial terms *Dean Clough* was considered an impossible project and turned down by every businessman who looked at it. Only a dream of the impossible could transform it. With an unattainable mission it becomes a project without an end. The process is the purpose. In so many ways waiting for some physical improvement can be destructive. Building a new 'Jerusalem' does not depend on roofs which do not leak. Increasingly I believe that the Arts, as well as Education, have become obsessed with the physical, at the expense of the spiritual. In our 'Practical Utopia', we have a Theatre, *The Viaduct*. It is a raw unrefurbished space beneath two great mills. It is inclined to be damp, it leaks. At first sight it might not suggest to some people a space in which magic can be created, but it is a theatre of miracles. It is also a marvellous illustration of one of the fundamentals in business; that there is no connection between cost and value. A growing belief in the power of our instinct will make us more aware of the proper balance between the material and the spiritual.

There is another powerful reason for the elevation of the Arts. We must always remember that it is only when we combine the Arts with enterprise that we create a civilised world. In a material-istic world, it is inevitable that making money has been elevated above its rightful status. The instinct of the artist is needed to remind us that survival is not enough, and only through discover-ing our higher purpose can we gain fulfillment. In place of the nineteenth-century concept of work as slavery and drudgery, we need to restore work to its rightful place as the realisation and expression of our unique being. In a world of real work, there is no retirement and no unemployment. In an industrial society, we need to make a conscious effort to develop our mystical senses. We must elevate the spirit above the intellect. Numeracy and literacy have never been regarded as more important as an aid to earning a living. This is understandable, but it is a love of the Arts which can remind us that a rising standard of living does not in itself make life worthwhile.

I understand the difficulties of overturning so many cherished ideas and how far away from reality these ideas may seem to be. We may feel powerless to change the system because our system is accountable. But the change we need is the transformation and development of those in power. Inspired teachers with the collective aspiration to push the human race forward, and with an awareness of how easy it is to hold it back, can transform the system within the system. Teachers with an unwavering belief and respect for the limitless power of every individual; teachers whose own inspiration leads them to respect the miraculous nature of each unique human being and who strive never to create a light for the few which creates a shadow in which so many wither.

I have already referred to 'Jerusalem' and I must make it clear that it is Blake's 'Jerusalem' of which I speak. Every schoolchild sings that great poem by William Blake, rarely, if ever, understanding its significance.

> I will not cease from Mental Fight,
> Nor shall my Sword sleep in my hand
> Till we have built Jerusalem
> In England's green and pleasant land

When Blake conceived his 'Jerusalem', it was his vision to create the Holy City of Imagination on Earth. He described those people, who strive to create it as 'golden builders'. That aspiration is the measure we should apply to our own careers. We need to dream extravagantly and to believe in our dreams. If we achieve this we can attempt anything. Can anything be more important than encouraging the human race to dream of creating a beautiful world and to give them the confidence to believe in their dreams? In place of allowing people to see themselves as victims, we need to recognise that it is the aspiration to be heroic which will create the society we need. These two aspirations — to behave heroically and to create a beautiful world — are the foundations of a civilised society. The role of the Arts is profoundly important to our society and civilisation. This new society will demand a new democracy, in which there is success, ability and inspiration for everyone. I believe that it is through the inspiration of great Art that people can discover their own genius and uniqueness and be better equipped for this new Society. In place of entrepreneurs intent on making money, we need entrepreneurs with a vision of greatness for their work. When we dream extravagantly, we are inspired to forge a reality beyond the straitjacket of practicalities. A true work of imagination and enterprise creates an image of perfection to which we can all aspire. It is the power to see beyond the limitations of an immediate reality which requires the *'learning of the imagination'*.

When the great industrial empires we revere are worm casts on the face of the earth, it will be the legacy of artists which will continue to inspire and be revered by our descendants. Perhaps in this post-industrial age, we can rediscover our purpose and place in the cosmos. Perhaps we can evolve into a society of 'golden builders' able to build Blake's new 'Jerusalem'; his Holy City of Imagination on Earth.

Biographical
Notes on Contributors

Menno Boogaard was born in The Netherlands in 1960 and studied music in Amsterdam and Utrecht. He is active as a performer of solo and chamber music and also as a repetiteur. He has combined a performing career with a keen interest in philosophy, especially relating to music. He is a passionate Wagnerian and studied in depth the writings of Schopenhauer. He explores the way in which philosophy and the practice of music intertwine, both through research and his own musical experience.

John Borstlap is a composer, born in The Netherlands in 1950, who studied in Rotterdam and Cambridge, winning prizes in Poland and Monaco. He now lives in Amsterdam and is a leading commentator on issues in musical life, founding a festival, the *Haarlemse Kamermuziekdagen* in 1998 and setting up a forum in 2000 to debate issues around the programming of contemporary music. His music has been performed in his own country, Germany and England. In 1997, Albany Records UK issued a CD — *Hyperion's Dream* — of chamber works. His music explores the continuing possibilities of the European tonal tradition, but in the light of twentieth century developments and made relevant to the contemporary world.

John Boyden has enjoyed great success as an innovator and entrepreneur in classical music in a career which spans 35 years. He has won numerous prizes and accolades, including the Billboard Trendsetter award and several Gramophone awards for his commercial recordings. He has launched the recording careers of, among others, Dame Margaret Price, Sir Simon Rattle and Julian Lloyd Webber. In 1970 he launched the Classics for Pleasure label for EMI with the industry's first commercial sponsorship deal. In 1975, he was appointed the first Managing Director of the London Symphony Orchestra and in 1992 reformed the New Queen's Hall Orchestra to recreate the sound and performance practices of the pre-1940 symphony orchestra.

Peter Davison is Artistic Consultant to Manchester's Bridgewater Hall; a venue he also helped to develop prior to its opening in September 1996. He has previously held posts with the Royal Liverpool Philharmonic Orchestra and English Bach Festival, more recently working as a consultant on many major Arts projects in the UK. He is a graduate of Cambridge University, specialising in the music of Mahler and a frequent contributor to journals and programme notes. In 1998, he was co-artistic director of a festival at Haarlem in the Netherlands, connecting contemporary music and the past. He has taught as a guest lecturer at the University of Manchester and the Welsh College of Music and Drama.

Sir Ernest Hall OBE DL went to the Royal Manchester College of Music (47-51), where he studied piano and composition. In 1961, he started his own successful business, and in 1983, with his son Jeremy, bought Dean Clough Mills in Halifax, developing them into a centre for business, the arts, design and education. He is also deputy-chairman of Eureka, The Museum for Children, Chancellor of the University of Huddersfield and a Vice-President of the RSA. In 1996. he won the Montblanc de la Culture award, and in 1997, the ABSA Goodman award. Sir Ernest Hall is a dedicated musician — a composer and pianist. In 94/95 he recorded the Bartók piano concertos and is currently recording the complete piano works of Chopin.

Robin Holloway, born in Leamington Spa in 1943, is a composer and music lecturer at Caius College, Cambridge. He studied composition under Alexander Goehr and was among the first to explore the territory of post-modernism, especially the reintegration of Romanticism, during the early 70's, in works such as his *Scenes from Schumann*. He has written extensively about Debussy and Wagner and taught a whole generation of composers at Cambridge University. His first symphony was performed at the BBC Proms in the summer of 2000.

David Matthews is a composer, born in London in 1943. His music includes five symphonies, nine string quartets, a large-scale *Vespers* for soloists, chorus and orchestra and numerous other orchestral, chamber and vocal works. His music is regularly broadcast and a number of his pieces have been recorded on CD. He is Artistic Director of the Deal Festival in Kent and composer-in-association with the Britten Sinfonia. He has also written extensively about music, including a book on Michael Tippett and an essay on the relationship of music and painting, *Landscape into Sound*.

Edward Pearce has written millions of words over 25 years for *The Daily Telegraph, The Guardian, The Daily Express, The Scotsman* and other major journals. His tenth book, the official life of Denis Healey, will be published in October 2001. He also appeared regularly for a period as a panellist on BBC Radio 4's The Moral Maze. Though a political specialist, he has written about music whenever possible and had a column in 'Classic CD'. He delivered the sole dissenting opinion on BBC Radio Three's tribute to William Glock.

Roger Scruton is a philosopher and writer who has held academic positions in England, America and elsewhere. He is the author of over twenty books, including works of philosophy, criticism and fiction. His *The Aesthetics of Music* is an account of the nature and significance of music from the perspective of modern philosophy. He has written widely on musical matters, and has also composed an opera, *The Minister*, performances of which have been well received, in addition to songs and instrumental music.

Robert Walker has been a professional composer for 25 years. He was formerly Professor of Composition at The London College of Music, but in the early nineties gave up the pressured life of a professional musician in Britain to set up home on the island of Bali, Indonesia. He built a remote house for himself, lived for nine years composing, thinking and playing in his local village gamelan. Due to political upheavals in Indonesia, he now lives in Bangkok where he is the Head of Composition at Mahidol University.

Robin Walker born in York in 1953, is a composer. He was a chorister at York Minister, where he gained his earliest musical education, and studied music at Oxford University. He went on to study composition at Durham University with the Australian composer, David Lumsdaine. Robin himself has taught at the Royal Academy of Music, the University of Manchester and the Royal Northern College of Music. He left full-time teaching in 1987 and moved to the Pennine village of Delph to concentrate on composing. His works often evoke images of the Pennine landscape as a metaphor of his own spiritual preoccupations, and several have been performed by orchestras such as the BBC Philharmonic and Manchester Camerata.

'Sea Sonata (Sonata no. 5 — finale)' by M. K. Čiurlionis

Publisher's Note on the Cover Illustration

The cover illustration is taken from a painting by the Lithuanian composer and painter, M. K. Čiurlionis (1875-1911), whose paintings attempt to re-create the experience of musical organisation through meditation on the natural world. This painting is the '*finale*' of a three-movement work entitled *Sea Sonata (Sonata no. 5)* (1908), and can be seen in the M. K. Čiurlionis Art Museum in Kaunas, Lithuania.

Čiurlionis's music, influenced by Chopin and also by native Lithuanian sources, is remarkable for its experiments with polyrhythm, modal and whole-tone harmony, and chromatic melodic line, and for retaining nonetheless an over-mastering tonal organisation. The keyboard works bears a resemblance to those of Scriabin, though without the intoxication of Scriabin's harmonic idiom. His paintings are lyrical landscapes and dreamscapes, in which the longing for order and harmony is expressed through musical analogies.

Coventry University

Index

Adams, John, 101, 161, 234
Adès, Thomas, 234
Adorno, Theodor, 3, 14, 63, 76-7, 78, 81, 170, 206
Amis, Sir Kingsley, 245f
Andriessen, Louis, 101

Bach, C.P.E., 195
Bach, J.S., 57, 66, 85-6, 90, 106, 170, 189, 194, 233, 237, 239, 240, 241, 245, 255
Bacon, Sir Francis, 247
Balzac, Honoré de, 62
Banchini, Chiara, 242
Bartók, Béla, 28, 94, 100, 163, 180, 182, 195, 196, 257, 259
Bartoli, Cecilia, 238
Beatles, The, 207
Beckermann, Michael, 29
Beecham, Sir Thomas, 214, 230
Beethoven, Ludwig van, 20, 31, 32, 44, 57, 66, 84, 87, 94, 100, 107, 180, 189, 194, 202, 204, 205, 208, 209f, 211, 225, 235, 241, 243
Benigni, Roberto, 33
Benjamin, George, 234
Berg, Alban, 14, 15, 60, 61-2, 63-5, 80, 84, 94, 167, 195, 202
Berg, Helene, 62
Berio, Luciano, 98f, 170
Berlioz, Hector, 44, 195
Biggs, Claude, 257
Birtwistle, Sir Harrison, 84, 99, 105, 135f, 167, 235, 238
Blake, William, 202, 247, 255, 256, 261-2
Blech, Leo, 222
Bloch, Ernst, 14
Boccherini, Luigi, 241-2
Bond, Capel, 241
Borges, Jorge Luis, 104
Boulanger, Nadia, 100
Boulez, Pierre, 46, 53, 64, 71, 78, 81, 84, 97, 153, 170, 201, 202, 208
Brahms, Johannes, 17, 19, 22, 56, 57, 66, 109, 169, 232, 235, 237, 245
Brentano, Bettina, 31
Britten, Benjamin, 1, 97, 129, 195, 211
Bruckner, Anton, 104, 105, 235, 236, 244
Bryars, Gavin, 232, 237, 241,

245
Büchner, Georg, 65
Burney, Charles, 217, 241
Butler, R.A., 235
Byrd, William, 117

Cage, John, 98, 135,
Cannabich, Christian, 241
Carroll, Lewis, 101
Carter, Elliott, 99
Casals, Pablo, 253
Celan, Paul, 167
Charlemagne, Emperor, 149
Chopin, Frédéric, 165, 195,
    259, 267
Čiurlionis, M. K., 267
Clifford, Max, 234
Connolly, Justin, 84
Cooke, Deryck, 200, 212
Cooper, Henry, 232, 239
Cornall, Andrew, 228

D'Arányi, Jelly, 221
Da Vinci, Leonardo, 155, 189
Damrosch, Walter, 229
Danzi, Franz, 240-41, 242
Davies, Sir Peter Maxwell, 105,
    201
Debussy, Claude, 8, 94, 95, 117,
    163, 165, 175, 180, 195
Del Tredici, David, 101
Derrida, Jacques, 48
Descartes, René, 247
Diaghilev, Sergei, 96
Dolmetsch family, 245
Dowland, John, 245

Dunstable, John, 245
Dvořák, Anton, 10, 210, 235

Einstein, Albert, 252
Eisler, Hanns, 14
Elgar, Sir Edward, 104, 211,
    223, 228, 235, 237, 244
Eliot, T.S., 110, 198
Ellington, Duke, 206
Fasch, C.F.C., 238f
Feldman, Morton, 167
Ferneyhough, Brian, 99, 105
Fichte, J.G., 32, 32
Finnissy, Michael, 99, 105
Fischer, Ernst, 123-4, 148
Foucault, Michel, 48, 53
Fragonard, J.H., 239
Freud, Sigmund, 157
Fricker, Peter Racine, 246
Furtwängler, Wilhelm, 221,
    225-7, 229

Gablik, Suzi, 188, 193, 198
Gauguin, Paul, 175
Gentili, Alberto, 238
Gershwin, George, 206
Gerstl, Richard, 58, 128
Gesualdo, Carlo, 195
Glass, Philip, 100, 234
Glock, Sir William, 234, 238,
    244f, 265
Goehr, Alexander, 109
Goldschmidt, Berthold, 245
Golther, W., 54
Górecki, Henryk, 108, 203
Gorowski, Jack, 225

Grieg, Edvard, 236
Gropius, Walter, 184
Grützmacher, Friedrich, 242
Gubbay, Raymond, 237

Hailey, Christopher, 60, 61, 81
Hall, Sir Ernest, 4, 5
Handel, George Frederick, 127, 189, 237, 239
Handley, Vernon, 244
Harrison, Beatrice, 229
Harrison, Margaret, 229f
Harvey, Jonathan, 194
Hašek, Jaroslav, 10
Hauer, J. M., 63-4
Haydn, Joseph, 32, 182, 1194, 211, 233, 235, 240, 242
Hegel, G.W.F., 31, 32, 76, 78
Heidegger, Martin, 132, 133
Heifetz, Jascha, 223
Hermstedt, Johann Simon, 243
Hickox, Richard, 244
Hildegard of Bingen, 256
Hoffman, Leopold, 241, 242
Holloway, Robin, 29
Holst, Gustav, 219
Housman, A.E., 237

Ives, Charles, 94

Janáček, Leoš, 1, 7-30, 196
Joachim, Joseph, 221
Joyce, James, 131, 200
Jung, Carl Gustav, 86, 116, 121, 130-2, 139, 146, 148, 202, 252

Kafka, Franz, 9
Kant, Immanuel, 32-3
Keats, John, 233
Keller, Hans, 209, 212, 244
Klemperer, Otto, 215
Kox, Hans, 194
Krommer, Franz, 241
Kuhlau, Friedrich, 241

Laing, R.D., 134-5, 148
Lao-Tzu, 173, 198
Lawrence, D.H., 157, 203, 212
Le Corbusier, 184
Lefaivre, Liane, 190f, 198
Leibniz, G.W. von, 32, 34
Lévinas, Emmanuel, 133, 148
Ligeti, György, 85, 97-8
Little Richard, 207
Lloyd Webber, Julian, 264
Lloyd, George, 245
Lumsdaine, David, 266
Lutyens, Elizabeth, 84

MacDonald, Malcolm, 81,
Machaut, Guillaume, 106
Magee, Bryan, 37, 40, 54
Mahler, Gustav, 11, 28, 44, 45, 61, 64, 75, 94, 99, 100, 101, 104, 106, 107, 195, 212, 205, 210, 235, 236, 237, 243f, 245
Mallarmé, Stephane, 98
Mann, Thomas, 55, 66, 81
Manze, Andrew, 239
Mao Tse Tung, 127
Marais, Marin, 239
Marriner, Andrew, 243

Martinů, Bohuslav, 210
McCartney, Sir Paul, 117, 207
Mellers, Wilfrid, 207, 212
Mendelssohn, Felix, 106, 245
Mengelberg, Willem, 221
Messiaen, Olivier, 85, 97, 106
Michelangelo Buonarotti, 189
Miller, Henry, 157
Mondriaan, Piet, 180
Monteverdi, Claudio, 105, 168, 195, 208
Moyse, Marcel, 222
Mozart, W.A., 17, 31, 32, 43, 44, 46, 95, 106, 194, 211, 233, 235, 236, 237, 238, 241, 243
Musil, Robert, 9-10

Nicolai, Otto, 243
Nielsen, Carl, 110, 235f
Nono, Luigi, 97, 170

Offenbach, Jacques, 106
Ogdon, John, 256f, 259

Pärt, Aarvo, 108, 203
Payne, Anthony, 104
Pergolesi, Giovanni Battista, 96
Pfitzner, Hans, 223
Picasso, Pablo, 131, 157
Picken, Laurence, 88
Plato, 35, 40
Presley, Elvis, 207
Price, Dame Margaret, 263
Prokofiev, Sergei, 103, 182, 195
Pruslin, Stephen, 136, 148

Puccini, Giacomo, 16, 194

Rachmaninov, Sergei, 110
Rankin, Ian, 237
Rattle, Sir Simon, 263
Ravel, Maurice, 95, 103, 163, 182, 195, 219
Read, Ernest, 213
Rebel, Jean-Féry, 239-40
Reger, Max, 95
Reich, Steve, 100-01, 161, 234
Rembrandt van Rijn, 155
Richter, Hans, 215
Rickenbacker, H., 243
Riley, Terry, 100
Rimsky-Korsakov, N. A., 217
Robson, Anthony, 239
Rochberg, George, 100, 103
Rolling Stones, The, 106
Roman, Johan Helmich, 239
Ronald, Sir Landon, 214-5
Rossini, Giacomo, 43, 44, 98
Rousseau, Jean-Jacques, 86
Rubbra, Edmund, 244-5

Saatchi, Charles, 234
Safranski, Rudiger, 31, 54
Sainte-Colombe, 239
Sargent, Sir Malcolm, 244f
Sartre, Jean Paul, 47-8, 132, 133
Satie, Erik, 94
Scarlatti, Domenico, 195
Schelling, F. W. J. von, 31
Schmidt, Franz, 104, 110, 244
Schnittke, Alfred, 208, 212,

Schoeck, Othmar, 110

Schoenberg, Arnold, 3, 7-30, 46, 52, 55-82, 83, 95, 100, 128, 129, 1132, 137, 157, 163, 169, 180, 200f, 202, 205f, 208, 212, 233, 236, 244

Schoenberg, Mathilde, 58

Schopenhauer, Arthur, 31-54, 90f

Schubert, Franz, 194, 211, 233, 235

Schumann, Robert, 100, 243

Scriabin, Alexander, 180, 195, 202, 267

Scruton, Roger, 2, 5, 54, 170, 208, 212

Sculthorpe, Peter, 202f

Semprini, 106

Shakespeare, William, 7

Shapey, Ralph, 99

Sharp, Cecil, 207

Sheppard, John, 245

Shostakovich, Dmitri, 97, 195, 245

Sibelius, Jean, 104, 206, 235, 236

Simpson, Robert, 194, 211, 235-6

Smetana, Bedřich, 10

Spohr, Louis, 242-3

Stamitz, J.W., 241

Stamitz, Karl, 241

Štědroň, Bohumír, 22, 30

Steiner, George, 182, 198

Stejskalová, Marie, 11

Stenhammar, Wilhelm, 104

Stockhausen, Karlheinz, 46, 84, 97, 168, 170, 201, 202

Stösslová, Kamila, 24

Strauss, Johann the Younger, 13, 95

Strauss, Richard, 28, 59, 90, 95, 101, 106, 127, 202, 223, 235, 244

Stravinsky, Igor, 28, 67, 70, 77, 78, 79, 81, 84, 85, 94, 95, 96, 100, 101, 102, 103, 105, 106, 110, 129, 137, 157, 163, 180, 182, 195, 196, 201, 206, 210, 219

Swedenborg, Emmanuel, 62, 74

Swift, Jonathan, 219

Szymanowski, Karól, 202

Tanner, Michael, 48, 52, 54

Tavener, Sir John, 108, 203

Tchaikovsky, P.I., 96, 168, 195, 238

Telemann, Georg Philipp, 238, 255

Terry, Quinlan, 103

Thatcher, Margaret, 242

Tippett, Sir Michael, 85, 201f, 206f, 211, 212

Torke, Michael, 101

Toscanini, Arturo, 215,

Trkanová, Marie, 11, 30

Truscott, Harold, 244

Tyrrell, John, 17, 30

Tzonis, Alexander, 190f, 198

Van Gogh, Vincent, 175, 180

Vasari, Giorgio, 149
Vaughan Williams, Ralph, 94,
    211, 228
Veracini, Francesco, 241
Verdi, Giuseppe, 106
Verlaine, Paul, 95
Visconti, Luciano, 237
Vivaldi, Antonio 189, 237-8,
240, 241, 245

Wagner, Richard, 3, 8, 31, 44,
    45f, 52-3, 54, 56, 83, 84, 93,
    106, 107, 112, 127, 180,
    182, 189, 195, 204f, 220,
    233, 236, 243
Walter, Bruno, 82, 215, 235
Watteau, Antoine, 239
Weber, C. M. von, 127, 240

Webern, Anton von, 46-7, 52,
    60, 61, 80, 183-4, 163,
    180, 202, 206
Weil, Simone, 140-2, 148
Welser-Möst, Franz, 244
Wenzinger, August, 242
Wesendonck, Mathilde, 45-6
Wilde, Oscar, 220
Wood, Haydn, 117

Xenakis, Iannis, 99, 170

Yourcenar, Marguerite, 150f,
    192, 198

Zemlinsky, Alexander von, 56
Zhdanov, B., 245
Zimmermann, Bernd Alois, 196